ON NORTHERN POLITICS

ON NORTHERN POLITICS

Advocating Change in Northern Ireland 1994-1998

NORMAN PORTER

Published by Perspicuous Press in 2023.

ISBN 978-0-6451422-9-7 (paperback)

Copyright © 2023 by Norman Porter

All rights reserved. No part of this book may be reproduced in any manner whatsoever without written permission except in the case of brief quotations embodied in critical articles and reviews.

First Printing, 2023

Cover Image: Celtic Knotwork Trivet by Sam Willcox

Contents

Preface   vii

PART ONE
TOWARDS RETHINKING UNIONISM

1   Northern Ireland: A "Unionist" View of the Way Ahead   3

2   Parity of Esteem and its Challenges to Unionism   23

3   Unionist Labour and Its Perplexities   42

PART TWO
ON RETHINKING UNIONISM

4   Why Unionism Needs Rethinking   68

5   A Civic Alternative   88

6   What's Wrong With Rethinking Unionism? A Reply   114

PART THREE
FURTHER THINKING ABOUT UNIONISM

7   Recalcitrant Unionism: Division, Unity and Febrile Spirits   137

| 8 | Unionist Degenerations and Beyond | 161 |
| 9 | Expanding the Unionist Imagination: Appropriating 1798 | 180 |

PART FOUR
THINKING MORE BROADLY

10	Politics: Blessing and Bane?	196
11	Reconsidering Reconciliation	224
12	Political Change in Northern Ireland	245

Afterword: Reconciliation and Its Unionist Critics   269
References   303

Preface

Most of the chapters in this book began life as oral presentations of one kind or another to a diverse range of audiences in Northern Ireland and (in one case) Australia. All of them, including the one that wasn't delivered as a talk or a lecture (Chapter three), were composed in Belfast during the years 1994-1998. These years were, in my view, the most promising in the history of Northern Ireland and stretched from the paramilitary ceasefires through to the signing of the Good Friday or Belfast Agreement and its ratification in referenda North and South. What has happened since is not my concern here, but I suspect it would be hard to show that the promise of the period 1994-98 has subsequently been matched, notwithstanding the short burst of light and surprising relief (2007-08) provided by the unlikely "Chuckle brothers" – the Democratic Unionist Party's Ian Paisley and Sinn Féin's Martin McGuinness, First Minister and Deputy First Minister of Northern Ireland respectively.

In spite of the disparate nature of its parts – diffuse presentations on several themes to various groups and pitched at different levels of complexity – a common thread runs through the book's chapters and gives at least a semblance of unity to the whole. Or so I hope. The common thread is, of course, the advocacy of political change of a certain kind as essential to the future prospects of Northern society. Two quick points are worth making now about the thread and my manner of handling it.

The first has to do with the practice of advocacy. I view it as part of the stuff of politics; in an ostensibly democratic society it's what citizens practice when they want to persuade other citizens that some course of action, or policy, or alteration of a controversial law, or whatever, would be good for their polity. And it's precisely as a citizen trying to convince fellow citizens that there are plausible, if not compelling, reasons for changing some of the ways in which we think and act in Northern Ireland that I understand what I'm principally up to in this book. I draw attention to this only because not everyone seems to agree that advocacy is integral to politics in societies such as ours. Apparently, what I call advocacy – which for me involves giving reasons for proposing this or opposing that – is a utopian, and possibly a dangerous, ploy to escape from obdurate facts of political life and to recommend the imposition of an unrealistic vision on a people whose interests it does not serve. I find this a very odd way of viewing political practice in general and what I'm doing in particular, and I have plenty to say against it especially in Chapter six and then again in the Afterword.

A second point is that, as a glance at the book's contents intimates, unionism is the main, albeit not the exclusive, focus of my advocacy. Attempting to persuade unionists that change may be a good thing rather than something to be feared and resisted is a necessary condition of political progress in Northern Ireland. Without unionist consent, it is unlikely that any change will be durable. But making unionists the target of my primary appeals has to do with another consideration besides. There is a deep-seated personal rationale involved; one that makes sense only against the backdrop of my family history. I'll restrict my explanation of the rationale and its historical entanglements to a bare minimum now because I have occasion to return to them at greater length later in the book (see Chapters one, ten and the Afterword especially).

Briefly, then, I'd left Belfast in late 1970 and though visiting it off and on over a period of years didn't return to live here again until July 1994 (a couple of weeks prior to the first IRA ceasefire). I didn't need to come back; to do so, in fact, was a wrench and a gamble – I resigned a tenured academic position at an Australian university (Flinders University) and I was responsible for uprooting my family (a wife and three children) at a cost I didn't foresee and continue to have serious regrets about (see the Afterword for a few details). Due in part to my activities and attitudes as a teenager, and in part also, to the legacy of my father's role as a leading Ulster Protestant during the 1950s and 60s, I felt implicated in the North's troubled experience. In returning to live here, I was driven to come to grips with my own heritage (Protestant and unionist) and also to understand the "other" side through meeting them, as far as possible, on their own terms – which became increasingly feasible as the paramilitary ceasefires created possibilities that would have been almost non-existent previously.

In the months following my reacquaintance with Belfast, I attended not only loyalist gatherings in the Shankill Road area, but also republican and nationalist occasions around the Falls Road in venues such as Conway Mill and Clonard Monastery. These experiences gave me a sense of local politics that was different from the sense typically found among most people from my background; it undoubtedly reinforced the desire to contribute to social and political life in Northern Ireland that had prompted my return in the first place. So, I wanted to contribute, which led to my joining the Ulster Unionist Party (UUP), but equally I wanted to understand, to make sense of myself, my family (especially my father), my history. In the process of becoming involved in the politics of the North, through party membership and through exposure to nationalists and republicans, I became convinced that unionism needed to be open to change, especially given the new spaces for exploration made available by the ceasefires. I started to advocate accordingly.

As should be evident, in doing so my motive wasn't to "do the dirty" on the UUP as some imagine, or to save unionists from their alleged stupidities as others speculate (see Chapter six).

It's appropriate now to explain the structure of the book and the character of its content. The book is divided into four parts, three of which are concentrated on unionism.

The first part (Chapters one to three) shows my groping towards the position I arrive at in *Rethinking Unionism*, although this isn't to say that its components lack integrity on their own terms. I certainly hope that they don't. The second part (Chapters four to six) is the centrepiece: it's focused on my book, *Rethinking Unionism. An Alternative Vision for Northern Ireland*, published in 1996, which attracted a modest amount of critical attention and confirmed my banishment to the outer reaches of the unionist fold. The third part (Chapters seven to nine) continues my engagement with unionism after its rethinking; two chapters underscore the depth of opposition within unionism to the type of rethinking I advocate, and a third probably tests the limits of unionist tolerance even further than my book does. A fourth part (Chapters ten to twelve) expands my focus beyond unionism by offering thoughts on religion and politics, reconciliation and initial issues with the Good Friday or Belfast Agreement. An Afterword provides some sweeping reflections on aspects of my experience in Northern Ireland and has as its focus, unionist rejections of my understanding of reconciliation which I fully articulated in a book, *The Elusive Quest*, published in 2003. I should add that I give more detailed introductions to each part and to the chapters contained within them, including remarks on the contexts in which they appear, as we proceed.

So much for structure, now for a quick word about the character of the chapters that follow. All but one originated as oral performances and for the most part I have tried to remain faithful to their initial mode of presentation – I have retained their sometimes quirky and casual style, and only reined it in when I judged that hyperbole was getting the better of me. And because I haven't tried to standardise the chapters into conventional academic form, there is an unevenness among them. Some are more tightly reasoned than others. That's fine by me since advocacy to be effective has to be tailored to suit different audiences. As should become clear, several audiences are addressed within the covers of this volume.

Finally, three further clarifications. I should signal (1) that an unavoidable element of repetition occurs as I attempt to communicate my major themes across audiences. I've tried to minimise its frequency and only hope that it doesn't grate too severely. I should also mention (2) that the bulk of book's content is being made public for the first time. It's true that occasional extracts from already published material make an appearance but it's only in three of the twelve chapters (two, eleven and twelve) that there is a manifest overlap between what is presented here and what is already extant. And the form in which these chapters are displayed in this volume reflects their original iteration. But if the gist of the book's content is already known, and if it's at times repetitive, it may be wondered (3) why I'm going to the bother of having it published. My justification is that by gathering together (and occasionally tweaking) previously unpublished writings I am, as it were, (and for my own reasons) settling accounts with Northern Ireland and therefore meeting an existential need; it is also simply because there is sufficient new material to warrant bothering about publication.

PART ONE

TOWARDS RETHINKING UNIONISM

The next three chapters indicate something of my struggle to make sense of unionism and, in one of them, a little of my involvement in its politics. They represent early pointers to my eventual attempt to rethink unionism. They also have their own rationales. Two of the chapters derive from my participation in Dublin-based events, respectively at Dublin Castle (Chapter one) and University College Dublin (UCD) (Chapter two). The other (Chapter three) derives from my experience of a particular facet of unionist politics in Northern Ireland. Each chapter was written during 1995, but not in the order in which they appear here. The second and third chapters follow chronologically, but I have decided to lead off with the chapter that was written last. I do so because in its two main parts it provides handy introductions to autobiographical details pertinent to explaining why I'm doing what I'm doing, and to the overall sweep of my understanding of politics in Northern Ireland.

I

Northern Ireland: A "Unionist" View of the Way Ahead

Upon returning from the 1995 British Labour Annual Conference at Brighton, I read a newspaper article written by a member of the Unionist Labour Group (ULG) executive committee (see Chapter three). In it he explained why no member of the UUP would ever attend the Irish government sponsored Forum for Peace and Reconciliation which was meeting weekly at Dublin Castle. I was unconvinced. My immediate response was to make a submission to the Forum which was accepted and led to my appearance (in a private capacity and not in my preferred role as a representative of the ULG) at Dublin Castle in October 1995.

It may be worth adding that I sent a copy of my submission to the new UUP leader David Trimble. I acknowledged that I was proposing to ignore the party's policy on non-attendance and gave reasons for doing so. I included a caveat indicating that if he found my case unpersuasive and advised against my attendance at the Forum, I would then withdraw my submission. He didn't reply. So, I went.

There are two parts to what follows below. The first is a text of the oral presentation I made to the Forum. The second is the paper I had submitted in advance of my appearance in Dublin.

Background and Obstacles

I should say from the outset how grateful I am to the Forum Committee for this opportunity to lay out some views on the political situation in Northern Ireland. I am delighted to be here. I should also emphasise from the start that, although a member of the Ulster Unionist Party, I appear before you in a purely personal capacity. But that, I imagine, is obvious.

Background

What may not be so obvious is who this person is who appears before you, and why he's here when so few other unionists have shown any inclination to come. Since I'm a total stranger to the vast majority of you, and since I'm representing nobody but myself, I'll try to satisfy any curiosity you may have about who I am and why I'm here through a few quick personal remarks. With any luck, these will provide a clearer picture of where I'm coming from and what manner of beast you're dealing with.

I was born into a staunchly Protestant and unionist family in East Belfast where I spent the first eighteen years of my life before emigrating to Australia with most of my family in 1970. My father was in certain respects the main influential figure in my life during my teenage years. He was an Orangeman, a Blackman and Apprentice Boy, but never a Freemason. He represented Clifton at

Stormont during the 1950s as an Independent Unionist. Prior to this, Ian Paisley and he set up the National Union of Protestants and from there he went on to become Director of the Evangelical Protestant Society. He was described by Michael Farrell, with probably only a touch of exaggeration, as being "active on the extreme fringes of Unionism". I inherited from him an intense identification with an ultra-Protestantism which I took to be synonymous with "true" unionism, but which in my case was not tempered by his evangelical faith. Prior to leaving for Australia, I was by any account an extreme loyalist and an explicit Protestant bigot.

The move to Australia changed my life and, most relevantly here, my attitudes to the politics of Northern Ireland. These attitudes were transformed quite early on, initially through the impact of exposure to a cultural and political way of life from which sectarianism had (by that stage) been more or less expunged. Australia quickly represented to me the chance of a fresh start; so much so that continuing in this new context to define my allegiances in ultra-protestant/unionist categories seemed more than faintly ridiculous. Northern Ireland and its quarrels appeared almost bizarre, and in every sense a world away. If that had been the end of the matter, of course, I wouldn't be living in Belfast now or appearing here today.

Northern Ireland and my interest in its affairs and attachment to its culture and politics weren't so easily disposed of, however. After my initial and almost embarrassingly swift rejection of them, they returned to puzzle and haunt me. Over a period beginning with a three-year spell as a postgraduate student in Oxford, England, from 1977-1980 and stretching through another spell in Australia from 1981 to mid-1994, I gradually acquired a sense of identity with Northern Ireland that is considerably subtler and more nuanced than the one I left behind in 1970. In particular, it is an identity that has no place at all for bigotry and sectarianism. It is also an identity that, as I now find, sits uneasily with some unionist senses of belonging, not least because it is one that happily accommodates a sense of Irishness. And I have to say that it was this growing identification with Northern Ireland, however vaguely perceived at times, that disrupted my life in Australia to the point where I decided to throw caution to the wind and return to Belfast with my family in order to come to terms with it. Shortly after my return the paramilitary ceasefires were declared, I joined the Ulster Unionist Party, became involved in the establishment of the Unionist Labour Group of which I'm Secretary, and through a twist of fortune find myself here today.

So why am I here today? There are two basic reasons. The first concerns a lesson I learned from my father: if you believe in a cause strongly enough and you don't think it's being adequately represented in public space, then, if you're serious, it's up to you to do something about it. Rightly or wrongly, it's my perception that the sort of unionist case I've tried to lay out in my submission isn't getting the press it should, that it isn't what most people most of the time suppose unionists to be saying, and so, given that I am serious about what I believe, I find that I've little option but to try to do something about it. And what better place to try than at the Forum for Peace and Reconciliation! Second, I'm here because I passionately believe that politics is a sham in the absence of dialogue. This is a point I want to return to shortly. But for the moment, let me put it like this: if I want others to hear my case I must also be willing to hear theirs; if I want to persuade others to take unionism seriously I must allow them to attempt to persuade me that I'm talking rot; if I lead with my chin then (if you'll pardon a blunt Belfast colloquialism) I must be prepared to receive "a dig in the gub" (metaphorically speaking, of course). So, I'm at the Forum because I believe in dialogue and because I think it's daft for unionist voices not to be part of a dialogue concerned with peace and reconciliation in Northern Ireland.

Synopsis of Submission

With these personal clarifications out of the way, I'd like to turn now to say a few words about my written submission. Its *central message* is quite simple: the best way ahead for all of us is to recognise that Northern Ireland has the potential to become the sort of society with which all its citizens may identify whether they consider themselves nationalists, unionists or neither. This potential may be realised by prioritising the quest for democratic and just institutions and practices, and by allowing non-sectarian, inclusive expressions of Irishness and Britishness to co-mingle to the benefit of us all.

Such a simple message is designed to have broad appeal and to gesture at a social and political vision to which everyone may be committed, even if it is true to say that a fair amount of *haggling* would inevitably be involved in working out its practical details. I've tried to give some intimation of the considerations and guidelines that I think should inform such haggling, but these aren't my major concern here. Indeed, I'm reticent to draw out any further the comments I've already offered about how an Irish dimension might be recognised within a context that respects the integrity of Northern Ireland. For even if we think that the Forum provides an admirable venue to tease out the details of such recognition, I'd have to say that I'm not the right person to be doing the teasing out.

There is another reason for not wishing to become too embroiled in difficulties attending the application of the main message of my submission: to do so would be premature, given that at this moment in time the big problem with my message lies with its reception. There are, it seems to me, serious *obstacles* standing in its path which have to be removed prior to quibbling over what it might mean in this or that instance. And it's to these obstacles I'd like to turn my attention. In doing so, I'll pick up on some of the points I raised in my submission but present them here with a slightly different gloss. In particular, I want to divide the obstacles into two different sets: those emanating from unionist sources and those from nationalist, and to concentrate on the former.

Nationalist Obstacles

With respect to nationalist obstacles to the reception of my message, I'll simply sum up the various points I covered in my submission in two propositions. First, various emotional attachments of nationalists prevent them from recognising the integrity of Northern Ireland and from identifying with it, but this obstacle may be surmounted by accommodating many of these attachments within an inclusive Northern Ireland that facilitates an Irish dimension. Second, there are also a set of nationalist beliefs which prevent my message being heard properly, but these are challengeable on intellectual grounds, along the lines I've already sketched, and on the grounds of political realism. These propositions are obviously controversial and warrant much more elaboration. No doubt aspects of them will be explored further during our discussion.

Unionist Obstacles

I'd like to deal in a little more detail with unionist obstacles. As you may glean from my submission, many unionists won't be particularly enamoured with my presentation of a unionist case. For example, I seem to be advocating dialogue with Ulster's so-called "enemies" without insisting on the satisfaction of a rigid set of preconditions. But, even worse, and more substantively, I am prepared to divest unionism of its Protestant connotations and to imply that majoritarianism isn't the only relevant consideration to bear in mind when deciding which organisational arrangements are best in a divided society like Northern Ireland. And, in addition, I don't simply dismiss nationalist sentiments as irrational and illiberal, as immature distractions to be transcended through a thorough embrace of membership of a pluralist British state.

There are, of course, in part, genuine political and intellectual differences between my version of unionism and other versions, just as there are between unionism and nationalism. And these have to be addressed as such, in the hope (however naïve) that they might be settled by the force of argument alone. But life is rarely that simple, and political life possibly never. For it just is the case that the waters are muddied here by fears, apprehensions, mistrust, anger, and bitterness; in other words, the presence of strong emotions in the politics of Northern Ireland makes it difficult for arguments to be treated on their merits, and for the most rational to win out. This doesn't mean that we simply despair of rationality and reasonableness, that we don't even bother to formulate good cases for our positions, but it does mean that more than fine words and clever arguments are required to assuage emotions like fear, anger and bitterness. And here is the rub: both governments and nationalists have to play an active role in helping to assuage such emotions because they present obstacles not only to my view of unionism, but even more so to the political aspirations of nationalists and to the governments' views as laid out in the Framework Documents. Or, put another way, if many unionists betray signs of a siege mentality or disposition, then certain sorts of deeds by nationalists in general, by Sinn Féin in particular, and also by the British and Irish governments are indispensable to their removal.

The deeds in question include not only action on decommissioning weapons, punishment beatings, the return of missing bodies, and the repeal of Articles 2 and 3 of the Irish Constitution. Sure, these are important, but equally important is the *context* within which words are uttered and deeds performed. And I'd suggest that in two crucial respects the current context within which much political talk and action occurs needs changing if unionism's renowned siege mentality is to be opened up. One is that much more explicit recognition has to be given by nationalists to the fact that unionists are the British presence in Northern Ireland, and that they have to be engaged as such. Confidence building measures, establishing trust, and overcoming fears are difficult enough tasks in a divided society without the added burden of the nationalist predilection to pressure the British, Irish and American governments to force unionism's hand. Unionists won't yet talk at all to Sinn Féin and will only talk on a limited agenda with the SDLP. Why? Partly because they are suspicious of the context within which the invitation to talk occurs. So, a move in the right direction would be to start changing this context by unambiguously recognising unionists as the British presence in Northern Ireland.

The present context of politics is also unhelpful in another respect which pertains especially to Sinn Féin: where words and deeds which point to a commitment to peace and nothing but the democratic process – and which are very welcome – remain too attached to a *culture of grievance*. Sure, the constituency Sinn Féin represents, and other constituencies too, received a raw deal under the old Stormont administration. But there is no monopoly of suffering and grievance, at least not now. More sharply, Irish republicans need to grasp that they have created victims, that they have visited suffering upon the people of Northern Ireland, that they have caused grievance. And one way in which they could demonstrate their responsibility for contributing to the mess that has been Northern Ireland for the last quarter of a century would be by admitting that they've done wrong; that, for instance, the Provisional IRA's key notion of a "legitimate target" was morally reprehensible. In this manner, the political context which, since the ceasefires, has facilitated little more than stalemate could be changed from another angle, and so hasten the facilitation of substantive political talks between all parties.

To conclude, then, there are various obstacles currently impeding political progress in Northern Ireland which require the urgent attention of us all. If we're serious about genuinely wanting a just and democratic society, then nationalists as well as unionists have to be more assiduous in their efforts to create the conditions which make it possible.

Northern Ireland: A "Unionist" View of the Way Ahead

The submission I'd like to make on the political situation in Northern Ireland divides into three categories which for convenience sake I'll describe as follows: distractions from politics; the focus of politics; and the aims of politics. Let me give a quick sketch of the principal entailments of each of these.

1. Distractions from Politics in Northern Ireland

- 1.1 To claim that there are distractions from politics, especially given that such distractions have the label "political" attached to them, prompts the question of what I take politics to be. Without engaging in prolonged definitional disputes, and without wishing to appear absurdly innocent of the corruptions to which political institutions and practices are always prone, I want to work with the following simple (democratic) understanding: *whatever else politics may be about, it's crucially about modes of interaction, organisation and decision-making in which dialogue among citizens and their representatives plays an indispensable role.* The spirit of this understanding traces back to the democratic experience of the ancient Athenians to which we in the contemporary West remain indebted, however much our experiences and circumstances differ from theirs, and received perhaps its most abiding articulation through the political philosophy of Aristotle. Arguably, Aristotle understood long ago what many in Britain and Ireland have in more recent times contrived to forget: dialogue matters to the quality of civic life, and its absence endangers the health of any polity.

- 1.2 A major distraction from politics currently appears in the preoccupation with the "political" issues of decommissioning paramilitary weapons, dismantling paramilitary organisations, ending punishment beatings and quibbling over the early release of paramilitary prisoners. To clarify, such issues are properly topics of political debate but, in a post-ceasefire situation, are improperly raised as obstacles to debate. This is not to say that it is unreasonable to expect immediate movement on the issues of weapons and beatings in particular; indeed, until such movement occurs there remains justifiable doubt about the democratic commitment of parties associated with paramilitary organisations, and about their grasp of elementary rules of justice. Nonetheless, it is to say that, however lamentable it may be, lack of movement shouldn't be allowed to paralyse the process of substantive political talks between parties, first, because lack of movement reflects a deep-seated mistrust which can't adequately be addressed independently of dialogue, and secondly, because paralysis exacerbates a loss of politics which adversely affects the whole of social and political life.
- 1.3 Another distraction from politics is inherent in the structures of direct rule and the Anglo-Irish Secretariat. These contribute to an acute "democratic deficit" in Northern Ireland which ought to concentrate political minds much more

firmly than it does. The peculiar structures of government here diminish the notion of political responsibility essential to democratic practice: they accord too much power to unaccountable bureaucrats, reduce local political parties to little more than "bit players", and undermine the functions typically associated with citizenship in a democratic polity.

- 1.4 A third distraction from politics is manifest in the advocacy of unrealistic options for the future of Northern Ireland. These options – which include those of a united Ireland, an independent Ulster, full integration with Britain and a return to a majority-rule Stormont – often appear in the form of impossible and unreasonable demands which create inflated expectations amongst their adherents and unnecessary fears amongst their opponents. It is precisely these interlocking phenomena of (exaggerated) hope and fear that tend to reduce politics to a zero-sum game and make substantive dialogical interactions between unionists and nationalists more difficult to imagine than they need be.

2. *The Focus of Politics in Northern Ireland*

- 2.1 Mention of this third distinction raises the question of what the proper focus of politics ought to be. An initial response is to say that political debate should have as its central focus enhancement of the quality of social and political life within Northern Ireland as it is currently constituted. The crucial phrase – *Northern Ireland as it is currently constituted* – requires immediate justification. It relies upon two basic premises: first, that any reasonable answer to the question of focus has to defer to democratic standards and thus cannot avoid conceding that the views of a majority of citizens cannot *legitimately* be overridden; and, secondly, given that a conspicuous majority in Northern Ireland expressly wish to remain part of the United Kingdom that wish must be respected. Accordingly, I claim that fruitful dialogue is distinguishable from idle political rhetoric in virtue of its refusal to pursue unrealisable dreams and its insistence on focusing on possibilities that occur within a context where the integrity of Northern Ireland is recognised.

- 2.2 The foregoing response to the issue of focus reiterates a common unionist line. But it remains seriously understated in several respects and in its present form is problematic. First, it occludes the different connotations unionists associate with a commitment to the integrity of Northern Ireland. Here it confronts the problem of there being more ways than one of describing a position as unionist. Secondly, it leaves utterly vague the meaning of the phrase *enhancing the quality of social and political life*. Here it confronts the problem of appearing vacuous. And, thirdly, it is silent about what space, if any, should be given to accommodating nationalist sentiments. Here it invites the understandable retort that all it offers is another curt denial of the validity of any nationalist stance and so is thoroughly unacceptable to a large number of Northern Ireland's citizens. I attempt to fill in the second and third of these gaps in my response and address the problems they suggest when dealing shortly with the aim of politics. It is to the first gap and the problem it presents that I'd now like to turn. I do so by identifying three sorts of unionist expression, and by explicitly endorsing only one of these.
- 2.3 To repeat, all three unionist expressions share what I'll now call claim (a): *that the integrity of Northern Ireland must be recognised out of deference to the democratic will of its people*. One unionist expression at least tacitly adds claim (b): *that the society's institutions and practices should reflect the cultural/religious*

affiliations of the majority. The other two unionist expressions reject claim (b) and agree instead on claim (c): *that a Northern Ireland worthy of the allegiance of all its citizens must not be shaped by exclusive cultural attachments.* A second unionist expression gives this claim a particular twist through a further claim (d): *that Northern Ireland should be viewed as an integral part of an inclusive, pluralist British state which respects equally the rights of every individual and tolerates cultural diversity.* A third unionist expression accepts the emphases on rights and diversity in claim (d), but objects that it doesn't take seriously enough the presence of a substantial nationalist minority within Northern Ireland. The assumption seems to be that the benefits of membership of a pluralist state should be sufficient to cure nationalists of their nationalism and turn them into good liberals – which is to say unionists. In rejecting this assumption, the third form of unionism substitutes claim (d) with claim (e):*in addition to guaranteeing individuals' rights and facilitating cultural diversity within the framework of the British state, a Northern Ireland worthy of everyone's allegiance must find space in its own institutional life for Irishness as well as Britishness.*

- 2.4 The third expression of unionism, which combines claims (a), (c) and (e), is the one I endorse. Put in other terms, it argues as follows. Northern Ireland shares much in common with Great Britain and, in virtue of their democratic mandate, unionists are entitled to insist that it remains within the United Kingdom. It also shares commonalities with the Irish Republic. But Northern Ireland is different from both and is in an important sense "a place apart". Its apartness is a constant source of friction not least because it is denied by those who like to suppose that it is as "British as Finchley" and by others who imagine that it is as "Irish as Cork". Both denials, though mirroring deeply held beliefs, are little more than first-class fictions which stultify genuine debate. Facing up to Northern Ireland's apartness does not imply an end to friction, but it does introduce the possibility of friction leading to creative outcomes rather than to perpetual stalemates. This possibility requires for its actualisation a devolution of significant powers to Northern Ireland which are shared among different political parties. In sum, an amplification of the initial claim that properly focused politics involves recognition of the integrity of Northern Ireland reveals that the Northern Ireland in question is one in which unionists, nationalists and others must have a meaningful stake. Fruitful dialogue about the future presupposes nothing less.

3. The Aims of Politics in Northern Ireland

- 3.1 Clarification of the question of focus has defined the kind of unionism I think has most to offer. It also has indicated the sort of space that unionism must be prepared to afford nationalism, even if more needs to be said about this. Before saying more, however, I want to consider what content can be given to the other claim I made in reference to the question of focus: that politics should be devoted to *enhancing the quality of social and political life in Northern Ireland*. I try to become clearer on this by laying out what I take to be the foremost aim of politics.
- 3.2 Generally stated, *the chief purpose of politics is to create, protect and sustain a way of life worth having*. Such a way of life is characterised, among other things, by certain sorts of political, legal, and socio-economic institutions and practices.
- 3.3 At a *political level*, a way of life worth having: (a) is comprised of institutions and practices with which citizens can identify and which command their allegiance; (b) is

maintained by an active citizenry whose words and deeds are integral to the institutions and practices that define the polity's way of life; (c) grants a particularly important role to political institutions by encouraging forms of political activity which are open to all citizens, by having on centre-stage public representatives who have real power to implement policies beneficial to society and who are subject to usual forms of democratic accountability, and by thus safeguarding a public space which is defined by inclusiveness and dialogue; (d) permits the proliferation in civil society of all institutions and practices that express the diversity of individuals, associations and groups – except those entailing a victimisation of others – and so guarantees toleration of difference.

- 3.4 At a *legal level*, a way of life worth having: (a) is constituted by legal and security institutions that are open to applicants of sufficient merit, whatever their background, are widely recognised as impartial, and therefore are acceptable to all sections of society; (b) institutionalises legislation guaranteeing protection of the rights of individuals and groups against discrimination, preferably through a Bill of Rights.
- 3.5 At a *socio-economic level*, a way of life worth having: (a) is distinguished by the presence of institutions geared to providing conditions conducive to the flourishing of all members of society, institutions not left to the mercy of market forces alone but reflecting acceptable principles of social justice; (b) is defined by structures suited to permit space and scope for the mix of individual/group/company/government initiatives and investments, especially in areas of acute deprivation, which are crucial to a thriving economy; (c) is characterised by the development of specific policies – in such areas as health, education, employment, social benefits, and so on – which are designed, first, to ensure that no persons or groups

are systematically discriminated against or forced, through unfortunate circumstances, to fall below acceptable standards of living, and, secondly, to provide for all persons fair access to and a share of society's resources and opportunities.

- 3.6 A way of life worth having shaped by the sorts of political, legal and socio-economic institutions and practices tersely outlined above captures, in broad terms, what I think we should be aiming to achieve through politics. And it gives some indication of how the quality of social and political life may be improved to the benefit of all Northern Ireland's citizens, unionist, nationalist and other.
- 3.7 The big issue arises of how nationalist concerns figure in such a putatively beneficial way of life for everyone. Nationalists are evidently being expected to acknowledge an image of Northern society – as "a place apart", for example – that is bound to rankle. Is this a remotely reasonable expectation? And, given nationalism's history of estrangement from much official public life in Northern Ireland, is it feasible to imagine a (seismic) shift here from alienation to identification which is reinforced through acceptable institutional arrangements? Three considerations may help by way of answers.
- 3.8 The first consideration expands upon the notion of Northern Ireland's "apartness" by suggesting that it implies the possibility of a successful, rather than a failed, political entity. Grasping this possibility involves (a) conceding that partition reflected different attachments of "heart and mind" which separated unionists and nationalists, and wasn't merely an arbitrary British imposition; (b) admitting that the legitimacy of partition can't be undermined by invoking either an abstract criterion of justice, since any such criterion is too abstract to admit of unambiguous application to the circumstances of Ireland in the first quarter of the twentieth

century, or a one-off election result in 1918, since its status isn't sufficiently privileged to trump subsequent election results and government agreements; (c) accepting that, despite official rhetoric, Westminster and Dublin perceive and treat Northern Ireland differently from other parts of Britain and Ireland; (d) acknowledging that under previous unionist rule Northern Ireland provided in significant ways a cultural, social and political environment uncongenial to nationalists; (e) acknowledging also that the way in which the Irish state developed, especially under Eamonn de Valera, made its cultural, social and political environment uncongenial to unionists; (f) recognising that Northern Ireland has undergone patterns of social and political development which have not only highlighted differences between unionists and nationalists, but also created a distinctive stock of common experiences, practices and interests which partly distinguish Northern Ireland's citizens from those in the rest of Britain and in the Republic of Ireland; (g) realising that in virtue of their unique history and circumstances, and given a determination not to repeat past mistakes, the people of Northern Ireland have an unrivalled opportunity to reshape their society (along the lines indicated in 3.3 – 3.6, for example), to exercise a control over their affairs that facilitates the emergence of a Northern Ireland to which everyone may be committed.

- 3.9 A second consideration takes up the theme of potential nationalist identification with Northern Ireland by submitting that it's appropriate for an Irish dimension to be granted some institutional expression. This is a tricky point which requires careful qualification: (a) its basic premise is that an Irish dimension must be accorded institutional recognition if nationalists are to be convinced that Northern Ireland is capable of becoming a polity with which they may identify;

(b) any recognition granted must be seen as an end in itself and not as a means to a further end (such as a united Ireland); (c) an Irish dimension deserving of institutional recognition must not be defined by sectarian features which serve to alienate unionists; (d) recognition must not be understood to amount to joint British-Irish sovereignty/authority over Northern Ireland, since this would contravene the democratic wishes of the majority.

- 3.10 A third consideration gestures at the kind of arrangements capable of accommodating institutional recognition of an Irish dimension. These include a type of power-sharing designed to curb potential unionist excesses, a symbolic expression of Irishness to complement symbolic expressions of Britishness, and various forms of North-South co-operation. To be acceptable, any such arrangements must be worked out against the backdrop of acceptance of Northern Ireland's integrity and difference, and the priority of establishing democratic and just institutions and practices. Accordingly, I suggest that deliberations here should proceed with the following guidelines in mind: (a) that attempts to facilitate an Irish dimension should serve the primary goal of creating, protecting and sustaining a democratic and just way of life in Northern Ireland (which, incidentally, is something not properly recognised in *Frameworks for the Future*, as evidenced by the paucity of references they contain confirming Northern Ireland's status within the United Kingdom, and by their readiness to countenance the implementation of undemocratic structures relieving citizens of control over their own affairs); (b) that a devolved assembly embodying principles of proportionality and weighted majorities, and eventually enjoying comparable powers to the old Stormont, should be viewed as a worthy goal which promises to nationalists (and others) a meaningful stake in political life; (c) that Irish and British symbols, shorn of their exclusive, sectarian connotations, should be permitted expression in an effort to underscore the uniqueness of Northern Ireland and to confirm that it is a society to which all of us may fully belong; (d) that, where appropriate in matters of mutual concern, interest, advantage and harmony, North-South bodies should be established, though only with circumscribed powers; (e) that East-West relationships should also continue to develop (since, beside their economic and political rationale, they help to break down British-Irish prejudices) with a proviso that some role be found within them for a Northern Ireland voice, at least on matters concerning its internal affairs.

4. Conclusions

- 4.1 The foregoing analysis has limited its attention to specific political factors which, in my view can't be ignored by any serious quest for a resolution of Northern Ireland's most acute problems. Although not expressly referred to, I hope that the thrust of my remarks touches upon important senses of the terms "peace" and "reconciliation". It certainly has been my intention to clarify political conditions crucial to a meaningful interpretation of these terms.
- 4.2 I'd like to conclude by underscoring the main theme I've been driving at and which I'll re-express as follows: what counts most in the search for durable peace and reconciliation in Northern Ireland is an unswerving commitment to build a just and democratic society capable of winning the allegiance of all citizens. It is in terms of this commitment that the interests and recommendations of the British and Irish governments should be judged, as should those notions of

unionism and nationalism which effectively make democracy and justice optional extras. To be committed to creating, protecting and sustaining a social and political way of life worth having in Northern Ireland adds an urgency to our efforts to overcome the sort of distractions from, or impediments to, meaningful politics I've already alluded to (see 1.2-1.4). And this faces both governments, all parties and all citizens with responsibilities that are too serious to dodge.

2

Parity of Esteem and its Challenges to Unionism

This chapter is based on a seminar paper delivered to staff and postgraduate students of the Politics Department at University College Dublin in February 1995. The original paper ranged more widely than the version I have provided here. But it had too many loose ends and half-developed ideas and, for the sake of intelligibility, warranted pruning. Many of the omitted ideas, and others besides, were articulated more fully subsequently. So, what's on offer below is an initial attempt to think about the concept of parity of esteem in the context of Northern Irish politics. A more comprehensive treatment of the concept in this context is developed in my book, "Rethinking Unionism" (1996), which incorporates much of the following material, and in another, "The Elusive Quest" (2003). I also offer a few critical comments on its applicability to Northern politics in Chapter five of this volume.

Introduction

The issue of parity of esteem in Northern Ireland is multifaceted and controversial. It is *multifaceted* because it is invoked as something like a guiding principle in many different areas of social and political life. It is cited, for example, in fair employment and equal opportunity legislation, resource allocation policies, youth employment and training schemes, and urban development plans. It is also called upon in demands to disband or reform the Royal Ulster Constabulary. A concept of parity of esteem underpins school programmes designed to promote Education for Mutual Understanding, as well as being pivotal to the push for more religiously integrated schools. Such a concept lies behind the decision by Queen's University Belfast (QUB) to stop playing "God Save the Queen" at graduation ceremonies. It is further at play in talk of cross-border institutions, in conceptions of possible power-sharing arrangements in an anticipated new Assembly at Stormont and, more generally, in suggestions that it is no longer acceptable to privilege the symbols of only one tradition in the North in the institutions of state.

The issue of parity of esteem is also *controversial*. It is heralded by the British and Irish governments; its virtues are extolled by ecumenical and reconciliation groups within the churches, as well as by the government-sponsored Community Relations Council and its offshoot, the Cultural Traditions Group. The concept of parity of esteem receives generally favourable press in local magazines such as *Fortnight* and *Causeway*. In addition, it is mentioned enthusiastically not only by the Alliance Party but also by the Social Democratic and Labour Party (SDLP) and by Sinn Féin. It is, however, treated with suspicion within unionist circles: ranging perhaps from mild suspicion within the loyalist Ulster Democratic Party (UDP) and Progressive Unionist Party (PUP) to extreme suspicion within the Democratic Unionist Party (DUP), with the Ulster Unionist Party

(UUP) registering mid-to-strong suspicion. It is not that unionists typically say that the idea of "parity of esteem" is in itself a bad thing – though many probably think it is – but more that it is used as a cloak to disguise any amount of anti-unionist, pan-nationalist mischief.

Such a situation is very suggestive. The way in which I have put matters makes it seem that there is general agreement among everyone except unionists on the indispensability of a concept of parity of esteem to a series of "progressive" social and political reforms. That may be true on specific concerns – the fuss that has accompanied QUB's decision to drop the British national anthem from graduation ceremonies, for example, has been created exclusively by unionists – but it is misleading to think that it is true on everything. At an obvious level, for instance, it is too much to imagine that those who explicitly endorse the concept agree on what they mean by it: what the British government believes "parity of esteem" consists in, say, is unlikely to correspond to what Sinn Féin believes. At another level, once the multifaceted uses of the concept of parity of esteem are seriously reckoned with a simple "unionist versus the rest" scenario appears patently absurd. These uses intimate that more is at stake than finding a fair balance between Catholic and Protestant or nationalist and unionist interests. Thus, it is reasonable to assume that whatever else the term may mean, lack of esteem or respect helped to justify discrimination in the past and that a call for parity is intended to prevent a repeat of past wrongs by insisting that people should be respected equally whatever their background. Accordingly, alongside attempts to do justice to Catholics now – and, some might say, to do justice to Protestants in the not-too-distant future – we might expect similar attempts to do justice to women, the unemployed, the working class, the disabled, and so forth. In short, the concept of parity of esteem in principle applies to any number of social groups and issues. And, precisely because it does, much more is involved in its employment than trying to overcome the problem of overt or residual sectarianism. That is why it's stretching credibility too far to suppose that on gender issues, for example, all unionists are the "bad guys" and all nationalists the "good guys".

Even so, it is unionists who are typically wincing when asked to embrace the language of parity of esteem. It is they who are most conspicuously squirming in discomfort when confronted by the adoption of this language in the official discourse of British, Irish, European and American governments and international agencies. This is probably because the development of an inclusive society at which such language gestures requires a seismic shift in attitude among unionists many of whom, in truth, may be more inclined to treat their traditional protagonists with contempt rather than esteem. Without denying that the same could be said of many nationalists' attitudes to unionists, it is with the latter that parity of esteem's challenges seem most acute and it's upon these that I wish to focus here. There is an obvious explanation why this is so: the very fact that the concept of parity of esteem has entered the vocabulary of political debate in Northern Ireland is at once an indictment of previous unionist bad practices. For, despite the extensive, almost profligate, use of the concept hinted at above, its present invocation centrally suggests that a lack of even-handedness has characterised the North's social and political life, that those from minority traditions or social groups have been treated shabbily in a unionist-dominated Northern Ireland and that rectification now has to be made to ensure that formerly discriminated against individuals, groups and traditions are accorded the respect or esteem they deserve. At the very least, a typical resort to the concept carries the inference that under the old Stormont regime Northern Ireland represented a social, political and cultural environment uncongenial to nationalists; and that however much its worst excesses have been remedied under direct rule from Westminster there is yet more work to be done.

Challenges: Individual, Cultural, and Political

The concept of parity of esteem, then, provides a focal point for expressing inescapable challenges to many unionists' view of Northern Ireland. But exactly what do these challenges amount to? I think they amount to three things.

Individual

In one case, we have what may be referred to as a demand for *parity of esteem for individuals* where the challenge is to end discriminatory practices against particular members of society. Here we're dealing with the sense in which the concept of parity of esteem translates most uncontroversially into the language of rights. Each individual regardless of his or her race, religion, culture or gender has a right to be treated with a respect equal to that due to every other individual. An application of this sense appears in fair employment and equal opportunity legislation recently implemented in Northern Ireland. It also lies behind the request supported by most local political parties for the introduction of a Bill of Rights. There are, however, two rather more controversial extensions of this "individual rights-based" construal of parity of esteem. First, there is the call for affirmative action in favour of those belonging to groups which were systematically disadvantaged by earlier bad practices - say, Catholics and women. The beneficiaries of such action, it should be noted, are individuals who are deemed worthy of special treatment in virtue of their membership of a disadvantaged group, whether or not such membership figures in their own self-definitions. Second, there is the idea that doing justice to individuals or respecting their rights requires the state taking interventionist action in the marketplace to correct injustices done to certain individuals through no fault of their own. This derivation of redistributive policies from a respect of individual rights is an idea that is prominent in much contemporary liberal political theory. These controversial extensions of a rights-based notion of parity of esteem may complicate the challenge to leave behind discriminatory practices, but its overriding concern remains unaltered: to secure the rights of individuals *qua* individuals.

Cultural

In another case, the emphasis shifts from individuals to cultural groups, traditions and social movements. Here the guiding motivation is to curb the real or potential all-pervasive power of the dominant culture from which various minorities feel excluded. And this motivation energises a conception of "*cultural parity of esteem*" which insists on adequate scope being given to the expression of minority voices. The challenge, then, is to create sufficient spaces in civil society for a plurality of cultural forms to flourish, for their adherents to articulate their own thoughts and to pursue their own ways of life. Or at least that is the general challenge. But given the peculiar circumstances of Northern Ireland, a concern with cultural parity of esteem presents a particular challenge too: being prepared to encourage understanding of, and accord equal respect to, the two main traditions in the North, whether we describe these as unionist and nationalist or as Protestant and Catholic. Such a challenge is responded to in school programmes in Northern Ireland designed to promote Education for Mutual Understanding. Facing up to its implications is integral to the rationale of the government-sponsored Community Relations Council and Cultural Traditions

Group, and to the activities of various church-based ecumenical and reconciliation groups.

Not surprisingly, the challenge to accord parity of esteem to Northern Ireland's two major traditions admits of controversial interpretations. Take, for example, a situation that may obtain when the notion of cultural parity of esteem is depicted in the language of rights: just as individuals have a right to equal respect so too have cultural groups and traditions. Now given such a depiction, when a tradition, or more exactly a group claiming to represent a tradition, chooses to exercise its right to cultural expression, it is simultaneously demanding that others respect that right. But it may happen that that demand is not acceded to because the cultural expression in question is perceived as offensive by those from another tradition, especially when it is imposed in a manner they cannot avoid encountering. In such a situation it is possible for both contending parties to invoke a concept of parity of esteem in defence of their respective positions, and to call upon conflicting claims to rights. On one side, the argument might be that cultural parity of esteem means tolerating traditional expressions different from one's own, and that all citizens have a general duty to respect others' right to such expressions. On the other side, the counter might come that cultural parity of esteem does not involve riding roughshod over the traditional attachments of a minority by asserting a dominant cultural form in areas where it is not welcome, and that minorities have a right not to have their lives interfered with in ways they find deeply offensive. Controversies over the routing of Orange Order marches bring into play both sets of arguments and provide a poignant illustration of difficulties involved in confronting the challenge posed by an idea of cultural parity of esteem. For my purposes here, though, the relevant question is whether unionism is prepared to concede that those arguments developed by its political opponents have any credibility whatever.

Confronted by the apparently intractable nature of the conflict between rival traditions, there is a temptation to give the idea of cultural parity of esteem a "neutral" twist, at least whenever possible. Seemingly, such a temptation proved overwhelmingly attractive to the Queen's University Senate when it decided in 1994 to stop playing the British national anthem at graduation ceremonies. In the interests of parity of esteem, it was considered prudent to cease privileging symbols of the majority tradition. The subsequent furore this decision provoked among unionists indicates that ostensibly neutral responses to cultural parity of esteem's challenge are not guaranteed a smoother reception than others. But the mere fact that a university institution was willing to meet the challenge in a fashion destined to arouse unionist ire is very revealing. It shows the discomfort unionists experience when faced with interpretations of parity of esteem that call into question their preconceptions. Beyond that it also reinforces a general point I shortly want to expand upon: cardinal assumptions of unionism are being disturbed not just by some "pan-nationalist front", but by broader forces and movements within Northern Irish society. The challenge to unionism's adaptability and credibility runs deep and wide.

Political

Unionism's difficulties are compounded by challenges engendered by a third sense of the concept of parity of esteem which is appropriately dubbed *"political"*. This sense is intimated in a recommendation of the Opsahl Commission's Report which conceived of parity of esteem "between the two communities" entailing "legal recognition of Irish nationalism" without denying the "Britishness" of unionists. Given acceptance of such a conception, the Report envisaged achieving what it termed "absolute parity of esteem" in the government of Northern Ireland where, as a matter of principle, "each community has an equal voice in making and executing the laws or a veto on their execution, and equally shares administrative authority" (Pollock, 1983: 112). At a minimum, such "absolute parity of esteem" anticipates power-sharing arrangements within Northern Ireland to which significant legislative and executive capacities are devolved. But as the recommendation of a "legal recognition of Irish nationalism" infers much more is anticipated besides. Here there may be a foreshadowing of the conviction lying behind the anthem decision of QUB – that it is inappropriate in a divided society to privilege the symbols of one tradition. Accepting such a conviction as basically sound does not, of course, imply a commitment to the kind of neutral alternative pursued by Queen's. Recognising the validity of both nationalism and unionism suggests, rather, the presence of public institutions reflecting the Irishness and the Britishness of Northern Ireland, an extension of North-South ties, and perhaps some sort of role in Northern Irish affairs for Dublin as well as for Westminster. These are suggestions already favoured by the Irish government, tacitly supported by the British, and echoed through the desires of many Northern nationalists. But again, it is worth remarking that they are suggestions for the future of Northern Ireland which are attractive not only to nationalists. Support for them also comes from an independent body such as the Opsahl Commission as a result of its canvassing of citizens' opinions within Northern Ireland.

A Non-Nationalist Challenge

Each of the foregoing suggestions, especially those prompted by a political rendering of the concept of parity of esteem, constitute separate challenges to unionists. But each in its own way also contributes to the overall challenge such a rendering forces upon unionist attention: to imagine a political future in Northern Ireland where matters of power and public identity are wrested from exclusively unionist control and expression and shared with nationalists and others. This is a challenge issued not just by external forces or nationalist "fifth columnists", but by actors within Northern Ireland who are not working from a nationalist script.

It is, however, relatively easy for unionists to caricature or to turn a blind eye to a non-nationalist challenge precisely because it neither makes much of an impression on unionism's electoral fortunes nor receives powerful external support. Indeed, with so much inter-governmental and international attention being devoted to mediating between the "two traditions" and to reconciling the "two communities", there is a (perhaps unwitting) tendency to marginalise even further those whose agendas are neither strictly unionist nor nationalist. Accordingly, the danger is that the significance of the above instances of non-nationalist concern about parity of esteem will simply be trivialised.

This danger is hard to avert if it is assumed that all that counts politically is conducted at formal levels of government, state institutions and political parties. It is in terms of such an assumption that many unionists think they can ignore criticisms from non-nationalist sources. But the assumption is questionable, and a non-nationalist challenge may prove more formidable than is initially supposed.

At first glance it seems odd to regard as formidable a challenge that is barely perceptible to many unionists. Its oddness diminishes, however, once we recognise that its real sting lies not so much in a direct confrontation of unionist sensitivities – as, say, in the Queen's University example - but in its indirect whittling away of unionist influence in various areas of civil society. As I have suggested, moves to end practices of discrimination and domination, to create spaces for cultural plurality, and to initiate in the manner of the Opsahl Commission new forums for discussion of Northern Ireland's future raise important issues connected to the concept of parity of esteem. But that does not exhaust their significance. In addition, such moves reveal the emergence of forms of action and debate that transcend the confines of typical unionist forms. They attest to the growing importance of what may be termed "a politics of civil society" which is separate from those formal levels of politics with which unionism is used to dealing. It is because unionism is not accustomed to engaging seriously in a politics of civil society – as evidenced, for instance, in its begrudging attitude and paltry contributions to the Opsahl Commission – that it may be oblivious of the real strength of the non-nationalist challenge and thus ill-equipped to meet it. And the essence of this challenge consists in the unsettling possibility that the character of Northern Irish society is increasingly being shaped independently of unionism; that various matters of social and political import within Northern Ireland are being pursued without regard to unionist opinion.

It could be objected that I am making something out of nothing here, since unionists can afford to be perfectly relaxed about a developing politics of civil society. That is to say, to the extent that unionists genuinely believe that Northern Ireland should be a fully pluralistic society, then it is entirely acceptable to them that various modes of social, cultural and political expression flourish independently of their control. More forcefully, it could be said that there is something insidious about attempts to keep too strict a check on the activities of civil society as the awful instances of political authoritarianism in the twentieth century amply demonstrate. Such an objection has a point if it is assumed that the alternative to a civil society independent of unionist influence is a civil society under unionist control. But this is not the only alternative, and it is not the one I have in mind. In spite of its apparent plausibility the objection falters on two counts, the second of which I think is decisive.

First, it is doubtful whether all unionists are so generously disposed to full-blooded pluralism as the objection supposes. Unionist practice during its years in power at Stormont gives us reason to doubt, as does the current practice of the DUP especially. At least for those unionists whose vision of Northern Ireland includes that of a society bearing the religious and cultural stamp of Protestantism, the non-nationalist challenge issued through a politics of civil society remains a powerful threat.

Second, the sanguine attitude the objection implies to the prospect of a politics of civil society being conducted beyond the reach of unionism betrays a cavalier approach to unionism's ongoing viability and a limited conception of politics. It is cavalier to suppose, for example, that unionism can thrive without loss even as it is marginalised from a raft of social and cultural issues that are being debated and acted upon within civil society. Being reduced to the role of spectator as socio-cultural dramas are played out before its eyes hardly constitutes evidence of unionism's vibrancy. It suggests, rather, a tacit admission that various concerns of social life are beyond unionism's ken. And this sort of admission arguably hastens the arrival of unionism's sell-by date. At work here is also a very restrictive notion of unionist politics which pares down unionism to a single-issue, constitutional creed. The idea that such a minimalist creed equips unionism to tackle the range of social and political responsibilities required of a political movement, party or government is, of course, absurd. But so long as a notion of political minimalism is fostered, it means that when unionism is forced to handle wider sorts of responsibilities, as it always has been, it can only do so either in an *ad hoc* way or in a way that is overdetermined by its constitutional priorities. To declare, even if only implicitly, the politics of civil society out of bounds is to suffer from myopic vision or perhaps a failure of nerve. And it is a declaration which derives small comfort from an invocation of pluralism once we eschew the simplistic distinction of "total autonomy" and "total control" regarding the life of civil society. To advocate that unionism participate in the affairs of civil society is not to urge that it endeavour to control those affairs; it is, rather, simply to say that in the absence of serious participation unionism consents to its own undermining and has few grounds for complaint if it is viewed by non-nationalists as a creed aspiring to obsolescence.

To summarise, the non-nationalist challenge of parity of esteem to unionism transmitted indirectly through a politics of civil society has a significance that far exceeds the electoral strength of non-nationalist political parties. Its general thrust is to query whether unionism has anything to offer to the resolution of the manifold social, cultural and political problems increasingly surfacing in the arena of civil society. If taken seriously, this general formulation issues a formidable challenge on two fronts: by casting doubt on the long-term possibilities of a unionism that avoids meaningful engagement with large tracts of social life in Northern Ireland; and by raising searching questions about the range and depth of unionist politics, including its guiding principles and strategies for non-constitutional political activity and its understanding of the relationship between a politics of the state and a politics of civil society. To allow such doubt to linger and to carry on as though these questions do not need answering is tantamount to confessing that unionism's political imagination is severely withered. It is also to add an element of credence to the ironical prospect of a Northern Ireland whose integrity may, as unionists wish, be respected, but whose character bears less and less resemblance to typical unionist images.

The Challenge of Accommodating Nationalism

If the challenge of parity of esteem's appearance through a politics of civil society isn't obvious to many unionists, the same can't be said of the challenge issued through its appearance in a demand for nationalist recognition in the cultural and public life of Northern Ireland. Here we encounter explicit unionist resistance to parity of esteem's extension into facilitating representation of an Irish nationalist identity in Northern institutions of state. A British identity alone warrants such representation, we are told, since anything more risks compromising Northern Ireland's constitutional status as a member of the United Kingdom. What lies behind such stiff, unrelenting reasoning which effectively mandates nationalist acquiescence to the unionist status quo? There are at least two sorts of answer: those reflecting unionism's familiar siege mentality, and those emanating from the conceptual framework of a particular type of liberal unionist thought. Let me briefly comment on both.

Siege mentality reasons account for much of unionism's suspicion of parity of esteem. By the term "siege mentality" I refer to a disposition shared to varying degrees among unionists of most persuasions. The disposition has deep historical roots in Protestantism's minority status within the island of Ireland as a whole. It is currently sustained by uncertainty over the constitutional future of Northern Ireland; an uncertainty that is fuelled by at least the following five factors: (i) suspicion of the political culture of the Irish Republic and of the Republic's intentions towards the North, not least given its claim to the territory of Northern Ireland and the fact that this claim has the status of a constitutional imperative; (ii) accelerating distrust of the British government's reliability which at times – such as that of the signing of the Anglo-Irish Agreement and, more recently, of the publication of *Frameworks for the Future* – spills over to accusations of betrayal by Westminster; (iii) unease at the growing confidence of Northern nationalists which is heightened by the unsettling realisation that unionists have been politically outmanoeuvred by nationalists for quite some time and by fear of their new bogey man – "the pan-nationalist front"; (iv) resentment at lack of international sympathy for the unionist case and at international levels, principally United States, interference in the affairs of Northern Ireland; and (v) despair of the cumulative effect of the other factors – for example, despair that, under strong United States pressure, the British and Irish governments are intent on pandering to the aspirations of Northern nationalists, placating republican terrorists, and generally putting the squeeze on unionists.

Given the prevalence of factors such as these in the perceptions of many unionists, it is scarcely exaggerating to say that unionism's siege mentality is alive and well. Unionists feel angry, hurt, disillusioned and deeply distrustful. Their destiny, despite repeated assurances about the principle of majority consent still being a trump card, seems no longer under their control. Yet again, many conclude, it is time to dig in, draw on their legendary powers of resilience and hold the line whatever the odds against them.

Against this backdrop it's not difficult to grasp why only a negative response greets requests for institutional recognition of a nationalist identity within Northern Ireland. Let me pick out three typical forms in which such a negative response appears. It appears in the claim that concessions to nationalist/Catholic grievances have gone far enough; in the affirmation that majority rule is the basic principle of democratic government, and that the political identity of the majority is solely entitled to expression in state institutions; and in the retort that the request adds insult to injury, since it is the unionist identity that is under threat and merits protection.

Now the first two of these forms may appear compatible with liberal democratic tenets. The principle of majority rule is as important to liberal democratic thinking as it is to unionist, and the notion that nationalists have received their due share of concessions could be construed in mainstream liberal democratic terms to mean that they deserve equal civil rights – which by and large they have now been given – but to no more than that. It may be the case that appeal to liberal values is a feature of some unionist thinking, as I'll consider in a moment, but there is room to doubt that liberal attachments run deep among those unionists whose siege mentality is a constitutive feature of their identity. One has to ask why concessions of equal civil rights to nationalists took so long to arrive, why British government pressure and legislation were necessary to secure them, and why they have been so grudgingly acknowledged by a large number of unionists. One wonders also about the strength of commitment to majority rule in the event of unionists becoming a minority within Northern Ireland. Padraig O'Malley, in his *The Uncivil Wars*, found even the seemingly moderate UUP leader James Molyneaux more than a little shifty of this issue (O'Malley, 1983). In view of such doubts, I think that the third form of negative response is the decisive one for siege mentality unionists; that it provides the backdrop against which the other two should be read. In other words, what matters most here is the maintenance of a unionist identity. Where this identity is vulnerable, as it is now, for its bearers to be exhorted to accord parity of esteem to a nationalist identity is almost the last straw. It is to ask too much because it appears, in the final analysis, existentially impossible for siege mentality unionists to agree to it. Or so we are effectively informed.

Is there a different story to tell with regard to unionists of a more overtly *liberal* persuasion? Yes and no. The answer is "no" in the sense that they too are opposed to granting political parity of esteem and sometimes for reasons similar to those I've been highlighting. Here it's apposite to note that a siege mentality is also discernible among those unionists who're inclined to wear their liberalism on their sleeve, so to speak. Take, for instance, remarks made during the last decade by the self-acclaimed champion of liberal unionism, Robert McCartney. In the 1980s he wrote of the "threat" to the Northern Ireland unionist not only from "within by the activities and violence of republican terrorists" but also from without by "a sectarian Republic which in its claim to his territory legitimises the internal violence and to which the minority look for support" (McCartney, 1985). Recent events have done nothing to soften McCartney's line. Even in the wake of the paramilitaries' ceasefires the language of threat and fear is still to the fore: the prospect of Irish unity threatens "government by an authoritarian theocratic and non-pluralist state", and unionists continue to "fear that their British identity and way of life will be subsumed in nationalist triumphalism" (McCartney, 1995a). The publication of *Frameworks for the Future* only heightens the siege aspect of his analysis, since the threat to unionism, already evident in the Anglo-Irish Agreement of 1985, is also underwritten and now made more acute by the British government and its "Fifth Column" (McCartney, 1995b). And so on.

In another sense, however, there is a difference between unionists for whom the category of siege is fundamental in their opposition to political parity of esteem and those others who, despite their attraction to the category, wish to present their opposition primarily in liberal terms. Sticking with McCartney, the liberal objection to parity of esteem for a nationalist identity apparently is that we're dealing merely with "Humespeak" for recognition of the legitimacy of the aspiration for a united Ireland. And, as such, speaking of parity of esteem here is muddled since it's asking not for something given to people, as is the case with genuine rights, but for something (inappropriately) given to an aspiration "which is contrary to the will of the democratic majority" in Northern Ireland (McCartney, 1995a). Its utterances betray, therefore, an intolerable objective running afoul of liberal democratic principles. Moreover, attempts to implement parity of esteem between the North's different identities, such as at QUB, are not examples of liberal neutrality at work but of official capitulation to nationalist propaganda. In sum, the request to institutionalise the legitimacy of a nationalist identity in the name of parity of esteem is impossible to meet: it violates basic liberal democratic standards the flaunting of which creates only confusion and mischief, as McCartney believes the recent decision by QUB amply demonstrates. And such confusion and mischief serve only to enhance unionism's siege mentality even among liberals.

Thus, we get the flavour of a liberal unionist line and glimpse how it eventually dovetails with unionism's disposition to a siege mentality. In both cases much is made of the notion of majoritarianism as if its invocation clinches the argument against political parity of esteem. What's missing is proper awareness of the pitfalls of relying too heavily on this notion, as anyone familiar with the great liberal thinker JS Mill's warning against a possible "tyranny of the majority" should realise (Mill, 1910), especially in the context of a deeply divided society. Although I don't have time to press the point fully, it seems to me that the unionist appeal to liberal democratic principles here is more than a little strained. Liberal unionist reasoning scarcely takes us beyond the anxieties of a siege mentality. In fairness, there are other arguments at liberal unionists' disposal, including McCartney's "creative" appropriation of Isaiah Berlin's distinction between "positive" and "negative" liberty (Berlin, 1969: 118-172) when trying to underline a rudimentary difference between unionism and nationalism that he thinks tells against political parity of esteem (McCartney 1988). Also worth a mention is Arthur Aughey's analysis of the different conceptions of citizenship and the state purportedly separating the Republic of Ireland and the United Kingdom, and allegedly counting against the case for cultural and political parity of esteem in Northern Ireland (Aughey, 1989).

Once more, unfortunately, a thorough evaluation of these additional liberal unionist reasons for rejecting a full accommodation of a nationalist identity in Northern Ireland will have to wait. But they are, I think, deeply unconvincing not least because the conceptual frameworks they rely upon are extremely restrictive and the Northern Ireland their unionism celebrates is worryingly inhospitable to non-unionists. And it's this latter point especially that unionists of all types so emphatically fail to grasp. Which is why a rather haunting hollowness characterises their attempts to resist the challenges posed by talk of parity of esteem. This is especially disappointing in the case of liberal unionists who appear curiously oblivious to the disquieting observation that their much-vaunted appeal to rational, liberal principles helps in practice to bolster unionism's more atavistic tendencies. Parity of esteem in all of its dimensions challenges unionism and sometimes severely. Thus far there is little encouragement to be found in unionism's responses.

3

Unionist Labour and Its Perplexities

Not long after re-settling in Belfast in July 1994, and shortly following the paramilitary ceasefires, I joined the Ulster Unionist Party (UUP). I did so in part because I read in a local paper of moves to set up within the party a labour interest group. I supposed that those attracted to such a group would not only be opposed to Thatcherite economics, but also be inclined to explore creative political initiatives in an environment where guns were mostly silent. I imagined that I'd find a measure of solidarity and common purpose in resisting unionism's customary conservative impulses and pressing for more progressive alternatives. I was, of course, supremely naïve.

Within a short space of time, I found myself on the committee of the Unionist Labour Group (ULG) in the role of Secretary. Full membership of the ULG was available to UUP members and associate membership was offered to other unionists. An official launch of the ULG in the Stormont Hotel gave promise of meaningful political engagement, as did occasional meetings with other left-oriented parties and representation at the British

Labour Party Annual Conference. But the early promise faded quickly, and little was heard of the ULG after 1996.

Below I offer some reflections on the ULG's prospects and difficulties which were written before its descent into oblivion was confirmed. That such a descent was its fate is hardly surprising in the light of these reflections, even if I hoped it might be otherwise. But, to state the obvious, trying to advance labour interests within the framework of the UUP was always going to be a strange, quite probably a foolhardy, venture. And yet, for a brief period in 1994-95, it seemed a venture worth pursuing; or so a handful of UUP members thought. It's hard to know why we did not least because as my reflections indicate little serious attempt was made to tackle issues that may have made a difference.

I should point out that in the analysis below I use the terms "social democratic", "socialist", "labour" and "leftist" interchangeably. In doing so, I am wilfully committing analytical inexactitudes for the sake of underscoring the important point that a unionist who identified with any of these political labels was welcome in the ULG. One merit of the ULG's Executive Committee was that it showed no appetite for indulging in the sort of doctrinal disputes that are sometimes the bane of left of centre political parties and groups.

Introduction

I begin by summarising the rationale of the ULG and then reflect on some perplexities it generated. As becomes evident, the sheer obduracy of these perplexities diminished any prospect that the Group would accomplish much of value. For the rationale, I reproduce a slightly modified article I wrote to announce the ULG's formation for the *Sunday World* (18 June 1995). For the perplexities, I draw on early musings and doubts I had written about the Group which I shared with some members of the executive committee. Throughout I suggest ways of responding to these perplexities in a spirit of optimism which, in retrospect I now see, nonetheless lacked any overriding confidence of their acceptance.

Rationale

The Ulster Unionist Party has been attracting members with a labour orientation to politics for most of the twentieth century. The voice of these members has not been consistently heard. It was particularly strong during the second decade of the century when it was influential in explaining the unionist perspective from a working-class perspective. A labour voice has been audible only intermittently within unionism since then. Loud echoes of its presence were evident during the 1960s, for example, but became fainter during the 70s and 80s due to prevailing constitutional uncertainty and ongoing violence. Much uncertainty still exists, of course, and undercurrents of violence continue to ripple through the social and political life of Northern Ireland. Several members of the UUP think, nonetheless, that a unionist labour voice has been silent for too long and that its silence is detrimental to the search for a stable, just and peaceful society. Accordingly, permission was sought from, and unanimously given by, the Officers of the Ulster Unionist Council for the formation of the Unionist Labour Group.

The Group believes that the Union of Great Britain and Northern Ireland continues to offer positive benefits to all citizens irrespective of their colour, class, religion, political affiliation, gender, or disability; that citizens' civil liberties are guaranteed by the British state. It also believes that all persons should be treated with equal respect and have access to those conditions necessary for following a plan of life of their choice. The ULG is convinced that these beliefs are compatible with, and in cases best expressed through, the pursuit of labour interests in Northern Ireland and throughout the

United Kingdom (UK). It recognises in addition the necessity of developing an international, and especially a European, profile. Thus, it seeks to co-operate with other labour groups, trades unions and related social democratic organisations for the purpose of advancing labour policies in parliament, an assembly and local councils.

These are policies which aim to achieve such objectives as a free and comprehensive health service; a right to work at a minimum standard wage; a guaranteed pensions and benefits system linked to the cost-of-living index; and socially acceptable housing provision which is available and affordable. The ULG also advocates the implementation of an investment programme to stimulate the economy, encourage industrial development and promote employment. It thinks that social and economic policies should be geared to meet Northern Ireland's special needs. And it is convinced that a Bill of Rights for Northern Ireland is essential.

The ULG is also aware that there is a discernible tendency among contemporary social democratic parties and movements to broaden their platforms to include more than the traditional labour concerns of the past. This has been particularly evident within the British Labour Party over the last five years. In part, these broadening attempts have been prompted by recognition of the need to address such issues as gender inequalities, the environment, the place and treatment of aboriginal peoples and multiculturalism. To an extent, because of the nature of politics in Northern Ireland, we have been mere spectators in debates about these issues. Regional and national differences aside, there are two lessons to be learned from the broadening tendencies of other Labour movements. The first is that we should be attentive to the greater range of issues that are now seen properly to belong on the agendas of social democratic reflection and action. A second is that we appreciate that there must be a shift from conventional thinking of rights merely as entitlements of individuals to a more expansive embrace of rights as possessions of groups as well. This sort of shift is particularly evident in debates about multiculturalism where a crucial concern is that of adequately facilitating the sense of "difference" expressed by cultural minorities. Admittedly, multiculturalism is hardly the challenge in Northern Ireland that it is in other parts of the UK. Nevertheless, the increase in ethnic minorities here makes the extension of the Race Relations Act to Northern Ireland imperative.

The sense of "difference" that is of acute relevance here, and to lesser extents in Scotland and Wales, is that expressed by nationalists. The great question is how it is justly to be accommodated. This question requires urgent attention. The ULG holds that the best prospects of its resolution occur within the framework of a Northern Ireland that reflects the ethos of a liberal and pluralist UK.

The foregoing views are, we believe, shared by a substantial number of citizens within Northern Ireland. The ULG hopes to offer a structure within which they may acquire adequate expression and representation.

**

So read the rationale submitted for public consideration in mid-1995. As hopes go, the one intimated in the preceding paragraph instantly seems quite utopian in several senses: that the rationale informing it could possibly be accommodated within the larger fold of the UUP; that the type of politics required by the rationale would be advocated by the ULG in defiance of the type practiced by the UUP; and that commitment to taking "difference" seriously would be sufficiently strong to facilitate advocating a just settlement with Irish nationalists which involved revising typical unionist priorities. These utopian elements collectively suggest that – absent radical thinking and courage – the ULG may be an inherently misbegotten enterprise. Whatever about that, each element highlights a different perplexity which merits comment. The ULG, I'll now maintain, is afflicted by perplexities of location, style and scope. I'll also intimate how I think the challenges these perplexities represent may be met and the ULG enterprise spared an ignominious demise.

Location

It is true, as mentioned above, that the UUP has contained members with labour inclinations throughout its twentieth century history. That doesn't mean, however, that the UUP is a political location to which leftists obviously gravitate. It isn't. From the outset, the inclusion of socialist tendencies within Carson's attempt to fashion a "New Unionism" – via the creation of the UULA (Ulster Unionist Labour Association) – was intended as an antidote to Bolshevik and republican tendencies within trades unions (Bew, *et al*, 1979: 48); it was designed to stymie a drift to Labour among the Protestant working class. Labour interests were circumscribed by overriding Unionist interests, which effectively meant that the UULA scarcely served as an antidote to sectarianism within Unionism or even as much of a check on the conservativism dominating unionist thinking. And, with perhaps the odd exception – such as the elevation to ministerial posts of figures like John Miller Andrews and later Harry Midgley in the old (pre-1972) Stormont – nothing much changed during the twentieth century, not even in the 1960s despite the slightly hyperbolic suggestion to the contrary in the rationale above. The political expression of Ulster unionism remained overwhelmingly conservative.

There is little reason to suppose that the current UUP offers brighter hope for labour prospects. It is doubtful, for example, whether more than a mere handful of the 600 plus delegates at the UUP's recent AGM would share labour sympathies. And the current appeal within the party of the right-wing Craigavon Society – including among party leaders and MPs – suggests the ULG will be hard pressed to make any impression within the party of mainstream unionism. It's tempting to conclude that the leadership of the UUP permitted the formation of the ULG precisely because it was not deemed to be a threat to dominant interests. Or, to add a more cynical note, the UUP hierarchy may have surmised that the presence of the ULG may even prove advantageous not only by enhancing the party's boast of being a "broad church", but also by providing an outlet for those few members of a socialist persuasion who may otherwise be tempted to join the more obviously left-oriented Progressive Unionist Party (PUP), its paramilitary baggage notwithstanding. Such speculation aside, an upshot is that, as things presently stand within the UUP, the Group runs the risk of being an irrelevant side-show.

Unease about labour interests developing within a conservative location or framework intensifies once we drill down to the micro-level of the ULG itself. Quite simply, the ULG is, I believe, already compromised by its apparent willingness to facilitate conservativism. And so, even in its infancy, the Group is handicapped in ways that suggest obtuseness and/or duplicity, infiltration and/or opportunism, or some combination of the lot. To explain, let me cite three examples of incompatible commitments. One is the fact that at least half of the Executive committee are members of the Orange Order (if not also in some cases the Apprentice Boys and the Royal Black Preceptory). Properly understood, I suggest that labour interests are anti-sectarian and it's difficult not to believe that they will invariably clash with many of the interests of the loyal orders. The proposition – which has seriously been put to me – that the Orange Order in particular offers a vehicle of solidarity for working-class Protestants and so should be welcomed by leftists is too preposterous to deserve comment. Another example is the strong suspicion that at least one member of the Executive committee is also a member of the Craigavon Society. A clash of loyalties here is simply inevitable. A third instance of incompatible fidelities is perhaps the most egregious, namely the absurd reality that one of the persons representing the ULG at a meeting with representatives of another political party and at the British Labour Party Annual Conference in Brighton is, by his own admission to me, a self-confessed Tory.

These examples prompt an obvious question: who is having a lend of whom here? Either the persons involved are too obtuse to recognise the contradictions of juggling left and right interests, and the necessarily divided loyalties such juggling involves, or they are duplicitous. Trust is essential among those starting a venture such as the ULG and yet it already looks like being a scarce commodity. Except for Orange affiliations, which, however ludicrously in my estimation, have long enjoyed cross-class expression within unionism, perhaps the other examples I raise are evidence of an infiltration, approved by senior party officers, that is designed to shackle any radical moves the Group may recommend. If such a conspiratorial line prompts wincing – and I'm certainly twitching at the mere thought of it – then maybe we are dealing rather with plain political opportunism, albeit of an especially bone-headed variety. To clarify, particularly in reference to the example of a Tory representing the ULG, the charge of opportunism implicates more than the individual involved; it also implicates his enablers within the ULG Executive. With respect to the latter, what could be their thinking? Possibly something like this: the Tory representative has influential contacts within the UUP; encouraging his participation in the ULG makes some pragmatic sense in terms of broadening the range of potential party allies, especially if the primary point of establishing the ULG is to find a niche within the party, to build a base of support within its membership that advances career opportunities and prospects; and if achieving this point requires a bit of ideological flexibility – to the extent of seeing nothing objectionable in promoting a Tory to champion the labour cause – then so be it. If such a depiction of their thinking is close to being accurate, then prominent members of the ULG Executive (the Tory's enablers) are taking the rest of us as mugs or else are assuming that we all share their cynically instrumental view of politics. But if it or something like it isn't the case, we are dealing with remarkable instances of political naivete, if not imbecility. No matter how we spin it, making the ULG seem dependent on the support of Tory members of the UUP is farcical. The issue of the ULG's location is more than a little perplexing if advancing labour interests is intended to be a serious matter.

Now it may be that I am so exercised by this issue, and perhaps sounding a little over-precious, partly because my route to the UUP has been unusual. I joined the Party in 1994 largely because I read about the formation of the ULG. It's quite likely that I wouldn't have joined otherwise. Consequently, my attachment to the UUP itself is rather shallow; it is (broadly understood) labour concerns that are my primary interest. I realise that this peculiar autobiographical detail places me in a different position from other members of the Executive. But then, I have lived most of my adult life outside Northern Ireland and haven't therefore formed deep allegiances to or within the UUP. Accordingly, I'm more easily inclined to be critical of the Party than are those whose commitments and attachments to it run long and deep. I understand, and I hope respect, these, since I don't believe they should ever be taken lightly, but I can't pretend to share them. Nor can I pretend to be so appreciative of their hold on other members of the ULG that I'm prepared to turn a blind eye to the deleterious effect acquiescence to conservatism is already having on how the Group imagines charting a meaningful path within (and beyond) the UUP. To sharpen the point, there must surely come a time when the ULG is prepared to call out the unacceptability of a lot of unionism's (right-wing inspired) political behaviour if it doesn't wish to risk emerging from the womb of the UUP effectively still born.

This raises the question of the relation of the Group to UUP policy in general. The ULG has expressed views only in areas where there's no conflict with Party policy, that is, areas where the Party doesn't have any policies (which in itself is quite remarkable). Such a situation betrays a large assumption the validity of which I doubt: that the Party is competent to devise policies in areas where the ULG chooses to remain silent in a manner that will satisfy those of a labour disposition. I doubt this assumption for two reasons. (1) I doubt the Party's competence to articulate a set of coherent policies adequate to the task of charting a convincing course for unionism in the aftermath of *Frameworks for the Future*. Its efforts so far have been less than impressive and have served more to confuse than enlighten the unionist faithful. (2) Even if it does get its act together, I'm doubtful of the outcome being sufficiently satisfactory from a labour perspective. This is because I think that a labour orientation to politics, which I interpret broadly as a quest for a more equal and just society, does impinge on areas the ULG is content to leave to the wisdom of the Party, and I find little reason to be confident in the latter's wisdom given that it will be unaided by labour insights. To continue in silence merely confirms the obvious: it is perplexing trying to figure out how to implement its rationale given the ULG's location within the UUP.

Style

A second perplexity arises here which I have labelled one of style, but which also touches upon matters of substance. I have hinted that the UUP's way of doing politics is, or should be, questionable from a socialist or social democratic perspective. What am I getting at? Manifestly, I am critical of the leadership of the UUP. It's unfortunate that such a remark is currently taken as evidence of one's sympathies with the right-wing of the party which has set itself against Jim Molyneaux. In my case, however, the remark is evidence of nothing of the sort. If the options are Molyneaux or a Craigavon society candidate, I've no hesitation in choosing Molyneaux. But this is a limited choice and I think it's lamentable that it's all we're faced with. I don't wish to offend those who're exemplary in their faithfulness to the leader, but I have to say why I can't share their view of the character of his leadership. In a nutshell, it's because I disagree profoundly with the image the Molyneaux leadership projects of what politics is about in at least a couple of respects.

First, the Molyneaux leadership promotes what may be dubbed (no doubt provocatively) a *politics of secrecy* in as much as it believes that much of the important business of politics gets done out of the public eye behind closed doors. For Molyneaux this means primarily working behind the scenes cultivating contacts and special relationships at Westminster and seeking to secure the Union by having changes made to the rules under which Northern Ireland is governed by Westminster – through winning a Select Committee for Northern Ireland affairs, upgrading the Northern Ireland Committee to Grand Committee status, and ending the Order in Council procedure for primary legislation in Northern Ireland. Here Molyneaux can claim some procedural victories and to his credit he has received rare accolades for honesty and decency among his parliamentary colleagues. But the price paid for such successes is high, arguably much too high for several reasons. For a start, Molyneaux's relative public silence leaves public space free of reasonable unionist voices of authority capable of appealing across the sectarian divide. Moreover, "public silence" as leadership leaves most citizens in the dark and suspicious of politicians, or, at best, indifferent to their activities except in times of crisis. Seemingly bereft of creative impetus, when unionists do attempt to enter public space, their efforts are overwhelmingly reactive and appear as a series of negative responses to the initiatives of others. And, if it's objected that this is an uncharitable caricature, the problem remains that insofar as inventive political moves are made by unionists they are done out of the public gaze and thus go unappreciated. The grim reality is that the results of secretive politics over the last couple of decades are decidedly unimpressive: unionism is now in a weaker position than it has ever been, and the procedural concessions Molyneaux has won from Westminster appear as a very slender consolation. In short, the politics of secrecy fails on its own terms: it can't deliver what it promises, namely a stronger unionism bolstered by public confidence in its stance and assured of British government support.

In addition, my claim is that the foregoing type of politics as secrecy is inimical to a politics of openness with which the left is properly associated. I'll say more about this shortly. Of course, it could immediately be objected that, whatever issues there may be concerning its efficacy, secrecy shouldn't in principle be problematic to leftist politics given the history of twentieth century socialism. Such an objection would be telling if we supposed that Soviet style communism – with its emphases on elitist, bureaucratic authoritarianism, suppression of dissent, suspicion of non-state prescribed cultural expressions and general politics of concealment – captured the socialist ideal. But once we say on the contrary that this, and various of its offshoots, is socialism at its most warped, the objection loses its sting. It shouldn't remotely trouble the ULG. But the secrecy practiced by the UUP leadership should.

Another difficulty with the UUP's political style, invited by its current inclination to secrecy but by no means dependent on it, is its *low-risk character*. This isn't terribly surprising since minimising risk has always been typical of a unionist politics obsessed with not surrendering, or giving an inch, but intent on defending its corner and nurturing its siege mentality. Thus, the reflex response to paramilitary ceasefires isn't at all to explore new possibilities for unionist-nationalist relations but to advocate caution and vigilance, to cultivate suspicion. And, above all, to play it safe. With tedious predictability, the UUP refuses to engage with other parties on the basis of *Frameworks for the Future* and proposes as an alternative – in *A Practical Approach to Problem Solving* – a procedural rather than a substantive way forward. But the difficulty engendered by this low-key approach is that it breeds confusing and ineffectual politics. *Confusing* because it leaves unclear precisely what the UUP's stance on substantive issues is. Recent events only compound this confusion. Take, for example, the ambivalence evident in attempts to achieve a semblance of unionist unity. On one hand, calls for a united unionist front to oppose *Frameworks for the Future* have come from the DUP, Friends of the Union, Robert McCartney, a group of businessmen and professionals, and some members of the UUP. The UUP has sent representatives to meetings organised by the DUP to see if agreement on unionist unity is possible, and there has been much talk in the media about the two parties burying the hatchet. On the other hand, we find Molyneaux trying to impose order in his own house and warning party members that criticism of UUP officers will be regarded as an act of intolerable disloyalty. And hope of unionist unity fades as sniping continues between McCartney and his supporters and prominent members of the UUP, diminishes further as leading DUP representatives accuse the UUP of endangering unionist unity by putting selfish party interests above the interests of Ulster, and dwindles almost laughably in the face of the current debacle (propelled by bad faith among different factions of unionism) at Belfast's City Hall. All of this leaves unclear whether the UUP does agree with the DUP on what a substantive response and alternative to *Frameworks for the Future* should look like. Under prevailing circumstances, low risk proceduralism makes for confusing politics.

It also makes for *ineffectual* politics. Quite frankly, beyond the insular world of unionist manoeuverings, the UUP's risk-averse strategy plays into the hands of nationalists, not least those of a republican persuasion. This point may be illustrated through reference to the *PIRA Position Paper* of late 1994. Two features of this paper are particularly striking. One is that PIRA's willingness to pursue the "risky strategy" of "total unarmed struggle" has so far reaped dividends for Sinn Féin which were previously unattainable. Its willingness to take this risk was based on its realistic assessment "that republicans at this time and on their own do not have the strength to achieve the end goal". There is a lesson here for unionists: they too, I suggest, need to assess realistically how effective their customary stances have been and to show the courage and judgement required of good risk-taking in order to reap rewards for unionism which have been missing for some considerable time.

A second striking feature of the PIRA paper is its assumption that unionists will do nothing of the sort. The paper certainly implies that it won't be too difficult to "effect the domestic and international perception of the republican position, i.e., as one which is reasonable" and, as a corollary, to expose unionism as intransigent and unreasonable. It never occurs to the authors of the paper that republicans may need a back-up plan in the event of unionists not acting as they're supposed to. Unionism has been type-cast as intransigent, reactionary and unreasonable and, so the reasoning goes, won't budge unless forced to do so by external bodies. Accordingly, PIRA should target the relevant bodies and seek to convince them of the reasonableness of its cause. Regrettably, I think that to a large extent PIRA is right in its analysis. Shackled by its low-key style which does nothing to offset its apparent "intransigence", the UUP offers little to dent Sinn Féin's image outside Northern Ireland let alone present a positive image of its own.

Only a reasonable unionism prepared to play high-risk politics has any chance of doing so. In short, low-risk politics, much like the politics of secrecy, seem ill-equipped to tackle the present problems in Northern Ireland. It is hard to believe that much improvement in the human lot – socially, economically or politically – has been achieved on its terms. One hardly needs to be revolutionary to think that high-risk politics would be better suited to Northern Ireland today. If there's to be any cause for optimism, it must come from some unionist group seizing the initiative and playing a high-risk game. If the ULG won't then I can't imagine who will.

What might this require? A *politics of openness* for a start. Here I am implying that the socio-economic core of the ULG's *raison d'être* – a minimum wage, adequate pensions, welfare and housing provisions, responsible investments, and so forth – points in the direction of a certain sort of politics. Admittedly, this is an arguable implication, since it's possible to secure acceptable socio-economic arrangements under a range of political regimes. Even so, I want to press the claim that what I'm calling a politics of openness more satisfactorily accommodates the ULG's socio-economic priorities than a politics of secrecy ever could. And it does so because underlying this sort of politics and these sorts of priorities there is an appeal to treating citizens as free and equal agents. At a minimum, the ULG's socio-political priorities aim at securing and maintaining material conditions for citizens that are sufficient to their being regarded as free and equal (in something like the senses intimated by Michael Walzer in his *Spheres of Justice*); whilst a politics of openness is concerned to ensure that citizens express their freedom and equality through having a meaningful say in how society is organised. In ways that Thatcherites and others of that ilk persistently fail to grasp, these remain properly intertwined goals for leftists.

To say a little more about my stress on openness, the politics emphasising it tries as far as possible to conduct its affairs in the public gaze, to encourage the development of an active citizenry, to promote inclusiveness and public dialogue. What I'm calling the politics of openness believes that public trust is built only by bringing the public along and by appealing beyond tribal boundaries. Unfortunately, it has never flourished within unionism but that doesn't mean that it couldn't. Or so I'd like to believe. In my view, it comprises a vision of society which includes at least the following features. It holds that a central purpose of politics is to provide access for all citizens to a way of life worth having. And this requires the existence of public institutions and practices with which citizens identify and which command their allegiance. Why? Well, not least because these defining features of a polity's way of life, in addition to any possible historical legacies they incur, are largely sustained by citizens' words and deeds rather than merely by bureaucratic procedures. The anticipation, then, is of a public form of life developing through political institutions amenable to the scrutiny and contributions of citizens; through the presence of public representatives who are subject to meaningful types of democratic accountability and who possess sufficient power to implement policies beneficial to society. Quite frankly, such an anticipation isn't available on the terms of a politics of secrecy, since these are inimical to the creation of a public space shared by citizens, detrimental to the cultivation of social and political trust, particularly among divided people, and oblivious to the indispensability of inclusiveness and dialogue to the health of a polity.

A politics of openness has other implications too. For example, it's conducive to encouraging diversity in civil society and tolerating difference. It appreciates that society's legal/security institutions must be open not only to applicants of sufficient merit, whatever their background, and be widely regarded as impartial; they also must be culturally inclusive. And to reiterate the point I made earlier about openness and socio-economic concerns, the aim is to create conditions that facilitate citizens' flourishing, including the development of an infrastructure permitting space and scope for individual/group/company initiatives and the implementation of specific policies in such areas as health, education, employment, social benefits which are designed to ensure that no individuals or minority groups are forced through unfortunate circumstances to fall below acceptable standards of living. In other words, conceiving of citizens as free and equal agents – an indispensable condition of a politics of openness - requires suitable socio-economic arrangements. The requisite politics and economics are mutually reinforcing; or at least they ought to be. And so on.

So inasmuch as the ULG demurs from objecting to a major strand of the UUP's current political style, the heartbeat of leftist politics – trying to create a just society of free and equal citizens – is effectively deprived of oxygen. This, I suggest, is more than a little perplexing.

Scope

As should already be evident, the perplexity of style hints at another perplexity: one of scope. A presumption within unionism is that labour interests *may* be tolerated if they don't impinge upon the constitutional issues which absorb unionist politics. The scope of ULG activity is circumscribed in advance. This is troubling both because unionism's present handling of its constitutional priorities is problematic from (my understanding of) a labour perspective, and because the rationale of leftist politics militates against this sort of circumscription of its scope anyway. Let me elaborate on these two emphases.

Take for a start unionism's current articulations of its *raison d'être*, maintaining the Union, within the context of paramilitary ceasefires. Here I'm not restricting myself to UUP politics but referring to defences of the Union found across the unionist spectrum.

These appear in two prominent forms. One – the most widespread – simply supposes that the Union is best secured by opposing any concession to nationalism on the grounds that all reform of Northern society supported by nationalists inevitably weakens Northern Ireland's position within the UK. Often at work here (although not invariably) is the almost stupefying assumption that Northern Ireland under the old unionist-dominated regime at Stormont was a decent society that was undone through Stormont's proroguing in 1972 when an ill-informed British government acquiesced to the propaganda of subversive nationalist malcontents. On these terms, culpability for a generation of conflict is to be borne by nationalism not unionism; unionism, rather, has been unfairly maligned in the court of an international opinion too susceptible to nationalist narratives; and unionism has also been betrayed by successive British governments through their unwarranted concessions to nationalism in the Sunningdale Agreement (1974), the Anglo-Irish Agreement (1985), the Downing Street Declaration (1993) and now *Frameworks for the Future* (1995).

Thus, the odd story of unionism's woes unfolds. But beyond the circles of unionism who believes it? Nobody much I'd venture. An obvious upshot is that unionists are expending their energy on debatable causes - vainly trying to shore up their position at Westminster, indulging in self-pitying cries about a lost world, and so forth – that do nothing to address the divisions that plague Northern society and that the ceasefires give us a chance to think about creatively. And this is what's so objectionable from a labour perspective. In virtue of its narrow focus on the constitutional question and the shrivelled way in which it's approached, unionism can't allow free rein to labour interests - which, crucially, extend to regard for all citizens and not merely unionists or Protestants – because they might (even if inadvertently) weaken the Union. Talk of equal rights and the like is fine if there's no constitutional threat involved; otherwise, it may be dangerous. Let's be clear: this is nervous, perverse stuff and it's the sort of stuff that seems to underpin current calls for unionist unity in face of the potential perils that silent IRA guns are (bizarrely) taken to represent. Leftist concerns must always play second fiddle here and can't be permitted to develop naturally for fear of upsetting unionism's fragile identity. And meanwhile politics in Northern Ireland, stymied as they so frequently are by unionist intransigence, stumble along.

Another form of constitutional defence, with significant pedigree but not majority unionist support, focuses on the idea of the Union. Its claim is that the constituent parts of the Union should be governed identically. Northern Ireland's exceptionalism – as the only one of the four parts to have experienced devolved government – should be ended forthwith. Reasoning along such lines is currently back in favour in Craigavon and other circles and is most compellingly articulated by Robert McCartney with a bit of help from Arthur Aughey. The appeal of McCartney's idea of the Union lies in its elegant simplicity: why shouldn't Northern Ireland be governed like the rest of Britain? Why shouldn't its citizens be granted the same political rights as other British citizens? Given that unionists form a majority in Northern society why should they be denied a full expression of their Britishness (which is what continuing devolution, especially since 1972, necessarily involves)? Since he thinks there are no convincing answers to these questions, McCartney reckons that the complaints which inform them are best resolved by securing the Union in the surest way possible, that is, via integration. A resolution which, in ushering in a full representation of Westminster's mode of non-sectarian rule, also apparently promises an overcoming of the sectarian problem that has haunted Northern Ireland's politics from the outset.

Now to an uninvolved observer the quest for integration, which was at the heart of the Campaign for Equal Citizenship conducted by McCartney and others in the aftermath of the Anglo-Irish Agreement, may seem a strange ploy to adopt given what we have known about British policy in Northern Ireland since 1985. But even in the wake of the recent *Frameworks for the Future*, McCartney is still trying valiantly to rally support for his idea of the Union and seems to believe its defeat is not yet final. Be that as it may, the point I wish to stress now is that his idea effectively marginalises nationalism's political manifestations. The price of (allegedly) transcending sectarian politics is a split in a Northern nationalist identity between its political and cultural dimensions with only the latter (in whatever emaciated apolitical form remains) permitted recognition. Requiring nothing less amounts to a serious overplaying of unionism's constitutional card from a leftist vantage-point. It isn't plausible to argue for justice and equality in Northern society while simultaneously demanding that nationalists cease to be nationalists and accept the legitimacy of *complete* British rule. Equal citizenship on McCartney's terms means unequal citizenship for nationalists who are deprived of having their political identity reflected in any of the institutions of the state. This isn't only unrealistic given the prevailing political circumstances in Northern Ireland; it is also unacceptable to a labour position which insists on doing justice to all citizens and not merely a (steadily decreasing) majority.

What I'm driving at here becomes clearer by elaborating why, given the political composition of Northern Ireland, leftists properly object in principle to a circumscription of their *modus operandi* for the sake of unionism's constitutional preoccupations. Here I want to pick up on an aspect of the ULG's rationale outlined earlier, and which has been at least implicitly present in much of my argument so far, when I referred to the broadening agenda of social democratic parties and movements throughout the West. There is a distinct tendency among such parties and movements to extend their platforms to include more than the traditional "labour" concerns of the past. This is currently occurring within the British Labour Party, for example, and it has been occurring within the Australian Labor Party and many others for quite some time. In part, these broadening attempts have been prompted by recognition of the need for a contemporary labour party/movement to address such issues as gender, the environment, the place and treatment of aboriginal peoples and multiculturalism. Of course, certain of these issues are felt more keenly in some countries than in others. Just as the problem of aboriginal peoples, for instance, is very important in Canada and Australia but of no importance in Northern Ireland, so there are problems of central significance in Northern Ireland which are unimportant elsewhere. To repeat a line introduced in my earlier summary of the ULG's rationale, there are, I think, two things to be gleaned from the "broadening tendencies" of other labour movements, regardless of their regional and national peculiarities. One is being alert to the greater range of issues that are now seen properly to belong on the agendas of social democratic reflection and action. Another is being equally attentive to the shift in emphasis some of these issues require from thinking of the treatment due to individuals to thinking of the treatment due to groups, including those which can't be understood exclusively, if at all, in class terms. This sort of shift is particularly evident in debates about multiculturalism where a crucial issue is that of adequately facilitating the sense of "difference" expressed by cultural minorities. Admittedly, multiculturalism is hardly the issue in Northern Ireland that it is in other parts of Britain, but what is pertinent here is the question of how the sense of "difference" expressed by nationalists is justly to be accommodated. And if we are attuned to the thrust of the "broadening tendencies" apparent in other labour movements, it becomes clear that this is a question that warrants the attention of the ULG. It can't satisfactorily be left to the UUP hierarchy to decide.

More to the point, to take seriously the imperative to do justice to nationalists calls into question some quasi-sacred unionist beliefs and practices. Northern Ireland was created to assuage unionist fears of minority status in an Ireland granted home-rule. For fifty years unionists enjoyed unchallenged control of the six counties under their jurisdiction in a partitioned Ireland with scant regard for nationalist sentiment and experience. The idea of doing justice to nationalists barely registered and when it appeared in modest form through the civil rights movement in the mid-to-late 1960s it was treated as a dangerous notion by large numbers of unionists. And, despite events of the last twenty-five years, it continues to unsettle many unionists even today. Protecting the Union and clinging to diminishing advantages over nationalism is what still matters most to the UUP and other unionist parties. I think this is massively short-sighted. And it gets things the wrong way around. A better way to protect the Union, I suggest, is to create a Northern Ireland in which nationalists feel at home and to which they can be committed. Accordingly, treating nationalists justly should be a priority. And not only because it might, ironically, deliver unionists more of the constitutional security they crave than all their naysaying and antics are ever likely to; but also, because it is the right thing to do. Or at least it is from a leftist perspective that's motivated by something like the "politics of openness" I alluded to previously. As things currently stand, the ULG shows little inclination to press a case along such lines in defiance of unionist convention. This is perplexing, not least because we ought, as people of the left, to be very uneasy with a prioritisation of the kind of constitutional politics which necessarily involves treating other citizens unjustly.

No doubt there is plenty to discuss about how this translates in Northern society today. However construed, I think the imperative to do justice to all Northern citizens is profitably pursued not by making it subservient to improbable or sectarian versions of the

Union and Britishness but by admitting basic features of our current Northern condition: that Northern Ireland (despite its place within the UK) is always going to be viewed by the rest of Britain as a "place apart"; that for the foreseeable future it's going to be viewed as a "place apart" by the Irish Republic too, and that there's anything but a serious desire for Irish unity in the Republic; that the society of the Republic is changing and that its state isn't the homogeneous, authoritarian one it once was; that the meaning of the Union is being searchingly questioned within the United Kingdom independently of the issue of Northern Ireland, and that a trend towards regionalism, encouraged by Europe and the British Labour Party's willingness to grant devolution to Scotland and perhaps to Wales, is likely to increase; and that within Northern Ireland the nationalist case has gained considerably over the unionist (often for good reasons) and that concessions granted to nationalists, in the name of equalising citizenship, are irreversible. These political realities ought to concentrate our minds and provide parameters within which the ULG attempts to implement its rationale however much its doing so runs against the grain of unionist orthodoxy.

Conclusion

To conclude by reiterating the obvious: the ULG has emerged from within the UUP, and risks being engulfed by larger conservative and sectarian tendencies within unionism. From the outset, it struggles to make a mark as I hope is now clear from the foregoing discussion of the perplexities of location, style and scope which it faces. The easy option is to shrug off such perplexities, fiddle around on the margins carefully avoiding controversy, and accept as canonical the UUP leadership's interpretation of what it means to strengthen and maintain the Union. But then why bother at all? To fall into line so meekly involves squandering the fresh possibilities for constructive politics that the paramilitary ceasefires open up. It implies swallowing the tired old guff about the Union being strengthened and maintained for fifty years through the unionist-dominated regime at Stormont and accepting the type of rear-guard politics this encourages. Or perhaps it entails seeing integration as being unionism's best bet for constitutional security. Either way, the ULG is hamstrung by unionism's reluctance to embrace the new political realities of our time and its refusal to entertain the type of politics that should be mandatory for those on the left. Quite frankly, seen in such a light, the future for the ULG already looks bleak.

Yet it needn't be. The perplexities of unionist labour don't have to signal fatal weaknesses in the project. The ULG could adopt a high-risk strategy by refusing to be hemmed in by the minimalist, reactionary, sectarian and negative tendencies so prevalent in unionism; and by engaging instead in what I've called a politics of openness which emphasises concern for the quality of life for all citizens in Northern society. This at least would give the ULG a sporting chance of being more than an irrelevant distraction and enable it to occupy the significant public space awaiting reasonable unionists which other unionist parties and groups seem more interested in closing off than entering. It would also offer a clear alternative to the dead-end politics encouraged by the Craigavon Society, McCartney, et. al. and show that unionist politics can be creative and positive. It could appeal further to a significant portion of the wider unionist population disillusioned with current unionist attitudes and strategies as well as to those of a labour persuasion who can't stomach the present unionist parties.

Or so one might hope in one's more optimistic moments.

PART TWO

ON RETHINKING UNIONISM

A little under a year following the publication of *Rethinking Unionism: An Alternative Vision for Northern Ireland*, the Workers' Education Association (WEA) organised a series of lectures and discussions in Belfast's Linen Hall Library on the topic, "Futures of Unionism". I delivered the first two of these lectures based on the main themes of my book – others were delivered by Jane Leonard, Feargal Cochrane and Arthur Aughey – and offered a short reply to the other contributions in a final session, which also included input from the Queens University Belfast (QUB) academics, Elizabeth Meehan, Richard English and Graham Walker. In what follows, modified and expanded versions of the lectures appear as Chapters four and five, and my extended reply (mostly to Arthur Aughey) appears as Chapter six. Since these chapters form a cohesive block, there is no need to preface each with further introductory information.

4

Why Unionism Needs Rethinking

Introduction

I should start by thanking Elda for her generous words of introduction and for organising this course. It's a rare privilege to have such a forum as this made available for a discussion of one's book. And I'm deeply grateful to Elda in particular and the WEA in general for making it possible.

I must add, though, that I also find the occasion a bit odd and more than a little daunting. I'm uncertain of my audience: I don't know most of you, I don't know why you're here or what your expectations are, I don't know who has or who hasn't read the book, I don't know what I can or can't take for granted, and, consequently, I don't know where to pitch my comments. My hunch is to take very little for granted and therefore to lay out the main arguments of the book from scratch as it were. I'll endeavour to do so by responding to three central questions: (1) what assumptions underlie the attempt to rethink unionism? (2) why does unionism need rethinking? (3) what might a rethought unionism look like? The first two questions will be dealt with in this lecture (chapter) and the third in the next.

Assumptions

Let me turn immediately to the first question: what assumptions underlie the attempt to rethink unionism? There are four sorts of assumptions involved in my endeavour.

Personal

Assumptions of the first sort are personal in nature and therefore peculiar to me. Accordingly, I'll make only brief reference to them, although it is probably worth indicating in advance that they only make proper sense against the background of a journey that led in various steps from my leaving Belfast in 1970 as a bigot to writing *Rethinking Unionism* in 1995-96 as, I trust, a transformed bigot. Important steps in this journey included a youthful identification with extreme loyalism followed by a (relative) loss of interest in the politics of Northern Ireland when moving to Australia. Such a loss proved temporary, however, and was succeeded by a rekindling of interest when I found I couldn't shake off the hold of my homeland. And this rekindling, in turn, prompted troubled reflections conducted from afar which cultivated a (seemingly) irrepressible desire to return "home" and become involved in the politics of this society. I realised the desire in 1994 when I moved back to Belfast with my family and joined the UUP. But then I experienced acute disenchantment with the conduct of unionist politics following the calling of the republican and then the loyalist ceasefires; a disenchantment which I've tried to articulate and go beyond through writing *Rethinking Unionism*.

If these are big steps in my personal narrative, what are the assumptions underlying them? Well, at least by the stage I'm up to now, two stand out. One is that, by virtue of feeling implicated in my unionist background, I considered myself obligated to identify with unionism and to contribute to the politics of Northern Ireland in whatever way I could from within the unionist fold. Thus, it would be as a unionist that I would rethink unionism. Another was that, given my first-hand experience of unionist politics, unionism couldn't make do without a serious rethink; that the type of (frequently appalling) attitudes to non-unionists that I found abundant evidence of within unionist circles couldn't simply be shrugged at; and that to cope with the growing discomfort I felt with conventional unionism I was either going to have to quit unionism altogether or try to offer some alternative.

The point of these personal assumptions is that I was, so to speak, "existentially driven" to write *Rethinking Unionism*. It wasn't a prearranged plan designed to tear strips off the UUP, as Jim Rodgers (a rather excitable unionist councillor) chooses to believe.

Political

These personal assumptions were informed by wider political assumptions which I'd acquired over the years, quite independently of unionism or the politics of Northern Ireland. Three were especially important. One was that in any contemporary democratic polity worth its salt, all members had to be treated as free and equal citizens: all should therefore enjoy the same rights, procedural entitlements and standing before the law as all others. A second assumption was that for a polity to be viable, to be immune to fragmentation and stultifying division, its most basic institutions and practices had to command the allegiance of its citizens. And a third assumption was that one of the principal things the ancient Athenians got right, and that Aristotle, say, articulated as well as anyone was that dialogue is central to politics; that in its absence politics becomes something of a sham and has to rely excessively on various means of manipulation and coercion if a basic amount of order is to be maintained.

Philosophical

These political assumptions were, in their turn, reinforced by broader philosophical assumptions to which I'd become committed. Stated very crudely these could be reduced to two claims. A first is that all acts of understanding in human affairs are irreducibly historical. This applies whether I'm concerned to understand myself and my own traditions, or the tradition of others, or the culture of those who seem "foreign" and puzzling to me. As I try, say, to make sense of my own unionist past and present or the past and present of Irish nationalists, I do so as someone who's already "encumbered": by my life history, by my cultural involvements, by my beliefs and values. And what's true of me in these respects is true of us all.

A second claim is that as humans we're self-interpreting beings. Put simply, this means we're beings for whom things matter and since what matters to us often changes over time we're inclined to evaluate/re-evaluate, interpret/re-interpret what does matter to us and why. We don't arrive in this life with a pre-determined set of beliefs, values and dispositions which remain intact until we depart it. On the contrary, we're all shaped in one way or another by our cultural, political and perhaps religious experiences and these give us our orientation to the world, to politics, to others, and so on. But the big point I'm driving at is that our orientations to these things are always open to change; that, indeed, the more seriously we take those things that matter to us the more prepared we may be to ask questions of them, and the more we ask questions of them the more willing we may be to revise them. Two things, in particular, seem to me crucial to understanding what it means to be a self-interpreting being. One is that I must admit that at any given moment my view of myself, say, or my view of politics may be defective; that they are in principle open to improvement, that others may have insights I lack and that I'd benefit from. And the other is that dialogue is indispensable to the business of self-interpretation; that it's through bouncing ideas off others, through listening to others, through being exposed to views/cultures/traditions different from mine that I'm aided in making better sense of my own life or of the life of my society. This sort of "making better sense" can't be done in sheer isolation; it's never a purely private achievement.

Political-Philosophical

Bringing together certain of the political and philosophical assumptions I've mentioned enables me to tease out three further assumptions which are decisive for the way in which I go about rethinking unionism.

First, and most obviously, I assume that dialogue plays a central role in my conception of what unionist (or non-unionist) politics should be. In my opinion, its importance to human affairs in general, and to political affairs in particular, is such that it can't be substituted by anything else, by any other means of communication. Thus, I'm unavoidably predisposed, as it were, to be deeply critical of any mode of unionist politics which appears not to rate dialogue highly.

Second, I assume that unionism should be related in the first instance to ways of life that unionists value, rather than, say, to a set of fears or to a siege mentality. This isn't to deny for a moment that unionists have fears or that many of them do display a siege mentality. It is simply to say that their fears and siege mentality reflect their perceptions of dangers to their ways of life. For my purposes, a way of life is primary. And it's primary for this reason: it's through their immersion in a particular way of life that's taken to be inherently unionist that unionists get their most rudimentary habits and customs and acquire most of their values and beliefs. In assuming the primacy of a way of life I'm concerned to ask questions of it: can it deliver all that's expected of it? And can it withstand external challenges?

Third, I assume that unionism and the ways of life with which it's associated is capable of, and requires, conceptual articulation. By this I mean that the often-implicit understandings of politics and the world unreflectively taken for granted in any way of life turn out to involve contestable claims which have to be spelled out and defended. Unionism, in other words, isn't immune from rational scrutiny and if, as unionists insist, it's up to scratch then it'll prove capable of providing a conceptual framework within which unionists can understand more clearly and deeply what they stand for and why.

Why Does Unionism Need Rethinking?

Given these assumptions, I turn to my second question, "why does unionism need rethinking?" I have already hinted at an answer which admits of a short and brutal formulation: because its ways of life and conceptual frameworks are grossly inadequate. Let me add several clarifications to this answer and then quickly try to explain why I think it is essentially correct in reference to what I take to be the two major forms in which unionism appears today.

On Ways of Life

The immediate clarifications I suspect are necessary relate to the emphasis I'm putting on unionist ways of life. One is that it's a reductive reference to the sorts of lives lived by unionists. It's not meant to be exhaustive: there's more to the lives lived by unionists than is captured by my term "a unionist way of life". This is simply to say that unionists share with nationalists and others in Northern Ireland all sorts of employment, consumption, entertainment, and many other patterns of life which are important to how they live. There is, however, another range of practices, values, historical memories, and institutional commitments which are presumed to be peculiar to how unionists live, and it's with this range alone that I am concerned here.

Another clarification underscores the importance of the notion of a way of life in my analysis: it indicates the *source* of a collective identity. I've already touched upon this, but it may be worth re-stressing if only to debunk the strong tendency among academic and popular commentators to locate unionism's identity in its famous siege mentality. This tendency (which I may inadvertently have given an impression of in Chapter two) latches on to something important, of course, when it draws attention to the mix of fears, insecurities and curious senses of superiority that are often present in many unionists' minds and inform feelings of being under siege. Even so, it's not obvious that questions of identity are reducible to psychological explanations. One difficulty of assuming to the contrary is that the psychological states typically gathered under unionism's "siege mentality" are unevenly distributed across unionism's different identities: they are very prominent in one, not quite so prominent, although definitely present, in another and almost without trace in a third. Or so an upshot of my analysis of unionism will lead us to believe. A further difficulty with attributing primacy to psychology here is the risk of promoting a distorting picture of unionists as maybe pathological or at least as unhealthily fixated on defining themselves in negative terms. I want to underscore instead the hint I've previously given about unionist negativity being derivative: the psychological traits unionists manifest are properly intelligible only when pitched against the backdrop of a world of significance comprised of institutions and practices with which they identify, of memories, commitments and allegiances that define who they are as unionists. Such a world of significance is what I'm getting at when talking about "a way of life" that is the source of unionists' identity and that gives them an orientation to politics. So, it's when unionists face disorientation through their way(s) of life being disturbed, threatened with disturbance, or imagined to be under threat of disturbance that elements of a siege mentality may appear. The mentality on display at times may be intriguing (to put it charitably); it is, however, parasitic upon those ways of life and their crises which give it sustenance. And, to repeat, it's upon these that I think the main focus should fall.

A final point deserving clarification is why I maintain that it's permissible to subject not only unionist theory but also unionists' ways of life to critical examination. Doing so may seem counterintuitive in this sense: a way of life is often a valued traditional inheritance which has withstood the test of time and should be respected as such, however congenial or otherwise it appears to others. Shouldn't critical examination, then, be off-limits? I don't think so. I agree that there is a *prima facie* case for appreciating traditional attachments, but these are not static and through the course of time may either suffer from internal strains or prove objectionable in various respects. And these are matters we are entitled to talk about and, where appropriate, even do so in a probing spirit. Or so I'm going to suggest as I turn attention to unionism's two major contemporary forms.

Cultural Unionism

The first of these forms I call *cultural unionism*. This is rooted in what I refer to as an 'Ulster unionist' way of life which is presumed to express a distinctive unionist identity; one that imagines that its two geographical referents (Northern Ireland and Great Britain) are similarly suffused religiously and politically and thus indissolubly united. And so, there emerges the picture of an identity located in six out of nine counties of one Irish province the political separation of which from the other twenty-six counties of Ireland was intended to guarantee an ongoing Protestant majority; a picture which (arguably) acquired consummate public expression in the old Stormont which served for many as a "Protestant parliament for a Protestant people." Also emerging is a portrait of an identity fashioned too by its political association with Britain and the conviction that the Britishness in which it shares historically has been, and (at least) constitutionally continues to be, shaped by Protestantism. Through such historical events as the "Glorious Revolution" of 1688, the Act of Union of 1801 and the Government of Ireland Act of 1920, the British dimension ostensibly helped define the way of life in which a cultural unionist identity developed by affording British institutions of state which ensured a Protestant monarchy, the sovereignty of the Crown in parliament, the rule of law, and civil and religious liberties; all of which were cemented through a Union of England, Scotland Wales and Ireland (subsequently reduced to Northern Ireland) in which each member was granted constitutional security.

And yet the amalgam of the two geographical referents, despite the avowed common bond of Protestantism, resulted in an identity unrecognisable elsewhere in Britain, with the possible exception of parts of Scotland (which is partly why some cultural unionists expand the reach of their way of life to include an Ulster-Scots heritage). No doubt the sheer distinctiveness of cultural unionism owed much to the experience of limited (yet highly significant) devolved government with its in-built assurance of unionist/Protestant rule, the belief (no longer reflected elsewhere in Britain) that Catholics were inherently disloyal, and the concomitant relevance of the loyal orders and their peculiar expression of a Protestant British ethos that romanticised the Reformation and the Empire. The result was a way of life unique to unionists living in six counties of Ireland (and perhaps to a lesser degree in tiny pockets of Scotland). Aspects of it overlapped, of course, with other British ways of life, especially those which registered positive attitudes to the monarchy, but not sufficiently to offset its strangeness to the British mainstream. It's hardly exaggerating to say that many of cultural unionism's manifestations and preoccupations seem increasingly anachronistic elsewhere in Britain where they represent little more than a form of unionism caught in a time warp.

Not surprisingly, then, various problems afflict cultural unionism's way of life. It suffers at one level from internal strains. The loss of the old Stormont and the guarantee of majority rule deprived cultural unionists of power to enforce their will, to dominate Catholics and prevent them from disturbing a valued way of life in which unionists called the shots; a loss compounded by the difficulty of accommodating within this way of life the presence of a large non-compliant minority in the North which is by definition seen as a threat or as 'other'. Of acute relevance too is the undeniable reality that (except in an arcane constitutional sense) there is no common factor of Protestantism binding together the two geographical referents and, consequently, Ulster unionism is out of step with Britishness in the rest of the UK. Moreover, archaic attachments (such as to the loyal orders), which have been historically important for advancement within the political ranks of unionism, lessen the influence cultural unionists may now hope to enjoy with unsympathetic or incredulous interlocutors in Britain and elsewhere. Which helps explain why, at another level, cultural unionism is subject to serious external pressure: its exclusive Protestant British ethos is challenged by UK and Irish governments, by European and North American governments and international agencies, as well as more diffusely by the increasing pluralisation of Northern Irish society which pushes cultural unionists' Protestant particularism more and more to the margins. It's impossible to believe that Northern Ireland's future can be decided on the kind of terms with which cultural unionists seek to trade.

Considering these terms a little more closely enables us to see how problems extend to the conceptual framework cultural unionists employ to articulate their political thought. This is a framework with concepts of liberty and loyalty at its heart. In the first instance, a strong link is posited between liberty and Protestantism, which suggests the latter is a necessary and sufficient condition of the former. This link is derived from the Reformation emphasis on individual spirituality, and at this level has some pertinence, even if exaggerated. But Protestantism isn't the only source of Western notions of individual freedom. Other sources include the development of capitalism and an introspective turn in philosophy which shifted attention from contemplation of humans' place in a cosmic order to reflections on the self and its consciousness. However much it contributed to its experience, it isn't possible to sustain the line that Protestantism is a necessary, let alone a sufficient, condition of individual freedom. And, at another level, where the emphasis falls on political liberty and freedom from despotic government, which we find in much Renaissance thought, there is no apparent indebtedness to Protestantism at all. The salience of these quick observations, which are developed much more thoroughly in my book, is to cast considerable doubt on the grounds on which cultural unionists typically claim political superiority over Irish nationalists and republicans: the case for claiming that Protestantism is required for freedom's access and protection, either individually or politically, quite simply fails.

Loyalty is the other crucial concept in the cultural unionist lexicon. Its invocation, however, occasions some confusion. For example, it is incongruous to many in Britain how unionists loudly proclaim their loyalty to the Union even as they openly defy the will of the UK parliament as they did in 1974 when rejecting the Sunningdale Agreement, then again in 1985 through their opposition to the Anglo-Irish Agreement, and now via their refusal to negotiate with nationalists through the auspices of *Frameworks for the Future*. So just what is this loyalty of which cultural unionists speak? In a sense the answer is straightforward: it is loyalty sworn to the Crown in parliament. This isn't absolute loyalty but loyalty that's qualified, that's dependent upon specific conditions being satisfied. At play here is the idea of a contract or covenant being entered upon by two parties each of whom incurs obligations and responsibilities. But this idea admits of different twists which complicate our understanding of cultural unionism's use of the concept of loyalty. I can't possibly attempt to follow these twists now and will have to settle instead on a very cursory summary.

What loyalty means, it transpires, hinges on which of three possible depictions of contractual or covenantal relations is being drawn upon. One depiction is that of a religious covenant drawn between God and his people (in this instance Protestants!) which involves the latter agreeing to submit themselves to (a divinely ordained) temporal authority. Loyalty is assured here to the extent that the temporal authority faithfully reflects its God-given brief through acting in accordance with divine law. A second depiction is that of a political covenant drawn, in this case, between Protestants and the

British Crown which involves the latter upholding and protecting Protestant faith and practices. Once more, loyalty is unproblematically given on the proviso that Protestantism is granted privileged status. A third depiction is that of a more general and secular idea of a social contract drawn between government and citizens where the latter promise to assume appropriate burdens and responsibilities in return for security and protection of rights. The loyalty expected here is the same for all citizens, those of all faiths or of none.

A rather large problem is that these depictions and their accompanying senses of loyalty scarcely cohere. The first (religious covenantal) depiction is rarely insisted upon strictly, but enjoys occasional airing in Paisleyite rhetoric, for example, when apocalyptically-charged language is deployed to remind governments of their religious failings and to alert Protestants to their higher calling of obeying God's law, even if doing so encourages contemplating disloyalty to a temporal authority (which is believed to have) gone rogue. Here there's a sharp contrast with the third (secular contractual) depiction which treats citizens as individuals with identical claims to rights and protection and with corresponding obligations of loyalty. Curiously, it's this depiction that sometimes characterises unionist dealings with the British government and yet often is set aside when responding to nationalists' demands for equal treatment in Northern Ireland. When "Ulster's" affairs are in the foreground the overriding imperative becomes that of safeguarding cultural unionism's way of life. And that means resorting to the second (political covenantal) depiction which is tantamount to saying that unionist entitlements outweigh those of nationalists precisely because nationalists are inherently disloyal; that the British government is duty-bound to facilitate a sufficient expression of an "Ulster unionist" way of life; and that where it's perceived not to be doing so (as has increasingly been the case since 1972) unionists' loyalty can no longer be assumed.

Lack of coherence among these different covenantal/contractual understandings is by no means the only or the most important problem. Of even greater consequence, I think, is that in practice an exclusivist translation of political covenantalism trumps the more inclusive type of liberal contractarianism and gives cultural unionists a rather deluded sense of when it's justifiable to be loyal and when it's not. But, as lack of comprehension of such a move in Britain (even within the ranks of monarchy's avid supporters) indicates, it is virtually impossible today to think of arguments that could possibly justify it. Political covenantalism's intellectual credentials are threadbare.

What we see nevertheless is an expression of cultural unionism which, in seeking protection of its way of life and claiming faithfulness to its understandings of liberty and loyalty, draws new lines in the sand with respect to loyal order practices. It refuses to engage those who find these practices intimidating or discriminatory. It also refuses to engage in wider political discussions based on *Frameworks for the Future*. Whatever the volume of its heroic noises, cultural unionism is in a bind, practically and theoretically. Absent a serious rethink, unionism appears moribund.

Liberal Unionism

Liberal unionism begs to differ. Thus, we may be told that there is already available a more than adequate form of unionism that avoids the pitfalls I've just been discussing. For a start, a liberal unionist way of life, which I call a "British political" one, is somewhat different. It ostensibly presents an acultural view of politics and, thus, aspires to a political way of life it certainly hasn't fully enjoyed since partition. Leaving aside the possibility that it's oxymoronic to think of an acultural way of life, let's say that we are dealing here with one which concentrates on the idea of the Union, emphasises a modern concept of the state, claims cultural neutrality in political affairs, celebrates plurality and appeals across the sectarian divide in a manner cultural unionism never could. As things currently stand, this is a way of life lacking proper expression so long as Northern Ireland is governed differently from the rest of the United Kingdom. An end to devolution and full integration into Westminster government is where the logic of this argument leads, at least according to its major proponents such as Bob McCartney and Arthur Aughey.

Two obvious practical-political problems are apparent, however. One is that Irish nationalists quite simply show no appetite for it and disbelieve its acultural claims, not least because liberal unionists seem very hesitant to advocate much reining in of controversial expressions of Protestant culture. The cause of unionist unity habitually inclines many a liberal eye to blindness of cultural excesses, even when they have more than a glimpse of sectarianism about them. Another problem is that the British government doesn't rate promotion of a liberal unionist way of life as a viable option for political progress in Northern Ireland.

If these are rather formidable practical difficulties, what about the liberal unionist conceptual framework? Are things more convincing at this level? I fear not, even granting that we are usually dealing with a higher level of theoretical sophistication than when discussing cultural unionism. Problems lie at the heart of the framework. These are evident once we probe its spins on history, liberty and citizenship.

The rallying cry of liberal unionism is "equal citizenship" for Northern Ireland; the plea that we here should enjoy the same burdens and entitlements as our fellow citizens in England, Scotland and Wales; that Northern Ireland should not be treated differently from elsewhere in the United Kingdom. A striking feature of this rallying cry is its association with a certain understanding of historical destiny. It is, we are told by Aughey, an idea "whose time has come" (Aughey, 1989: 157). Let's briefly conjure with this. Whereas republicans live in the hope that their day will come, liberal unionists are announcing that theirs has arrived. Which means, of course, that republicans got it wrong. To indulge a play on the republican mantra of *Tiocfaidh ár Lá* ("our day will come"), it's as if Gerry (Adams), Martin (McGuinness) and company have been "out-Chuckied", so to speak, by Arthur and Bob. This is close to seeing "equal citizenship" in our time as analogous to a type of realised eschatology. But only, it seems, to the eyes of faith and those eyes, it turns out, are very few. This is conceptually vexing: an idea whose time has come, much like a realised eschatology one suspects, needs to be obvious not merely to the few, but to the many who rely on nothing more than their normal faculties to spot it. Unless, of course, I'm barking up the wrong tree and it's a contemporary form of Gnosticism that Aughey is calling upon – in which case it's only the few who will ever be privy to its insights. Whatever relief from an epistemic conundrum this offers isn't, however, enough to offset a lingering problem of efficacy. The idea "whose time has come" is doomed to wither on the vine unless its imminent manifestation falls within the purview of the British government at least. There is no sign that this is occurring.

And then, of course, there is the equally troubling question of agency. If destiny has arrived, how did it get here? Clearly, Marx's revolutionary proletarians haven't been at play. Perhaps, though, it's Hegel's "cunning of reason" that's involved; perhaps *Geist* has been working its teleological way through British and Irish history and has finally declared its hand in favour of unionism (which is possibly another – albeit unorthodox – way of saying God was a "Prod" all along!). In the absence of convincing metaphysical demonstrations, however, there is sadly nothing to say for this. It is little more than idle kite flying.

Nestling up close to the concept of equal citizenship, we find another take on the concept of liberty, one ostensibly stripped of overt Protestant connotations. Part of the attraction of equal citizenship, it appears, is the added guarantee it provides to individual freedom. Or so runs the logic of McCartney's appropriation of Isaiah Berlin's famous distinction between "negative" and "positive" liberty. The barebones of his argument are these: (1) Negative freedom means removing as many obstacles as possible, within the boundaries of the rule of law, that inhibit individuals from living lives of their own choosing, whereas positive freedom circumscribes the choices available to individuals and, in the name of a higher good, compels them to conform to prescribed patterns of life. Positive freedom, thus construed, seems to licence "forcing people to be free" and in truth offers servitude rather than freedom. (2) Britain is a bastion of negative liberty whereas the Irish Republic is a haven of positive freedom, an authoritarian state hostile to liberalism. (3) Securing equal citizenship, which, to repeat, entails Northern Ireland's full integration within the British system of government, is the ultimate protection of individual liberty precisely because it at once removes the threat of a united Ireland and its accompanying authoritarian rule.

This is unimpressive stuff. Even if we buy Berlin's depictions of negative and positive freedom, it is close to ludicrous to imagine Britain as the embodiment of the former and Ireland as the embodiment of the latter. Just sticking with the liberal unionist polemic against the Irish Republic, it's perverse to glide over the Republic's de-clericalisation and liberalisation during the last two decades, its ongoing transformation through membership of the European Union, and so on. It is simply prejudiced not to recognise Ireland as a liberal democracy comparable to Britain. And an important spin-off of this prejudice is a misreading of nationalist reluctance to embrace or identify with various British institutions in Northern

Ireland: the reluctance doesn't spring from some deep-seated illiberalism, but from the conviction that much institutional life in the North reflects a cultural British particularity uncongenial to many with Irish sensibilities. Let's be clear: it's delusional to think that, in the context of Northern Ireland, unionism represents liberalism whilst nationalism represents authoritarianism.

Now my objection to liberal unionism here isn't merely that it makes a bad fist of applying its conceptual framework to local political conditions. It's also that there is something wrong with the framework itself, or, more specifically, that its concepts of liberty and citizenship are questionable. For instance, I think that we shouldn't buy Berlin's characterisation of positive freedom (in its political guise) as a subterfuge for tyrannical control of individuals. What Berlin severely downplays is positive freedom's association with the very democratic notion of citizen self-rule, that is, with the idea that the more citizens contribute to shaping the collective fate of their society the freer they become from manipulation by elites. I'll say more about this a little later (see Chapter five). Moreover, such downplaying of freedom's link to self-rule feeds into a quite thin and one-dimensional concept of citizenship; one which may have the virtue of insisting on our having equal rights and protection of individual liberties, but not much else. What's missing is proper appreciation of the dimension of citizens' identification with the basic institutions of government and society; the sort of identification that commands their allegiance and instils a willingness to engage in practices of self-rule. A merely procedural model of citizenship can't adequately accommodate this dimension. And, anyway, we may wonder how many unionists remain unionists only because they are individualistic rights-loving liberals whose attachment to British institutions has no other rationale or lacks any further cultural depth. On strictly liberal logic here, the moment it could be demonstrated that Ireland offered more negative liberty than Britain support for the Union would collapse. But I rather suspect none of us would expect to witness any liberal unionist stampede southwards under such circumstances. Why not? Well, in part because, as cultural unionists understand, allegiance to the Crown, say, invokes cultural resonances of an almost primordial sort amongst most unionists, including liberals. Liberal unionism, then, is not only practically challenged, but also, in several crucial respects, conceptually blind. It scarcely offers a promising way forward for Northern Ireland and seems every bit as unlikely as does cultural unionism to secure agreement with nationalists. The case for unionism's rethinking remains.

Conclusion

So, I'm saying that unionism needs rethinking because, in what I've called its cultural and liberal forms, it's tied to ways of life that are out of kilter with realities in Northern Ireland, Britain and the Republic of Ireland. More than that, these are ways of life that are inherently too exclusive and that are related to conceptual frameworks that are much too narrow.

As I have suggested, cultural unionism involves a way of life defined by a Protestant-British ethos which at once makes unionism anathema to those not sharing this ethos; and it employs a conceptual scheme which wrongly assumes that Protestantism is constitutive of our ideas of liberty and loyalty and so is closed off to the other strands of thought in Western history which make these ideas what they are for many of us. Liberal unionism, for its part, invokes a British political way of life which simply can't accommodate non-unionist allegiances in Northern Ireland; and it works within a conceptual scheme which thinks of citizens *purely* as individuals whose rights and liberties need protecting and of politics mainly as a procedural device for securing such protection. In doing so, it removes a good deal of the stuff of politics and yields, in my view, an absurdly individualistic account of citizenship which is particularly ill-equipped to handle the conundrums that afflict the politics of our society. The question thus obtrudes: is this all that unionism can offer?

5

A Civic Alternative

I now turn to considering whether unionism can offer more than either its cultural or liberal expressions seem able to provide and, if it can, thereby answer the question of what a rethought unionism might look like. I want to begin with a quick recapitulation of my criticisms of unionism's typical offerings by relating them to some of the assumptions which I admitted underlay the writing of *Rethinking Unionism*. Doing so enables me to throw into sharper relief tasks which are required of any adequately rethought unionism and which I then use as guides in my process of rethinking.

Recapitulation

I have in mind here four specific assumptions which facilitate a succinct exposure of what needs fixing in unionism and give hint of a more feasible form of unionist thinking.

First, there's what I'll call the *liberal assumption*: namely, that all members of a polity should be treated as "free and equal citizens" and that all should, therefore, enjoy equal rights. Now liberal unionism has no trouble in principle agreeing with (at least a weak version of) this assumption, but cultural unionism has. Sure, cultural unionists often enough play lip-service to something like it but what may be termed the "covenantal" dimension of their thought tends to clash with it and in practice override it.

Second, there's what I'll call – with some hesitation and at the risk of enormous misunderstanding – the *(civic) republican assumption*: namely, that to be viable a polity must be characterised by institutions and practices capable of commanding the allegiance of (the vast preponderance of) its citizens, that is, institutions and practices which we regard as "ours". Unionism, in the history of the Northern Ireland's government, has never seriously sought to satisfy this assumption. And neither cultural nor liberal unionism show any prospect of seeking to do so now. Antipathy to Catholics and/or non-unionists guarantees that. Which is partly why I think their visions for our future remain gloomy, whatever the up-beat rhetoric of defiance or prophecy sometimes accompanying them.

The third and fourth assumptions interlock. Let's call the third the *democratic assumption*: namely, that a democratic mode of politics privileges the practice of dialogue (I understand that not all such "democratic" modes do so but, since I'm not interested now in analysing democracy's inferior renderings, I'm sticking with a characterisation of what I take to be its superior articulation). Here the guiding idea is that it's only as we engage one another, listen to one another, challenge one another, address each other's concerns, put up arguments, amend arguments, retract arguments – in short, deliberate together – that we can expect to reach enduring political agreements. Agreements capable of winning our consent or even (on a good day) reflecting a consensus. In the absence of dialogue, it's hard to see how we'll ever begin to overcome the divisions that corrupt our politics or develop bonds of trust and understanding with those who are different from us. And this applies to how we may conceive of a workable devolved assembly involving a form of citizens' self-rule almost certainly through power-sharing arrangements between unionists and nationalists (and others). If we never allow ourselves to be taken beyond purely instrumental relations with our political rivals, which is what's happening when dialogue's importance is scorned, our governing arrangements are doomed to remain fragile – operating as they must under the perpetual threat of imminent breakdown.

The fourth assumption I'll call the *interpretative* one: namely, that we (as individuals or as members of a cultural/political tradition) have to admit that our understandings of ourselves/ society at any given moment are always open to revision. Implicitly or explicitly, we interpret and reinterpret what counts for us and why. And here, I suggest, the whole business of interpretation/reinterpretation, evaluation/re-evaluation finds its locus in dialogue. It's through checking out, say, the intelligibility of our own views with others and being exposed to (what might initially strike us as) the strangeness of theirs, that we arrive at deeper, fuller understandings of what matters to us and why. This interpretative assumption also makes dialogue central. In doing so, it reinforces the democratic assumption: dialogue is beneficial for us politically and, more generally, as human beings. To borrow from an old Guinness advertisement, dialogue, with or without the aid of the black stuff, *is good for you*.

A politics based on these assumptions and reflecting the complex British/Irish condition of Northern society is, I contend, conducive to achieving a decent future beyond sectarianism, stalemate, and division. Yet, I'm also maintaining, there's little to suggest that either cultural or liberal unionism show much interest in them. Democratic and interpretative assumptions which underscore the indispensability of dialogical practices are, on the terms of both liberal and cultural unionists, more of a nuisance than a guide. And, at root, that's because both (wrongly in my opinion) think it's enough to reduce politics to a protective tool which is utilised in the service of some version of *correct thought*; it is (so they imagine) the possession of such a device that equips unionists to avoid pitfalls which may be entailed in risky dialogical encounters. One problem is that a merely protective tool proves feeble when an exploration of creative political possibilities is required, and another problem is that insisting on the purity of correct thought (besides very probably betraying an unhelpful approach to reality) is futile when the healing of a society's debilitating divisions necessitates facilitating the views of others.

By restating my argument thus far in relation to these assumptions, it is possible to highlight tasks to be performed by any unionist expression aspiring to overcome the inadequacies of conventional unionist offerings. Three tasks stand out. One I'll call the *non-discriminatory task* which is entailed in the liberal assumption: ensuring that no impediments prevent individuals of whatever background or tradition from being treated as free and equal citizens. A second, I'll name the *inclusive society task* which is bound up with the civic republican assumption: creating and sustaining institutions which are owned by all citizens and with which they may identify. And the third I'll refer to as the *dialogical political task* which is integral to the democratic and interpretative assumptions: cultivating a type of citizen-centred politics which involves citizens in the business of governing and helps to break down barriers between them. When we recast the issues at stake in these terms, we may see that it is impossible for either cultural or liberal unionists to perform the second task, since their attachments to their respective ways of life commit them to kinds of exclusivism which make them blind to elementary conditions of inclusion. It's therefore not surprising that they also lack the conceptual acumen to grasp what might be required of the task of guaranteeing an inclusive society. And things aren't much better when considering the other tasks. Liberal unionists may be capable of tackling the first, at least in principle, but not so cultural unionists: the latter's way of life precludes a full embrace of any principle of non-discrimination and puts the first task beyond them. With respect to the third task, there's little hope of its being completed by these forms of unionism. Their conceptual frameworks which are heavily loaded on the side of protection, simply don't easily enable the performance of creative politics with all the risks and openness that dialogical engagement suggests.

A big upshot here is that the three tasks I've highlighted may be impossible to perform not only without an adequate conceptual framework, but also in the absence of a way of life permitting their performance (not to mention encouraging the articulation of the requisite framework). So, I'd like to turn now to teasing out what some of this means in the hope of offering an alternative vision of unionism which succeeds where other visions fail. I start with a sweeping overview of the way of life and framework I associate with this alternative to which I give the title "civic unionism". I then focus on an idea of *due recognition* which is at the heart of my attempt to handle the problematic second task, and finally, take up the notion of *citizenship* which bears most obviously on discharging the third task.

Civic Unionism: An Overview

To start, then, with an overview, I need to be upfront about the way of life I'm envisaging and its relation to unionism.

A "Northern Irish" Way of Life

I want to call this for convenience a "Northern Irish" way of life which, to be frank, may readily appear too elliptical to be useful. It instantly sounds parochial and perhaps lacking in the grandeur of an unapologetic British way of life that not only invokes ties to other nations (England, Scotland and Wales) but also memories of Empire and relations within the British Commonwealth. It also seems to pale in comparison to familiar romantic images of an Irish way of life; it may easily appear as an insipid player on a stage dominated by the literary, musical and mythical attractions of an Irishness which is also capable of playing on a history of oppression and capturing the sympathies and imaginations of international audiences. And perhaps worst of all, it risks being mistaken for a strangely narrow "Ulster" way of life whose champions seem weirdly unaware of the general distaste others have of their dour dispositions and charmless, uncompromising attitudes (even if deep down they really are great *craic* – and I should know since it's among such people and within this way of life that I was brought up!).

At any rate, the way of life I'm associating with civic unionism is more diffuse and inchoate than these others; it is based more on signposts than on settled destinations, more on possibilities than on definitive forms. It struggles for adequate expression because its potential is easily stifled by its powerful rivals and their simple, but reassuring, myths of undiluted Britishness, Irish destiny, and Protestant heritage. As I put it in *Rethinking Unionism*: "That Northern Ireland, in all its complexities and contradictions, might be the site of a way of life that is peculiarly its own is a disturbing thought to those whose sights remain firmly set on Westminster or Dublin, and one distorted beyond recognition by those who claim 'Ulster' as the exclusive home of their tribe or tradition" (Porter, 1996: 171). But what exactly is it that I'm appealing to here?

A short answer is *an interest in making Northern Ireland work*. This interest, I'm claiming, can't be realised sufficiently without a shift away from conventional obsessions with either maintaining the Union or agitating for a united Ireland. Of course, it could immediately be objected, why should nationalists care about this since it's scarcely in their interest to want Northern Ireland to work or to cast around for some (probably undesirable if not fictitious) 'Northern Irish way of life'? A fair enough rejoinder, I suppose, albeit one that is in my view a little hasty. But my beef here isn't principally with nationalists, although I do hope to muddy the waters enough to indicate that the springs from which they draw aren't always as clear as they may seem (surely, one might conjecture, it's only possible to think of the North as merely a "lost green field" if the water supply has been affected, even if ever so slightly!), and to suggest that a rethought (civic) unionism may be worthy of their consideration. Whatever about that, it's with mainstream unionists that my quarrel is presently concentrated. They most certainly do have an interest in making Northern Ireland work and yet their thoughts and actions would almost make us believe to the contrary. If the nationalist case typically downplays British factors in the North, most unionist cases typically downplay Irish factors. As a result, we end up with distorted visions of what Northern society is, that is, visions that obscure its complexity and therefore are shut off from the possibility of it possessing an alternative way of life. So, an important step in the argument I'm trying to develop is to clarify what I take Northern Ireland to be.

The image of the North I'm depicting is of a society that is different from Great Britain and the rest of Ireland, and I do by drawing upon two metaphors. The first is that of the North as "a place apart" – neither as British as Finchley nor as Irish as Cork – but not because it is closed off from other British and Irish expressions but, rather, because it is peculiarly open to both. Which leads to the second metaphor, borrowed from Edna Longley, of the six counties as a "cultural corridor" open at one end to British influences and at the other to Irish. Combining these two metaphors yields something like what I call a "difference *through* openness" thesis: Northern Ireland is different from other parts of Britain and of Ireland *because* its corridor is open at both ends. This picture of an open-ended corridor invites a challenging scenario: as the influences flowing from both of its ends meet, mingle, fuse and clash something distinctive emerges which (if viewed through exclusively British or exclusively Irish lenses) may seem maddening, frustrating, unacceptable and maybe unworkable; or, alternatively, (if our lenses are suitably ecumenical) may appear promising, brimming with possibilities, and hinting of creative opportunities to fashion a fresh future for a much-maligned society.

We may begin to get a handle on what I'm gesturing at by acknowledging that Northern Ireland is a place apart in the sense that politically and administratively it's different from its closest neighbours. Obviously, since partition, and despite their geographical location within the island of Ireland, the North's government and bureaucracy have been independent from those of the Republic of Ireland. Equally obviously, Northern Ireland is not only geographically separate from Britain, but also politically and legally distinctive: from experimenting with 50 years of devolved government until 1972 and subsequent (thus far unsuccessful) attempts at power-sharing through to enjoying a separate judiciary and statute book, its place within the UK has been unique. Following Ireland's partition, the North has to some degree taken its own route. It's also a place apart in the sense that its citizens have been subject to extraordinary pressures and worries that have been different in kind from those familiar in other liberal democracies, Ireland and Great Britain included: since the recent years of conflict from 1969 especially, Northern citizens have shared a harrowing "troubles-related" experience – however widely varying its expressions and unequally distributed its effects – that accentuates their difference from other British or Irish citizens.

With the exception possibly of those who dream of an independent Ulster, there is considerable reluctance to ascribe much positive meaning to Northern Ireland's apartness. It is a problem to be overcome by those seeking a united Ireland and by those seeking an integrationist solution to unionism's woes. That's grand up to a point I suppose – inasmuch as it's clearly reassuring to plenty of unionists and nationalists to have pleasant dreams of victory for one's side – but when the price to be paid is perpetual stalemate if not overt violence, then maybe it's time to give pause to these sorts of dreams. This isn't to say that everything about them should be discarded, but that their respective identifications with Britishness and Irishness may be accommodated in other ways, especially those not dependent upon zero-sum logic. Which is where it's important to introduce into our deliberations the second metaphor of a cultural corridor which links the North to Britain and to Ireland.

In a sense, doing so is merely a bland statement of the obvious: given its location and history, the North cannot help but reflect a range of British and Irish influences. What can be denied though is that these should be appropriated – at least in some measure – culturally or politically. We're painfully acquainted with insular efforts to live as if one or other end of the "cultural corridor" has been closed off and unwanted British or Irish traffic banned from entry. And even when this doesn't happen quite so blatantly, even when there's apparent broadminded acceptance of cultural traffic coming from both directions, there is plenty of resistance to cultural openness ramifying into political openness. For example, on matters political, insist avowedly tolerant liberal unionists, Northern Ireland's cultural difference doesn't warrant any political translation. But this is far too facile. Much of the cultural complexity ingrained in Northern society is politically charged through and through and can't be depoliticized by the wave of a procedural wand.

An implication of the preceding reflections is that appropriating the metaphors of "a place apart" and a "cultural corridor" entails allocating proper space to cultural diversity and allowing the possibility that we're all shaped in various ways by an interweaving of British and Irish forces. It also hints at political arrangements that facilitate such diversity and reflect Northern Ireland's difference even as they remain open at both ends to Westminster and Dublin.

So, to some extent, I'm saying that there's already a semblance of a particular Northern Irish way of life in operation; one of course that overlaps with other British and Irish ways without being reducible to any of them. But it's frequently choked in its development and because it lacks full representation it's easily overlooked or disparaged. Neither unionism's nor nationalism's conventional conceptual frameworks equip us to recognise it. To offset their baneful influences, we need to think differently about our Northern circumstances, which we may do by imagining a dialectical interplay between a more appropriate conceptual framework that opens up our latent Northern Irish way of life and accommodates its proper expression, even as this way of life in turn enables an articulation of such an appropriate conceptual framework.

Civic Unionism

The conceptual framework in question is what I'm calling civic unionism, and it rests upon two premises: (1) that enhancing the quality of social and political life in Northern Ireland is the major priority (rather than, say, upholding the Union or striving for a united Ireland); and (2) that, given this priority, achieving a way of life worth having for all citizens is the fundamental goal of political action. This second premise is one that assumes much of what I've already mentioned regarding a Northern Irish way of life but is an indication of the need to add conceptual depth and detail in respect to its civic and unionist components.

I'll say a little more about the latter component shortly and for the moment it's enough to remark that in lieu of a democratic decision to exit the UK by the North's citizens, it's reasonable to advocate a political vision which accepts Northern Ireland's current constitutional status. This evidently weighs things in favour of Westminster but not in such a manner as to preclude involvement by Dublin.

On the civic component, the point is to stipulate more of what I mean when referring to a "way of life worth having". Given the ground already covered in my criticisms of standard forms of unionism, it should be clear that by such a life I'm referring to one in which we are all treated as free and equal agents, enabled to enjoy a sense of belonging through institutional arrangements that reflect who we are, and permitted to have a voice in how things are organised. Accordingly, there is an emphasis on both the entitlements of individuals and the entitlements of citizens to have a significant say in the shaping of their personal, cultural, social and political lives. To acknowledge both sorts of entitlements means advocating the development of a Northern society that incorporates at least four features: *devolved institutions of government* in Northern Ireland that are based upon principles of power-sharing and that are sufficiently inclusive to guarantee citizens' identification and allegiance; a *tolerant and pluralistic civil society*, that is, one in which institutions and practices that express the diversity of individuals, associations and groups – except those entailing a denigration of others – are encouraged to blossom; *acceptable legal and security institutions* that protect the rights of individuals and groups against discrimination, that are widely recognised as impartial, and that, through their inclusive symbolic emblems and uniforms, are seen as representative of all citizens and not merely one tradition; and, finally, *socio-economic institutions that are geared to providing conditions conducive to the flourishing of all citizens* and, therefore, that are not left to the mercy of unregulated market forces alone but that are answerable to principles of social justice. To add a few quick comments on this fourth feature what's required is conceiving of structures suited to permit the mix of individual, company and government initiatives and investments, especially in areas of acute social deprivation, that are crucial to a thriving economy. It is also imperative here to conceive of political measures being taken in such areas as health, education, employment and social benefits that ensure that nobody is forced, through unfortunate circumstances, to fall below certain acceptable standards of living. And it is further apposite to conceive of policies that provide for all citizens fair access to, and an equitable share of, society's resources and opportunities, not to mention (as few do) policies geared at cultivating among citizens habits conducive to good practices of self-government.

Accepting the entitlements of individuals and citizens in these ways intimates that the civic component is intended to appeal to all of us, whether we consider ourselves unionist, nationalist or neither. To concentrate attention on such matters could open up new possibilities and put old animosities under pressure. Common ground could be discovered by citizens devoted to making Northern Ireland work. New forms of citizen identity and attachment might appear alongside traditional ones. Is such talk dismissible as a mere pipedream? Well, it assuredly is to those who are unwilling to allow their imaginations to exceed the narrow boundaries which define the interests of their tribe or tradition. And, admittedly, within unionism at least, such people currently have the numbers. To yield to their uninspiring view of things is, in my opinion, no longer acceptable. It is tantamount to underwriting a tyranny of "what is" in which we are boxed in by old prejudices and doomed to live according to scripts that are a testimony to little more than human fear and intransigence. But it needn't be like this, especially if enough of us are willing to subscribe to something like what I'm calling civic unionism.

Okay, then, let me quickly take stock of where I'm up to in laying out an alternative form of unionist thinking. I've so far tried to support claims of this sort: only by redescribing what Northern Ireland is are we opened to the possibility of full enjoyment of a Northern Irish way of life; only then are we able to articulate a conceptual framework commensurate with its basic features and indicative of its potential for development (as a "way of life worth having") in directions beneficial to all of us in the North; and only this framework (civic unionism) equips us to perform the tasks I earlier suggested were necessary to reformulating unionism in a fashion that gives Northern Ireland a chance of working adequately. More now needs to be said about the three tasks I identified in order to bolster these claims. Or at the very least more needs to be said about two of them. I'm going to assume that enough has been said about civic unionism to render the first *non-discriminatory task* of us all being treated as free and equal agents/citizens unproblematic on its terms. But I don't think that's true of the second and third tasks. These require more attention which I now hope to provide by recourse to concepts of recognition and citizenship.

Due Recognition

To recall, the second task is that of creating and sustaining an *inclusive society* comprising institutions which are owned by all citizens and command their allegiance. This has never been achieved in the history of Northern Ireland and there's little question that the brunt of the blame here must be borne by unionism. The sheer fact that Northern society is riven with sectarianism and division makes tackling this task very difficult. And at the heart of the difficulty is the unavoidable problem of significant nationalist/republican alienation from government institutions. Without substantial change Northern Ireland simply can't work sufficiently, as a recent generation of violence has often cruelly underscored. The current emphasis on the language of parity of esteem – pressed by the British and Irish governments – is intended to address this problem. But is this the best language for helping us think our way through things here?

Difficulties with "Parity of Esteem"

Although I've been critical of unionism's responses to the challenges posed by demands for parity of esteem (Chapter two), I'm not convinced that sticking with this concept is the best way to proceed. I don't want to make too much of my unease here because for the most part I support the main point it's trying to make, namely that an even-handedness needs to characterise arrangements in Northern society; that desires to seek advantages for one tradition should be curbed by respect for the integrity and entitlements of the other. But does agreement with this point necessarily involve *esteem*? There seems to be a presumption at work that esteem can unproblematically be accorded to another traditional identity simply by virtue of its significance to those who bear it. But what is it that we're being expected to accord? Acknowledgement of others' entitlement to an expression of their identity doubtless, but maybe also an affirmation of the intrinsic worthiness of that identity and the way of life with which it's associated. If the latter is required then, as I maintained in *Rethinking Unionism*, the emphasis on esteem is pushing its luck. "To expect Catholics to esteem an Orange culture they perceive to be inherently anti-Catholic and triumphalist is as far-fetched as expecting unionists to admire a nationalist culture that expresses itself through such slogans as 'Brits Out'" (Porter, 1996: 188). And, considering *parity*, once we press beyond the point of objecting to prejudiced and unfair treatments of minority cultural forms are we saying, as some unionists fear, that unionism and nationalism must be given strictly equivalent political treatment? Or, simply put, does a political translation of parity (of esteem) entail the implementation of some type of joint (British and Irish) authority in the governmental arrangements of Northern Ireland? For, if it does, unionists regard this as a bridge too far; it is, they think, an undemocratic ruse in which fears of majoritarian tyranny are over-compensated to the point of stripping the majority tradition of its proper democratic prerogatives.

Introducing Due Recognition

In response to such worries, I propose exchanging the concept of parity of esteem for that of due recognition. For a start, *recognition* is a term with a philosophical pedigree that equips it to do much heavier and more important lifting than does the term esteem. Bluntly put, *to be deprived of esteem is to be slighted, whereas to be deprived of recognition is to be blanked out*. Esteem is something we are entitled to request, but recognition is something we are entitled to demand; it is something that, unlike esteem, is at its core non-negotiable. In reasoning along these lines, I am, of course, recalling insights from the most celebrated section on the master-slave dialectic in Hegel's otherwise frequently impenetrable *Phenomenology of Spirit*. Resisting the temptation to digress into discussion of the varied, rich connotations of Hegel's analysis and their potential to undermine standard Enlightenment, and especially Kantian, approaches to epistemology, moral philosophy and political theory – not to mention their impact on Marx and subsequent developments in Marxism – let me settle for two more accessible points.

One is that relations of domination and subjugation don't work out well for anyone in the basic sense that all parties in such relations fail to have their personhood affirmed; absent reciprocity – which is precisely what's missing in master-slave interactions – nobody enjoys an assured grasp of identity. Why? Well, because it's not pre-given, because none of us arrive in the world as fully developed, self-contained selves; rather, we appear as beings crucially dependent on others; beings requiring others to recognise (a likeness of) themselves in us and of us in them. To be denied recognition is to be treated as a thing not as a person and to treat others as things isn't just to de-humanise them but also to inflict harm on ourselves, since we need their affirmation as much as they need ours, and only persons (not things) can meet such need. Warped power relations distort elementary facets of our humanness. Recognition's denial is a travesty of the intersubjective condition of personhood which hangs on mutual acknowledgement of a dignity we share equally as human beings.

By extension a second point presents itself: what's true of an understanding of self-awareness at the level of an individual is true also at the level of a group or a collective. We define ourselves not merely in reference to our personal traits and qualities but also in reference to our larger allegiances of family, religion, culture, nationality, politics and so forth. Recognition of these allegiances is vital too as we only have the sense of ourselves that we do by virtue of them. That's why being denied expression of, say, our religion is such a big deal to believers: it's tantamount to others wanting to eradicate the core of our identity. And this is intolerable. Similar points may be made of our other types of group identity, not least of those most relevant to us in Northern Ireland today. For example, attempts to minimise or, worse, to suppress expressions of Irishness in the North arguably involved refusing to recognise dimensions of a cultural-political identity that were and still are essential to nationalists. To resort to language I mentioned a few moments ago, this was equivalent to wanting to *blank out* of Northern society's public space any hint of a nationalist presence. But nationalism's public erasure in the past is the problem that's trying to be corrected now. And I'm suggesting that replacing the term esteem with that of recognition strengthens the force of the argument: it becomes a matter of rudimentary justice which makes demands (and not simply requests) of us. It is only when our institutional design and our endorsed public practices reflect the fullness (and complexity) of who we are that Northern Ireland has any prospect of functioning properly and winning the support of citizens across the board. Insisting that our major traditions are appropriately recognised here is therefore a crucial step in ensuring that this occurs.

"Appropriately recognised" is of course a key, and controversial, qualifier, which leads me to explain the stress I'm putting on the notion of *due* in this context. Two additional considerations may help. A general one is that recognition necessarily comes in grades. At its most basic, as I've been arguing, it is unqualified, that is, where non-recognition is impermissible precisely because it would involve a denial of personhood. And here I include an understanding of persons not only as moral and spiritual individuals of intrinsic worth but also as cultural beings (in the broadest sense). So due recognition at this level involves appreciating the importance of, say, traditional identities and their cultivation; it accepts a *prima facie* case against moves to crush or stultify these, or to deny them representation in the public life of a divided society. Matters shift a little when other deliberations arise, such as if we are expected to endorse the entirety of a tradition's various manifestations or agree to its preferred range of exhibitions; it is here that practical judgements need to be made about what's "due" (or just, warranted, permissible) in the varying circumstances of social and political life. This is to pick up a point I made in the previous lecture (Chapter four) and developed in my discussions of cultural and liberal unionism, when I said that our ways of life (and thus the traditional identities bound up with them) aren't immune from critical inspection; it's also an extension of my emphasis on why "esteem" can't automatically be granted on request. As it happens, we're often unavoidably caught up (unofficially) in an exercise of grading recognition claims or of talking about degrees of recognition, especially when some expressions of traditional identities entail a misrecognition of others by promoting images of them that utterly distort these others' own self-understandings. There's plenty of evidence of this to be found in popular manifestations of unionist and nationalist cultures that we hardly need reminding of, but the main point I'm stressing now is that there should be no question of recognition extending, say, to a public ratification of distortions of this kind; no such traditional misrepresentation of others is "due" that sort of recognition. And it's also likely that in the name of "due" recognition limitations will be placed on the acceptable range of a tradition's public display, which is clearly a relevant reflection bearing on the matter of disputed marches in Northern society. Sure, the traditional identity demanding expression through parades is entitled to recognition, and within areas where it is welcomed that should be relatively unproblematic (although even in these contexts we might shift uneasily in the face of its more excessively acerbic exhibitions). But what isn't granted is licence to its untrammelled display in every conceivable venue, including formerly traditional ones. This is not its "due". Good sense or judgement suggests that where it is deemed offensive its presence should be limited. And so on.

A second, more particularly political, consideration involves the application of due recognition in the organisation of Northern society. I've made clear that by invoking a concept of recognition I think there's a compelling case for British and Irish factors featuring in the public institutional life of Northern Ireland. And, in part, this is to concede that Ireland's partition was a messy, tragic affair that would've benefitted from more delicate handling, not least in the treatment of nationalists who were forced to comply with arrangements they very much opposed. But does that mean that British and Irish factors should now count equally? Not quite. Although the thrust of my argument for civic unionism entails questioning the centrality of constitutional concerns, the fact remains that Northern Ireland is constitutionally part of the UK and not Ireland. And given that more Northern voters prefer the current constitutional status quo to any of its alternatives, and that Northern Ireland's legitimacy is recognised in international law, British factors are presently "due" more recognition than are Irish. A mistake is to think that a majoritarian principle – which is of course what's being relied upon when deferring to the volume of voters' preferences – can be pressed too far beyond its crucial constitutional role. For instance, it can't convincingly be utilised to justify any or all exclusions of Irish identities from institutional representation, of minority nationalist parties from political power, or of the Irish government from any input into aspects of Northern political life. Due recognition, as understood in the civic unionist terms I've been presenting, counts not only against (some) nationalist proposals of joint sovereignty, but also against (many) unionist endeavours to marginalise the symbolic, practical and institutional instantiations of nationalism within public life in Northern society. It's hardly surprising, then, if civic unionism seems odd to other unionists, if not also to most nationalists. My claim is that it offers the prospect of an inclusive Northern Ireland in a way that other unionist positions cannot match; and that this prospect is enhanced by having at one's conceptual disposal a notion of *due recognition.*

Expansive Citizenship

Finally, we come to the third task which derives from the democratic and interpretative assumptions I drew attention to earlier. I've depicted this as a *dialogical political task* which is concerned with encouraging a citizen-centred political focus; one that involves citizens in the processes of self-government and helps to break down barriers between them. At heart, what's required here is a conception of citizenship adequate to the task. In briefly trying to meet this requirement, I'll call upon (my notion of) an *expansive* understanding of citizenship, that is, one that extends beyond more common (and inadequate) understandings of the nature of citizens' activity, and finish by considering an objection to it.

On the Nature of Citizens' Activity

There is, in my opinion, a dreadful inadequacy in attempts to restrict the focus of citizen-relevant activity to protective causes. This isn't true only of those unionist attempts I've already criticised, but also of typical liberal endeavours to think of citizens' interests in utilitarian or procedural terms. If we conceive of individuals primarily as desire-maximisers, for instance, it is a short move to think of citizens as consumers; or if we conceive of individuals primarily as rights-bearers, it isn't too difficult to think of citizens as procedural sticklers preoccupied with rules of due process (or their equivalent) and not much else. In either case, the nature of activities appropriate to citizens is protective in kind and the activities themselves are frequently performed on their behalf: safeguarding citizens' scope for consuming whatever they fancy without any reference to whether what they fancy is worth fancying on one hand; or, on another, maintaining procedural conditions necessary for the realisation of citizens' entitlement to pursue plans of life consistent with principles of right and justice. Nothing wrong here, we might think. And in a sense, there isn't: we all consume and the more we're allowed to do so without restriction the more agreeable we typically find things (even if sometimes to our longer-term regret); and many of us are keen on having our rights protected in such a way that we're able to follow a principled course of life respectful of others. And yet there's something missing. The activities that citizens are freed up to do – consume goods or lead principled lives – are not essentially (or perhaps even remotely) political in nature. Here politics, with its focus on citizens' predilections to consumption, rights and so on, is about making possible other things in our lives that we might value. But there are no activities required of citizens that are inherently political, especially when even the minimal activity of voting is optional. No mention, then, of the necessity of dialogue, of practices essential to self-government, or of moves to foster a common citizens' identity; these are virtually surplus to requirements on the terms of much contemporary liberal political theory. What I've called a third *dialogical political task* becomes close to irrelevant. And if we think this task shouldn't be cast aside so lightly – since it might mean devaluing the importance of multi-party talks to sort out our future in Northern Ireland and thereby present us with exceedingly grim political prospects – this is despite, not because of, the foregoing liberal attitudes to concerns of citizens *qua* citizens.

I think this is unfortunate, to put it mildly, precisely because it invites us to glide over difficulties at the core of Northern Ireland's politics and to be radically unprepared in knowing how to tackle them. It's to be cut off from insights that are accessible only through dialogue; it's to overlook the fact that trust, the cultivation of which is crucial to overcoming problems in a divided society, can't be engineered in the absence of interactions in which all participants are allowed to speak in their own voices – not even through encouragement of shared consumption habits, bureaucratic protocols or good laws, for none of these are adequate substitutes. All of this is to say that in addition to its necessary protective dimension, the nature of citizens' activity is profitably conceived of more broadly to include a creative, specifically political focus. As I argue in the final chapter of *Rethinking Unionism*, resources for such a broader conception may be found in a classical republican tradition of political thought tracing back to Aristotle. What's particularly germane here is thinking beyond the confines of negative freedom – which stultify the political imaginations of many liberals – by recapturing freedom's "positive" association with the self-government of citizens. The basic impetus is to avoid despotic rule – whether "hard" as in tyrannical dictatorship or "soft" as (arguably) in the types of bureaucratic administration we experience in Northern Ireland due to our dysfunctional politics; it is also to escape manipulation by elites (which is always a danger in any society which panders to the interests of global capital) by granting citizens control of their collective fate. So, it's only as we exercise control over our affairs through our common deliberations about what course we should take, what goals we should pursue and which should be prioritised, about what policies we should adopt and so on, that we are free in the positive sense of the term. And this is the stuff of citizens' activity. Moreover, since the freedom it makes available is that which we realise together as citizens, it requires inclusive public spaces open to the disparate voices in society. It is by arguing with and listening to one another, by proposing and counter-proposing, agreeing and disagreeing, evaluating and judging together, that we may hope to reach decisions about our collective life with which we may all live and to which we may be committed.

This classical republican citizen-freedom nexus is what I'm trying to recapture here. Once central to Western, especially European, understandings of politics, it has increasingly been pushed to the margins and probably appears unfamiliar to most contemporary citizens. Thus, it bears repeating that the nexus goes beyond a purely protective conception of citizenship – which effectively makes freedom "freedom from politics" as Hannah Arendt pithily puts it (Arendt, 2000: 443) – and intimates a wider conception which links citizens' activity to the achievement of a free society. And so, via such an alternative perspective on citizens' activity we may grasp that crucial sense, overlooked by many liberals and unionists alike, in which what's on offer is freedom through politics.

An Objection

There is, however, something potentially misleading about how I've just framed the contrast between liberal and classical republican views of citizenship; something we may get at by raising the objection that the latter view becomes hard to imagine outside the world of small (ancient Greek or Renaissance) city-states. What I've failed to mention so far is that we're living in representative democracies where the direct participation of citizens in issues of government simply isn't possible. Two quick clarifications here will have to suffice by way of a reply. First, considering matters from the angle of institutionalised decision-making, it's obviously representatives who are explicitly responsible for decisions taken at formal levels of government as well as at such events as multi-party talks on Northern Ireland's future. But these representatives are also citizens who are accountable to other citizens whom they represent – which is why we have such practices as elections, referendums, and the like. And the rationale informing their deliberations (far from being different in kind from) presumably reflects that found among the wider body of citizens. The classical republican-inspired view I'm advocating (taking its cue from the ancient Athenian notion of citizens as those who rule and are ruled) stresses continuity in the representative-citizen relationship. Accordingly, it cautions against political representatives assuming a kind of autonomy considered the preserve of "experts" that prompts an imposition of technical or bureaucratic fixes to political problems; fixes invariably bypassing the messy business of building trust among divided citizens. Not least because its attitude to citizens' activity scarcely requires it, there is, I'd argue, much less reason to advise such caution on conventional liberal terms. So, to the extent that we think that caution against deferring to technocratic expertise at the expense of citizens' judgement matters (and it's feasible to think like this without lapsing into a Neanderthalic replica), a classical republican view, far from appearing obsolete, continues to instruct.

Also of relevance is a second angle where the focus shifts to the role of citizens operating outside the formal channels of the state. This is an angle which is available to us only against the backdrop of our habitation of a contemporary Western social and political world which reflects a distinction between the state and civil society unknown in pre-modern times. And this may strike us as initially unpromising to the degree that acknowledging the backdrop seems to put the "proper" business of politics – conducted at the formal level of the state – out of most citizens' reach, or perhaps worse makes the state principally appear as a set of bureaucratic institutions from which citizens are necessarily alienated, or worse still, encourages an image of the state as the source of coercive authority with an array of disciplinary measures under its control which render citizens powerless. No doubt there are very real tendencies in late modern Western societies that give credence to such impressions. But they don't tell the whole story. And here it becomes possible to be upbeat about what our second angle can offer. If, for example, we think that one of the defining features of modern civil society is that it makes available public spaces for citizen activity independent of state control, then another way of thinking emerges. Latching on to opportunities afforded by the presence of such public spaces – which started with the introduction of newspapers and the proliferation of coffee houses in the eighteenth century, and has now spread in previously unfathomable directions through ever-developing new media, as well as through a myriad of voluntary associations, community groups, religious organisations and so on – citizens are able to contribute to public affairs even when their access to government is limited. Thus, even if their deliberations aren't guaranteed to make a direct impact on decisions made at a state-level, they may still count in helping to shape public opinions that governments ignore at their peril. It becomes possible to think that through working together with other citizens at these more "informal" levels, barriers between citizens may begin to be overcome, some common purposes discovered, and civic habits conducive to good self-governing practices developed. And, besides, there's always the prospect that those (representatives) entrusted with the power to effect decisions at state/government levels may themselves have been formed (at least in part) through participating at more informal civil society levels; a prospect which permits a projection of a potential congruence of the two angles insofar as these representatives realise that it is not possible in the longer run to conduct the business of government without taking seriously citizens' concerns in civil society. Accordingly, how we conceive of the nature and goals of citizen activity matters a great deal. The old classical republican view of what it means to be a citizen lives on in a different form; one that enables it to facilitate satisfaction of requirements entailed in our third task.

Conclusion

To wrap up, I've tried to show that an alternative form of unionist thinking is conceivable; one that draws from a Northern Irish way of life – inclusive of all citizens – that facilitates (and requires) a conceptual framework I've called "civic unionist". Operating within this framework, it becomes possible to imagine performing tasks beyond the competence of standard unionist approaches, especially those of creating and maintaining public institutions acceptable to the wide range of Northern citizens, and of articulating a citizen-centred mode of politics capable of taking the sting out of our differences and gradually building trust between citizens who are also members of our major traditions. I've suggested that our ability to tackle these tasks is enhanced by drawing on a concept of recognition and an expansive understanding of citizenship. Equipped with these, there is a basis of hope for the future of Northern Ireland. The rather formidable challenge remains of persuading unionists (and others) that this is the case.

6

What's Wrong With Rethinking Unionism? A Reply

Introduction

Rethinking Unionism has received many reviews – some positive, others not; some illuminating, others bewildering. One impression I'm left with is that not everyone who claims to have read the book seems to understand it. But I suppose I have to say something like that since if I were to take seriously all the reviews I've read, I'd have to plead guilty to holding incompatible opinions and to committing sins of the widest assortment. Of course, it's always possible that my opinions are just confused and contradictory, and that certain reviewers grasp them much better than I do. And it's equally possible that I've not only committed many sins I'm barely aware of, but also that I'm such a compulsive sinner that my sins have become both brazen and hugely inconsistent.

Openness to these possibilities notwithstanding, I find it difficult to concede that I've written a book which simultaneously seeks only to shore up the Union and seeks mainly to undermine it (by pandering to nationalists); one, moreover, which is stymied by my Protestant attachments and is guilty of betraying them. For the record, I've tried neither to shore up nor undermine the Union; tried neither to pander to nor dismiss nationalist concerns. I am left wondering too about which of my alleged Protestant attachments clouds my judgement, especially since the one of hyper-individualism attributed to me by one reviewer leaves me mystified. As for accusations of betrayal, I suppose I should be chastened on learning that, as the headline to Alex Kane's review in the *Belfast Telegraph* put it, I'm an "intellectual Lundy". As I struggle to ascertain how best to convey a chastened spirit, I also have to factor in the revelation that, as Brian Feeney told readers in the *Andersonstown News*, I'm merely "a souped-up Alliance man" (which I assume is an insult not intended literally given that I've never had any association with the Alliance Party). Then just as I'm close to bowing to the penetrating "insights" of Kane and Feeney and conceding that we're very fortunate to have in Belfast such fair-minded and reasonable unionist and nationalist political commentators with whom one may bounce off ideas, along comes an Irish American reviewer to put everyone in the shade. From him I learn that I am opposed to all things Irish and particularly hostile to the Republic of Ireland, and yet that (poor benighted unionist though I am) I have somehow managed to write a "relatively sane" book. Evidently, the Irish American's ability concurrently to excoriate and to humour a target (me) indicates a master dialectician at the top of his game; evidently too, it suggests Alex and Brian have their work cut out playing catch up.

Obviously, I'd like to hope that I'm now addressing an audience much savvier in its understanding of *Rethinking Unionism* than most of the reviewers I've referred to. Given the lectures on unionism that have been delivered over the last five weeks, there is a sporting chance of this being the case. And yet I hesitate to take it for granted. In part, this is because not all the lectures in this series enhance the understanding I'd have preferred. To clarify, I don't have in mind the lectures given by Feargal or Jane – there was nothing in either to which I'd take exception. The same can't be said of Arthur Aughey's lecture but that's not surprising given that I've been expressly critical of his views of unionism in my book and in the lectures I delivered here. Aughey finds plenty of faults in my position as became clear in his lecture and his review in *Fortnight* (Aughey, 1996: 31). So, in what follows I propose to offer a reply to his attempt to tell me what's wrong with *Rethinking Unionism*, not least because of the wide range of issues he brings up. The reply focuses on three sorts of differences between us. Differences of the first sort are, I think, relatively trivial and concern misunderstandings about what I'm claiming or not claiming. The second and third sorts are more substantive and refer respectively to differences that are philosophical and political in nature. Let me quickly say something about each sort in turn.

Misunderstandings

To start, I want to tidy up a couple of misunderstandings about what I'm claiming or not claiming. According to Aughey, I not only disagree with other unionists but cast aspersions on their mental capacities. As he put it in his *Fortnight* review, I regard unionists as "an object of ill-concealed contempt" and treat them as though they "suffer from mental deficiency or Bourbonic stupidity". Aughey's lecture a couple of weeks ago also made clear that he thinks I ask and expect too much too soon of other unionists. In saying these sorts of things, I don't think he gets me right.

On the "contempt-stupidity" issue especially, there is a gross misrepresentation of my position. There is no evidence cited from my text where I subject other unionists to any derogatory insults of this kind. It may be cute to make claims of this nature – I suppose one way to undermine the book's argument is not to engage seriously with its content but instead make its author appear insufferably arrogant – but in the absence of any supporting textual references it is, let's say, a rather less than charitable thing to do. Or, if I may put it this way, anyone curious to discern my intentions in writing *Rethinking Unionism* could scarcely do worse than consult Arthur Aughey. The relevant argument I do make against standard forms of unionism is that they typically operate within conceptual frameworks which I think are restrictive in the sense that they screen out too many of the realities of our current situation in Northern Ireland that can't plausibly be screened out. Here it would be more appropriate to say that I accuse a lot of unionists of being blind to a lot of things they ought not to be blind to. But this accusation doesn't in any way imply contempt of other unionists (though I do admit that it does at times express exasperation with some of their attitudes and practices) or suggest that they are stupid.

All of this is worth pointing out for a very important reason. I tried, however inadequately, to take other unionists seriously on their own terms. That meant taking seriously their beliefs and the reasons they offered for why they believe what they believe. Now I happened to disagree with most of those reasons and attempted to explain why. In doing so, I imagined I was treating other unionists with respect not contempt; and in engaging them in such a fashion I thought I was appealing to their mental capacities not bemoaning their cerebral deficiencies. Moreover, I might add, in conducting myself in this fashion, I supposed I was (at least in this sense) being impeccably Kantian: I wasn't trying to force or manipulate others into seeing the world as I see it; rather, I was offering reasons why they might consider my view and leaving them to make what they liked of those reasons. As Kant convincingly argues, giving other persons reasons for why one is advocating this or criticising that is integral to treating them with respect.

On the issue of inflated expectations, I again fear Aughey is wide of the mark. Far from expecting too much too soon from unionists, I don't expect anything. In fact, expectations are about the last thing I have of politics in Northern Ireland. I thought I had made that clear enough in the book. For example, I explicitly stated that "settling a theoretical argument rarely settles all that requires settling". And I expressly wrote that: "It is not at all that I expect something like a civic unionist vision to be quickly adopted in Northern Ireland" (Porter, 1996: 212). The real issue at stake isn't whether I expect too much too soon, but whether I ask too much too soon. And that's an issue that can only be judged in the light of other differences between us.

Philosophical Differences

One bundle of such differences is appropriately labelled "philosophical". The trouble is that getting clear about what it consists in is an intricate, time-consuming exercise; it is, frankly, one that is probably out of place in this forum. And yet to say nothing about our philosophical differences would be unfortunate. So let me try out a compromise: by drawing on Aughey's lecture and his *Fortnight* review, I'll indicate in a very schematic way where I think he distorts the philosophical position I subscribe to and why I regard it as important to respond to these distortions, albeit briefly.

Plato's Cave-Sun Metaphors

Aughey finds my approach quite Platonist, although he raises doubts about whether I measure up to Plato's standards for a philosopher. The idea is that my approach fits with Plato's famous cave-sun metaphors, not least because I allegedly "make much of my intellectual journey towards the sunlight" and my "return to the cave in Northern Ireland".

This is all quite entertaining and it's a pity to spoil the fun by pointing out that it's really twaddle. Perhaps the best response is simply to say in good Belfast language, "catch yourself on Arthur". But in case that doesn't suffice allow me to add that I don't make that much of my journey away from Belfast and then back again, and whatever I do make of it I wouldn't think of describing in terms of "sunlight" and "cave" metaphors (unless, of course, I'm merely making a cheeky allusion to a bright/overcast contrast between Australian and Irish skies!). The little I do make of this journey is meant to underscore that my perspective on Northern Ireland changed over time partly because my experience of life broadened. But this isn't to say that something similar wouldn't have happened even if I'd never left Belfast. We'll never know. But that's why the sun-cave stuff is inappropriate and misleading. And, on a more serious note, this is even more the case for two other reasons. One is that I eschew the Platonic metaphors here because I don't think of my relationship with unionists or others in Northern Ireland in categories of enlightenment and darkness. I don't imagine that I possess superior wisdom. And I don't think along such lines for the further reason that I disagree with Plato on the relationship between philosophy and politics. On this relationship, my sympathies lie much more with Aristotle: *practical wisdom* (which is the sort required in politics) derives from experience, from being involved, being implicated, engaging in dialogue with other citizens, and so on. It doesn't come from contemplative basking in the sun.

Philosophe (Imposter?)

Anyway, even if I did fancy myself as a philosopher in the Platonist mould, there are apparently grave doubts about whether I qualify. Aughey canvasses the possibility that I may be more of an "imposter" on the following grounds: (1) I have a vision (civic unionism); (2) I have a mission of political redemption; (3) I have "an object of ill-concealed contempt" which is to be redeemed; (4) and, finally for good measure, I exhibit the give-away contradictory trait of an "openness of mind yet certitude of judgement" which "is evident throughout the text".

I'll say something about each of these grounds, but first I think it's appropriate to make a general observation about the mode of Aughey's critical approach. Instead of dealing with specific arguments made in the text, he reinvents the case he wants to oppose and, having done so, he then, perhaps inspired by the spirit of many Australian cricket teams, "sledges" away at his mark (in this case me) presumably to his own merriment. And thus, the general problem: his approach seems to aim at niggling and unsettling his target but at the rather exorbitant price of relying upon a figment of his own imagination. Reading Aughey's reading of what I'm up to leaves me incredulous; it's disingenuous stuff.

Turning very quickly to the grounds on which my philosophical credentials may appear dodgy, my reply is this: (1) yes, I have a vision, but it's tentative and provisional and not a blue-print; (2) I don't think I'm on a redemptive mission – that is more Ian Paisley's slant and *maybe* Aughey's chum Bob McCartney's too – unless, I suppose, we buy into a sceptical conservative line which (bizarrely) attributes messianic ambitions to *any* attempt to improve the human lot;

(3) I've already dealt with the accusation about contempt, which merits nothing more in response than a wry shrug (even if it raises questions about Aughey's approach to intellectual sport – assuming that's what he thinks he's playing); (4) and on the charge of being open-minded but full of judgemental certitude, I must say I find it a rather inflexible indictment (not least because it's made without any qualifiers such as "perhaps" or "maybe") which makes me wonder if we have an instance of the pot calling the kettle black, so to speak. At any rate, it's difficult to know what to make of the charge, since the only proof offered in its support is that I'm apparently guilty of it "throughout the text". Perhaps (to employ a qualifier) in Aughey's mind this makes the charge unanswerable, but frankly I think it's a sweeping generalisation which amounts to little more than a sleight of hand designed to maximise mischief. For what it's worth, I'll simply point out that I am persuadable by good reasons but try as I might to be convinced by his rhetoric, I don't think anything Aughey says here qualifies as one. And, if, however mistakenly, I think that I have good reasons for advocating a position on unionism, say, then I'll back them until I'm shown to be wrong. In which case I'll be obliged to change my mind. Backing (what one takes to be) good reasons in this spirit isn't, to my understanding, quite the same as certitude, and there is nothing contradictory about making judgements for which one believes good reasons can be produced and being open-minded. And to reiterate my earlier point: offering reasons to other unionists is a sign of respect not contempt.

Hermeneutics and Enlightenment

So, I protest. But my complaining isn't done with yet. According to Aughey another philosophical contradiction lurks. And it's this. I appear as a stock Enlightenment figure even though I claim that my approach is hermeneutical and therefore historically situated rather than abstract. Thus, we get the delicious ironical rub: I'm an Enlightenment figure who is loathe to acknowledge "any debt to Enlightenment thinking". And besides, debts to the Enlightenment are to be paid everywhere whatever hermeneutically inclined thinkers suppose; and my analysis of unionism turns out to be unhistorical and abstract anyway.

How confused must I be? Not nearly so much as Aughey I'm going to suggest. As it happens, I'm glad to acknowledge debts to the Enlightenment. Contrary to the impression created by Aughey's unvalidated smears, I make any number of favourable mentions throughout *Rethinking Unionism* to thinkers like Kant, Hegel, Rawls, and Habermas which, I would have thought, are sufficient evidence of such acknowledgement. The fact is that I'm critical of a particular Enlightenment strand often associated with Anglo-American utilitarianism and positivism, and, to a lesser degree, a strand that runs from Kant to Habermas (even as I admire many of the discerning analyses it prompts). But this hardly amounts to a rejection of the Enlightenment *per se*. Three other points are pertinent here: (1) the history versus abstract contrast is not a useful way of distinguishing non-Enlightenment from Enlightenment intellectuals once we include among the ranks of the latter such historically-minded thinkers as Hegel and Marx; (2) it's possible to be indebted to the Enlightenment without insisting that the approaches to life and society typically identified with it offer insights into the human condition that don't require supplementing, correcting and adjusting; (3) and, for the record, hermeneutics *isn't necessarily* radically anti-Enlightenment. Versions of it may be – Richard Rorty's, for example – but the version I explicitly identify with (initially articulated most fully by Hans Georg Gadamer and developed further by Charles Taylor) isn't. This is especially the case with Taylor to whom I owe most here (perhaps unsurprisingly since he was my doctoral supervisor at Oxford). He treats "philosophical hermeneutics" as an alternative mode of thinking that falls between modernity's uncritical supporters on one hand and its explicit (pre-modern or post-modern) opponents on the other. To repeat, embracing this sort of stance does not imply antipathy to the Enlightenment as such. In short, then, once more we see Aughey attributing deep contradictions or problems to my position based not on arguments I present but on concoctions he falsely attributes to me. Continually having to point this out is a little tiresome.

Unhistorical on Unionism

A central charge remains to be answered, however. My discussion of unionism is allegedly unhistorical, and my alternative vision is abstract. There is a cluster of issues that need sorting out here. Let me pinpoint Aughey's specific claims: (1) I lack an appreciation of the "historical conditioning of unionist politics", even if my argument is "insightful and illuminating"; (2) but I offer a caricature of unionism by treating most unionists as mentally deficient or suffering from Bourbonic stupidity; (3) civic unionism has no traditional roots and is therefore merely an abstract model; (4) and I'm politically irresponsible or naïve by recommending that Northern Ireland should be understood via an "openness through difference" thesis which embraces the idea of the North as a cultural corridor open at both ends to British and Irish influences, since in practice it would result in the British end of the corridor eventually being sealed off due to the insatiability of nationalist appetites.

Well, it's nice to learn that despite my failure to appreciate unionism's historical conditioning, not to mention my demeaning caricature of its supporters and the abstract nature of my alternative, I offer an argument that is insightful and illuminating. Exactly how I manage to do so in the face of such formidable flaws is something of a mystery, however. Maybe it's by magic. Whatever about that, Aughey through his (almost) maniacal desire to accuse me of regarding other unionists with contempt, and of saddling them with stupidity and the like seems to display an unfortunate overreaction to criticism whereby insulting motives are assigned to a critic (in this instance me) whenever genuine disagreements are aired. Besides giving a jaundiced account of my intentions, Aughey underplays the tragic element I try to reveal about (many) unionists clinging or aspiring to ways of life that aren't fully available, which is to say that in my opinion their plight is partly existential. Their plight is also, in my view, partly intellectual, which is why I go on at length about my disagreements with typical unionist priorities and conceptual frameworks. I'm not sure I grasp what is so "unhistorical" about these lines of analysis. But then, Aughey is more obsessed with recasting what I say rather than with dealing directly with any of my specific arguments. Sure, I could have written a different sort of book which narrated the historical twists and turns of why unionists said this or acted like that; one which tried more assiduously to situate unionism and its responses against the backdrop of the vicissitudes of cultural and political life in the Republic of Ireland, Northern Ireland and Britain. By not doing so, I obviously haven't written a political history of unionism. Accordingly, I suppose that in not doing something I'd no intention of doing, I'm susceptible to the (rather lame) complaint of undervaluing unionism's historical particularities. Even so, that doesn't mean that I lack historical understanding in the strong sense inferred by Aughey. My account of unionist ways of life, for example, includes various historical referents and frequent allusions to unionist relations with nationalists. And more to the point, it's historical and not at all abstract in the sense that it tries to show why these ways fail on their own terms precisely because they don't fit with our current realities. But Aughey isn't distracted by this line of reasoning.

More strongly, my claim is that the realities of political life in

Northern Ireland point to the inadequacies of standard unionist attempts to capture and deal properly with them. It is these realities that scream out as it were for more adequate understandings and conceptualisations; it is these that prompt my attempt to articulate the alternative I call civic unionism, which is, in my opinion, the antithesis of an abstract model (about which I'll say more shortly) that I've simply imposed (inappropriately) on the unsuspecting world of Northern politics. It's entirely fine for Aughey to object to civic unionism's emphases and the arguments I advance on their behalf. It's more than a little cock-eyed, however, to depict what I'm trying to do as an exercise in abstraction. It isn't. If Aughey doesn't grasp this, he's utterly missed the point of what I'm up to.

Political Differences

I suspect that underlying the gulf between us here is a difference of conviction about what is entailed in appreciating unionism's historical conditioning which extends into a rudimentary political disagreement. For Aughey, the appreciation in question implies a sensitivity to unionism's potentially perilous minority status on the island of Ireland; a sensitivity which ends up justifying the appropriateness of "masterful inactivity" given the political conditions in which UUP leader Jim Molyneaux found himself; and one which endorses the applicability to an understanding of Northern Ireland of Carl Schmitt's reduction of politics to a struggle between "friends and enemies". I disagree that historical sensitivity is sufficient to afford any such justification or endorsement. To infer, therefore, that Aughey's judgement is more historically attuned than mine doesn't follow. It's more that we have very different views of politics which shape what we think is appropriate or inappropriate granted our historical circumstances.

Friends and Enemies

I don't think it's necessary to rehearse my criticisms of the politics of masterful inactivity, but I do wish to comment on Aughey's embrace of Schmitt in this context. The fact that many unionists are suspicious of political reforms welcomed by nationalists is said to be understandable because they fear that acceding to them may hasten the arrival of nationalists' ultimate aspiration of a united Ireland. It makes sense for them to resist reform rather than co-operate. And, to add analytical heft to this sort of thinking, it's expedient to draw on Schmitt for intellectual support since in his view a friend/enemy distinction is basic to politics.

What makes perfect sense from one angle, however, makes uncomfortable reading from another. Given that historical sensitivity is apparently a big deal to Aughey, let's factor in from the outset at least the following: Schmitt opposed the Enlightenment (!); he was a high-ranking Nazi supporter and a leading theorist of fascism; and he remained virulently anti-Semitic even after World War II. Given the horrors visited upon the world, and upon Jews in particular, by those enamoured by Schmitt's take on politics during his lifetime wouldn't we hesitate (in the name of historical sensitivity at least) to commend it in a society as divided as Northern Ireland's (or, I would add, anywhere)? Apparently not. In fairness, Aughey is not alone in seeing great insight in Schmitt's friend/enemy distinction: thinkers across the political spectrum from right to left continue to be attracted to it. And I'm not suggesting that in resorting to it, Aughey is approving fascism or indeed anything that the "historical Schmitt" was into. I would conjecture though that recommending Schmitt's concept of politics whilst lying low on how it shaped his political practice involves bracketing his Nazi and other entanglements; and that as a result Aughey becomes implicated in acclaiming (what on his own terms must look like) a suspiciously *abstract definition of politics*. Leaving that conjecture aside, let's consider more closely what Schmitt's appeal is to Aughey and what it might mean to buy into Schmitt here by reflecting on his notions of the nature of politics and of political authority.

At a glance, once his unsavoury political commitments are ignored, we might think it makes obvious sense to draw on Schmitt. Given that the North's politics have often been conducted along the lines of a friend/enemy split, appealing to a thinker who has made such a split a central theme of his work promises to throw light on our situation by providing helpful analytical tools with which to interpret it. Difficulties arise, however, once we ask whether a friend/enemy distinction is a political inevitability. Clearly, I approach it in the spirit of a problem to be tackled – by querying the assumptions on which it's based in Northern Ireland, by suggesting why I think it sells us short in how we understand ourselves as citizens and in how we view what's politically possible, and so forth. To operate solely within the confines of the framework it affords, in my opinion, implies accepting bad practices. And, in large measure, that's why I'm motivated to criticise its acceptance and to seek alternative ways of thinking about the type of politics needed in a society as divided as Northern Ireland's. As is already transparent, Aughey supposes that what I'm proposing smacks of some kind of misguided messianism. Which is how it *may* appear (to a suitably sceptical conservative mind) if a friend/enemy binary is accepted as an unavoidable feature of politics, since we should then be obliged to work within the limits it imposes, that is, limits I transgress. And herein lies Schmitt's attraction: he offers the strongest possible reinforcement of the binary, which has wide-ranging consequences for how we think about politics, not only in Northern Ireland but generally. So, let's spell out what Schmitt is offering here.

Take his concept of the political. "The specific political distinction to which political actions and motives can be reduced is that between friend and enemy" (Schmitt, 1995: 26). In so saying, Schmitt underscores the strength of his conviction that politics thrives on conflict. Conflict is constitutive of politics; it's the criterion that demarcates what's distinctive about politics. Absent conflict we don't have politics. So, there must always be an enemy, a public adversary; a group we can demonise as strange, foreign, alien, a threat; a group we (friends) must consolidate ourselves against. What forms consolidation should take obviously depends on circumstances, though it's important to note that war isn't to be shied away from because it would signify a failure of politics, rather, on Schmitt's terms, war appears more as a continuation of politics and a perpetual possibility (as it must be if a friend/enemy binary is the defining feature of the political). Who, then, decides these things; who makes the call on how enemies should be treated, on what lengths we should go to in order to avert the threat they represent? To answer, we need to add to the mix Schmitt's notion of political authority. Every group, we are told, requires a sovereign who has the task of making decisions in exceptional or extreme circumstances, including the decision of what situations qualify as extreme or exceptional. This sovereign is the ultimate source of authority; there is no higher court of appeal beyond the sovereign's decision, which, accordingly, "terminates any further discussion". So weighing up the perceived threats (ethnic, cultural, religious, civic, or whatever) to one's group is the prerogative of a sovereign who in effect defines who we are and who we are not – and it's in the light of these definitions that determinations are made by the sovereign about the manner of the threat posed and about the actions appropriate to counteract it, including those of extreme measures if circumstances warrant invoking a "state of exception".

I must confess that my initial response to Schmitt's emphases here is simply to say, "oh dear"! I'm going to assume (correctly I hope) that Aughey is proposing (at least in the context of Northern Ireland politics) only a (further) sanitised version of Schmitt for our consideration, that is, a Schmitt whose view of political authority is shorn of the dictatorial connotations that made it so attractive to fascists, and whose depictions of the "enemy" have been sufficiently trimmed of their demonising tendencies to make elementary civility a possibility. Even if he is, there's still a lot to take issue with. Let me start by laying out (some of) what's wrong with *Rethinking Unionism* from a (sanitised) Schmittian perspective: striving to overcome our acute divisions in the North, seeking mutual understandings between members of different traditions, engaging in dialogue, pressing for a common citizen identity, asking unionists (and nationalists and republicans) to reflect on what they're about and how they understand themselves, and so on. Bluntly, rethinking unionism is folly; it is an absurd venture. Accepting that, what then should our priorities be? Avoiding defeat, not compromising, not shirking the conflict, pressing for victories, not being deceived by ambiguous and duplicitous language, sharpening tactical tools – these are the things that matter politically. Forget rethinking, just grasp that unionists (and nationalists) are what they are; grant that, work with it, move on. Conflict can be managed at best, not resolved.

The issue at stake here boils down to this: Schmitt isn't merely offering a handy explanatory device to account for what's going on in conflict societies; he is submitting a more fundamental claim which Aughey purchases and I don't – conflict is (allegedly) the warp and woof of politics, and, as such, is a unique ontological given that shapes how we think and act politically. I reply that conflict or struggle is manifestly part of the mix; but add that it finds its place alongside other things such as humans' propensity for co-operation as well as their quests for a good society, for justice, for virtue – quests integral to the Western tradition of political thought, which also appear anathema on Schmittian terms. The question thus arises:

why privilege conflict, why make a friend/enemy distinction basic? A possible (theologically controversial) answer is to say because of the effects of original sin, and another (very contestable) answer is to say because of the innate tendencies inherent in our putative dependence on (the strange notion of) a selfish gene. I'm not sure these answers are on offer, and, even if they were, neither would settle matters anyhow. My worry is that I'm not convinced there is an answer beyond "just because"; and in asking for a deeper reason, I suspect I'm more likely to get a lecture on the inappropriateness of rationalism in politics than to be provided with one. Let's recall that a feature of Schmitt's idea of political authority is that it invokes "decisionism" as its final criterion: (understanding that it makes no difference here whether sovereignty is the possession of an individual or a collective) a sovereign's decision on issues of supreme political consequence is its own justification and doesn't have to prove itself through giving reasons out of respect to others (goodnight Immanuel Kant!) or be subject to reason's interrogations. So, perhaps the same logic applies here: an (arbitrarily privileged) ontological given doesn't require reasons for its acceptance; (uncritical) compliance will do nicely.

Where does this leave us? To reiterate my earlier point, it leaves me disputing that the disagreements I have with Aughey reflect a lack of historical attunement on my part; it is much more that our diverging responses to the historical circumstances of unionists (and others) in Northern Ireland are rooted in our very different conceptions of politics. And, obviously, I'm unpersuaded by Aughey's attempt to reduce the project of *Rethinking Unionism* to little more than an irrelevant tilting at windmills. Furthermore, I struggle to take seriously the notion that his Schmitt-indebted alternative is a historically grounded, normatively innocent, realist antidote to my (alleged) flight into utopian fantasy. On my reading, it is, rather, a massively controversial, question-begging, departure from the best traditions of Western political thought; one, moreover, with potentially disturbing ethical and political ramifications which offer bleak prospects to citizens in the North. At best, Aughey gives hope merely of a continuation of a politics of constitutional stand-off, with the ever-present threat of a descent into violence lingering in the background. This, from my perspective, is a diminution of politics, an implicit acceptance of sectarianism, and an unrealistic orientation to political realities in Northern Ireland today.

Civic Unionism, Abstract Ideals and Nationalist Appetites

Finally, let me return extremely briefly to the accusations that what I call civic unionism is merely an abstract ideal as well as an open invitation for nationalists to go for broke and deliver a united Ireland. On the latter point, this is bogus reasoning where the worst possible outcome (from a unionist perspective) is predicted of, say, recognition of an Irish dimension in the institutional life of the North – by ascribing to nationalists voracious appetites and suspect motives – and using it as an excuse to oppose the granting of any such recognition. By implication, this means that issues of justice or fairness and the like are never decided on their own merits; rather, everything is calculated along the friend/enemy spectrum. The supposition of unionists that this is political realism in action is very peculiar because it seems to imagine that nationalists will somehow come to acknowledge that they can't expect more than unionists are prepared to offer and, therefore, will eventually accept that the North remains unionism's domain. Perhaps the kindest thing to say is that this is a type of unionist hocus-pocus whereby "we" (unionists) best protect the British character of our wee country through incantations of loyalty which our enemies (despite being fellow citizens) cannot share, but which they will nevertheless accede to. The hope is that it's highly improbable that other parties to negotiations on Northern Ireland's future will be mesmerised by such magical charms and buy into a zero-sum logic which, rather than delivering peace and stability, risks pitching us back into civil strife.

As to the assertion that my alternative vision for Northern Ireland remains an abstract pipedream (partly because it makes unreasonable requests of unionists), I'll simply add the following retort to what I've already said. The notion that making a case for common citizenship and institutions capable of winning the allegiance of our major traditions asks too much too soon of unionists – because it presupposes conditions of stability which don't exist – gets things back to front. Without striving for these goals, that is, without committing ourselves to the search for common positions beyond sectarianism stable conditions will never exist. And, anyway, what would it take for stability to exist on Aughey's terms – the defeat of nationalism (whatever that means)? If so, the right time for my approach is never likely to arrive. When it comes to requests to compromise, to consider things from a different angle, to acknowledge that others may have legitimate entitlements that require a bit of give from unionists, it's never the right time. A familiar, and very jaded, unionist refrain is that it's always too soon to expect much from them, and that whatever is expected is always too much. This is a refrain that makes little sense if we think of politics in civic republican terms, for example, where the incentive is to seek common ground citizens may share. In repeating the refrain, Aughey is effectively caught in the steel trap of thinking of nationalists not as political opponents and fellow citizens but as the enemy to whom concessions are not willingly granted.

But what about civic unionism, is it an inescapably abstract ideal, nonetheless? I've already tried to indicate why I don't think that it is. To finish, I do concede that the way of life and mode of thinking to which it appeals lack support among unionists. But, I claim, it draws on traces, hints, partial manifestations from Northern Ireland

and broader Western thought and experience; it is underdeveloped admittedly but it's not a flighty apparition (heavenly or otherwise) owing its presence to too much time spent cloud watching or star gazing. It is offered as a set of possibilities worth pursuing and not as an abstract model; it suggests a fresh set of priorities for unionism suited to the times in which we live, a set open to revision and not delivered in a spirit of certainty.

At the last, I suppose I'm appealing to something on which Aughey seems to put little value: that humans (including unionists!) indebted though they are to their history are not merely its inevitable products; they are also creative, responsible agents capable of critical reflection, self-inspection, political evaluation and so on. Unionist priorities need revising for good and for prudential reasons. I don't accept that saying this is to ask too much of unionists. Rather than provoking doubts, Aughey convinces me of it, however inadvertently.

PART THREE

FURTHER THINKING ABOUT UNIONISM

Following the publication of *Rethinking Unionism*, I received numerous opportunities to comment on the politics of Northern Ireland, especially in reference to unionist attitudes and behaviour. In addition to the "Futures of Unionism" series (see above Chapters four to six), these resulted in my speaking at such diverse venues (among others) as a conference in Dublin on the theme of 1798 and its legacy, summer schools (John Hewitt and Merriman), universities (UCD, University of Ulster), local branches of political parties (UUP, SDLP, Workers' Party), special interest groups/organisations (Glencree Centre of Peace and Reconciliation, Meath Peace Group, New Ireland Group, Irish Association), as well as Irish government committees. Not surprisingly, there were lots of overlaps in the speeches, talks and lectures I gave at these venues, and it would be needlessly tedious and repetitive to reproduce each of them here. I've chosen to include (in Chapter seven) a synthesis of my remarks at a number of these venues, the unedited texts of presentations made at two others (in Chapter eight), and a slightly extended script of a stand-alone lecture (in Chapter nine). I say more about the circumstances and content of these selected performances in separate introductions to each chapter.

It is worth pointing out that the overriding theme of the following three chapters is that of continuing thinking about unionist politics during a period that runs roughly between late 1996 through to the end of 1997. Accordingly, I am commenting and reflecting on attitudes in evidence and on events occurring not only during the time of a breakdown of the PIRA ceasefire but also after the ceasefire's reinstalment. Multi-party talks, excluding and then including Sinn Féin, were in (a sort of halting) progress with the support (or maybe, more accurately, the acquiescence) of some unionists and the conspicuous opposition of others. At no time during this period was there any reason to believe that an agreement among the North's political protagonists was in the offing.

7

Recalcitrant Unionism: Division, Unity and Febrile Spirits

This chapter is unusual for several reasons. The first is that unlike other chapters, it incorporates content spread across a range of talks at different venues but divests the text of specific references to any of these. Second, it is, consequently, the most heavily edited chapter in this volume. And third, although it divides into two clear parts, I suggest that they exhibit a coherent thematic unity despite their quite different focuses once they are linked to an overarching narrative. (I try something similar in the next chapter but in a much looser fashion.) Whether the suggestion works (in this chapter or the next) I'll leave to the reader to decide.

Introduction

At present, one division of potential consequence within the house of unionism is that existing between unionists prepared to engage in multi-party talks about Northern Ireland's future, and those not. This isn't a simple division. All unionist parties agree that talks shouldn't proceed on the basis of the Framework Documents but, unlike the DUP and the United Kingdom Unionist Party (UKUP), the UUP is willing to attend talks in the hope of not being bound by the Documents' categories. The UUP is also open to the loyalist parties, PUP and UDP, being present at talks whereas the other two unionist parties aren't. This latter disagreement ostensibly is about a matter of principle: whether talks should be restricted to "constitutional" parties or be open also to parties with paramilitary connections. Even here, however, the waters are a little muddied since it's unclear how the DUP's innocence of paramilitary association (even if "unofficial") could successfully be defended. So, unionist unity on the most pressing issue of the day – how and under what terms fresh arrangements for Northern Ireland should be decided – isn't guaranteed; yet it reappears momentarily in concerted opposition to Sinn Féin's inclusion in talks about this issue. In the wake of the breakdown of the PIRA ceasefire, this is an easy unity to uphold. Should the ceasefire be re-instated (as seems to be expected) such unity may be strained. I suspect the UUP won't follow the other unionists' line if Sinn Féin is invited back into the talks process; it will, though, probably vociferously object to Sinn Féin's inclusion and attempt to subject republicans to conditions that underscore that they are unworthy political participants. Thus, even if I'm right in conjecturing that there may soon be a tactical difference between unionist parties over how to deal with Sinn Féin, it's unlikely that the UUP's language towards republicans will suddenly be less vitriolic than the DUP's or UKUP's. There still will be a limited anti-republican kind of unionist unity the uncertain consequences of which may eventually demand serious reckoning.

This quick summation of unionist division and unity suggests a rather dreary picture, and yet an intriguing one. It is dreary from the perspective of those (like me) who think unique political opportunities are opening up and should be seized upon as a matter of priority; to watch unionists resort instead to carping and quibbling is a depressing sight. Where, then, is the intrigue? Perhaps perversely, I think it's intriguing nonetheless to witness the contortions of unionist thought and action in the context of (what most unionists regard as) deeply disagreeable political circumstances. When we explore unionist responses to division and unity there emerges a strangely complex picture of political ineptitude accompanied by far-fetched, at times hysterical, interpretations of events. And if unionist spirits aren't consistently febrile, they are inclined to the odd burst of delirium which seems to grip even those from whom it may least be expected. Thus, we witness unlikely political accounts which often rely upon invective as an assured tool of persuasion. And what's curious or intriguing here is how a peculiar type of feverish action and/or language use is seen by unionists of most varieties as a suitable accompaniment of (what I think is implausible) analysis.

As may be expected, this is most conspicuous among those unionists who are opposed to the current talks-process; those for whom pragmatism is a foreign concept, a sign of weakness, of loss of faith, and so on. Febrility is a constant temptation here. Keeping balance between unionism's different moods is a challenge; yet it's one that only those with (at least) occasional pragmatic tendencies are capable of discerning. For the others there's nothing to balance; there's only a faith to defend, a cause to uphold. Division between those vulnerable to pragmatic overtures and those deaf to anything of the sort thus has a hint of inevitability and suggests potentially conflicting orientations. At best merely tactical agreement on some issue of the day – say the routing of Orange Order parades or denouncing republicans – is the most that may reasonably be hoped for as things presently stand within unionism. And yet desperation to achieve a semblance of unionist unity persists, especially among non-pragmatic unionists. Thus, we may be intrigued by what once would have seemed a very unlikely alliance between the liberal unionism of Robert McCartney and cultural/fundamentalist unionism of Ian Paisley; an alliance that seeks to extend its reach by appeals to David Trimble and the UUP to join it (even if only informally) and mount a united front of unionist defiance capable of staring down nationalist opposition and the resolve of two governments. Recalcitrance, though not named as such, is the big card for such unionists, and the pitch is for all to join in its playing. And so, the call is for unionists of all stripes to refuse to engage on the terms agreed by the other parties at the Stormont talks; to dismiss outright any suggestion that a view of uncompromising non-pragmatic unionism is less than authoritative for true unionists; and to vilify any unionist who dares to think otherwise.

McCartney's Febrile Imagination and Recalcitrant Politics

Pertinent illustrations of what I'm driving at here may be gleaned from McCartney's recent contributions to political debate in Northern Ireland. Focusing on these has the advantage of underlining my observation that it's intriguing that delirious outbursts aren't merely confined to unionists of fundamentalist inclination (though Ian Paisley and his supporters have been amply demonstrating for many years that they're in plentiful supply there) but are now commonly found among those who think of themselves as exemplars of non-sectarian, liberal conviction. Take, for instance, McCartney's latest call for unionist unity (*Belfast Telegraph* 14/5/97) which arises from a narrative indulging an array of conspiratorial and paranoid claims; one suggesting the activity of a febrile imagination rather than that of a finely tuned rational mind; and one underscoring not so much liberal unionism's credentials as recalcitrant unionism's ineptitude.

McCartney's Story

Let's rehearse McCartney's story. Unionism's enemies are everywhere, within and without the unionist fold. Those without include nationalists of all persuasions, as well as significant sections of the political and media establishments in Britain, Ireland and the USA. In their various ways, these external enemies aim to subvert the Union, to hasten the arrival of a united Ireland. The evidence of anti-unionist contrivance is allegedly everywhere. Republicans have proved adept at manipulating confrontations between the RUC and pro-Union supporters (not least at Drumcree) – to the detriment of both. There is a steady erosion of the Britishness of Northern Ireland through education for mutual understanding. This erosion is accelerated by the increasing denigration of Union symbols and their display, such as at QUB. An insidious "social engineering" is at work to facilitate Irishness and to marginalise Britishness. Such social engineering is supplemented by political machinations. The Downing Street Declaration, the Framework Documents, and the terms of multi-party talks compound unionism's difficulties. Behind their fine sentiments, they betray one overriding purpose – to lull unionists into a united Ireland.

Not all unionists seem to recognise their imperilled condition, however. Certain business leaders are particularly culpable. They too easily succumb to a Northern Ireland Office (NIO) political agenda for the sake of their own petty gain. Most alarmingly, according to McCartney, the UUP walks oblivious of unionism's danger, or maybe more accurately exacerbates it. As he claimed during the recent general election campaign, one of its documents written in 1992 during the Brooke-Mayhew Talks served as a "prototype of the Framework Documents". Apparently, *Democratic Realism* was produced by the UUP with occasional assistance from the NIO. The document indicates that as early as 1992, UUP negotiators were willing to accept almost every idea that appeared subsequently in *Frameworks for the Future*, including the proposal of North-South bodies with executive powers. The content of *Democratic Realism* remained hidden from the electorate and from the vast majority of UUP members. Its disclosure now, McCartney believes, reveals a deviousness within upper echelons of the UUP. Thus, there is a hollow ring to the UUP's subsequent opposition to the Framework Documents, and to its ostentatious refusal to enter negotiations on their basis. Whatever its protestations to the contrary, UUP actions during recent multi-party talks have confirmed its tacit commitment to *Frameworks for the Future* – actions that purportedly include the production of "a secret Hume-Trimble document" on decommissioning which guarantees Sinn Féin's being let off the hook. More importantly, McCartney charges, the UUP actively "failed to oppose agreement of rules which confirmed the Framework Documents as the essential parameters within which any final settlement could be achieved". This, it transpires, is no ordinary failure since those same documents "provide for Irish unity by instalments".

The enormity of the UUP's perfidy is now transparent. In McCartney's story, the UUP continues to deal in a secretive, underhand way; it remains wedded to the Framework Documents and, as a consequence, it is prepared to pursue a course that can have one outcome only – a united Ireland. Accordingly, its public pronouncements about the non-negotiability of the Union and of the unacceptability of the Framework Documents are inherently untrustworthy.

That needn't be the end of the matter, however. McCartney's invective against the UUP doubles up as an appeal for unionist unity; the UUP's dressing down also amounts to a summons to

David Trimble and his supporters to join Ian Paisley and him in a resolute stand against the anti-unionist tide. This means engaging in determined action to defend the rights of lawful marchers, to avoid confrontations between the RUC and unionists, to reclaim the moral high ground, to resist all attempts to diminish Northern Ireland's Britishness and to undermine the Union, and to refuse to participate in a talks process that's already loaded against unionism's interests.

Some staggering claims are contained in McCartney's story. These require two kinds of responses: one kind dealing with issues he raises about unionism, and another kind attending to more general aspects of his narrative. I'll start with the latter, which may be dispensed with quite swiftly.

A General Response

McCartney's narrative trades in sweeping generalisations that don't withstand scrutiny. It lumps together as agents of conspiracy such diverse actors as (some) unionists, republicans, international and local media, the British, Irish, and American governments. And so forth. In doing so, it also links entirely separate events – such as the national anthem dispute at QUB and controversy over an Orange Order march at Drumcree – as illustrations of an extant anti-unionist conspiracy. And loitering in the background there's at least a faint hint that the hand orchestrating the anti-unionist agenda may be located in some republican dirty-tricks department. Not, I should add, in the sense that the Army Council of PIRA is explicitly dictating terms to other agents of conspiracy, but more in the sense that republican spin has hoodwinked actors who should know better and has resulted in their acquiescence to an agenda hostile to unionism and implicated them in what appears (to minds like McCartney's) as an overarching conspiracy. Unfortunately, we wait in vain for evidence capable of supporting this bit of McCartney's story. It is hard to take seriously, which isn't surprising given that absent a predisposition to paranoia it makes little obvious sense to connect such a disparate array of actors let alone events with quite different rationales. To live in McCartney's world implies never accepting anyone (other than perhaps sycophants) at face value; it entails rejecting any explanation of an event that doesn't fit into his conspiratorial scheme. Good luck to those wishing to inhabit it.

Consider too the wild claims about Irish unity McCartney expects us to believe. That a united Ireland is being subtly promoted, say, through programmes – such as Education for Mutual Understanding – designed to encourage reconciliation between the North's different traditions. Or that non-unionist political parties have appetites capable of satisfaction only through the achievement of Irish unity. In one case we see a plainly daft attempt to attribute ulterior motives to even the most innocent reconciliatory venture in Northern Ireland which introduces children from unionist and nationalist backgrounds to perspectives other than their own. And in another we are required to ignore the fact that every non-unionist political party (with the possible exception of Sinn Féin) accepts that unionists cannot undemocratically be shunted into a united Ireland; or, more pointedly, that most nationalists and the Irish government would buy a settlement that falls far short of unity. The McCartney story's conspiratorial framework can't accommodate such inconvenient facts. Its inability to do so stretches credibility beyond belief.

It's worth remarking further that a crucial part of McCartney's story relies upon an absurdly mechanical form of logic. Thus, we get the implausible formula: accepting a particular set of negotiating rules necessarily entails accepting the Framework Documents which, in turn, guarantees Irish unity. Given this formula, unionists have no place at the current multi-party talks. The rules governing the talks already predetermine the outcome. Hence the invective against the UUP about which I'll have more to say shortly. The truly worrying point now is that McCartney's mechanical logic divests politics of contingency. The deliberations and arguments of political actors don't count for much. Dialogue is incidental. But that's not unexpected given the pattern of his thinking. McCartney's analysis leaves little scope for the practice of politics; it requires rather (his version of) correct thought. Since nationalists, on his terms, cannot meet this requirement (their thought is by definition incorrect), it is impossible to envisage an accommodation of their concerns, at least in any form they would find remotely acceptable. Accordingly, McCartney can promise only a bleak political future of perpetual stalemate in Northern Ireland. His political views are aimed at heralding the putative superiority of unionism not at tackling the problems of a divided society.

To be frank, this is pretty chilling stuff and a recipe for more appalling politics. McCartney's analysis is chilling because, as I've argued, it feeds a paranoia that defies reason. It gestures at conspiracies. It mocks efforts at accommodation and compromise. Consequently, it risks raising the temperature of political discourse close to boiling point and reducing politics to an instrument of defiance unsuited to exploring creative possibilities. That all of this is done in the name of liberal unionism disturbs. One consolation is that it appears more recalcitrant than liberal (although it's not inherently contradictory to think that it's possible for it to be both) and in its manifest inability to convince very few, if any, non-unionists it may be judged as politically inept. But it's too soon to relax with such a consolation. McCartney's story is intended for a unionist audience; it is fellow unionists he's seeking to win over, and it may be that my accusation of political ineptitude is wide of the mark here. Perhaps his story hits a nerve among unionists and is capable of rallying them under one banner.

McCartney and Unionism

Which brings us to the issues McCartney raises about unionism. For a start we might wonder just how seriously his claims about UUP perfidy are intended. At an initial glance, they seem counter-intuitive and comical. Perhaps we should congratulate McCartney for injecting humour into the dour world of unionist politics. Admittedly, as funny lines go, the one about David Trimble's UUP being so wobbly on the Union as to be complicit in its undermining doesn't quite fit into the side-splitting category. But it may be enough to raise a few giggles, even though it's probably not so much humour that we're dealing with as it is an electioneering stunt. Perhaps, in the run up to the recent General Election, the aim was to create discord within the UUP and to whip up support among wavering unionist voters in North Down.

Yet McCartney protests his earnestness. And I must admit that I can't be sure of what precisely to make of it. I'm not privy to sources that might facilitate definitive judgement. This doesn't mean being rendered mute, however. It's possible to pursue various lines of reasoning that permit tentative conclusions on some matters and more confident ones on others. And, as I hope I've already established, there's little doubt that McCartney is prone to over-egging the pudding, so to speak, and it's reasonable to read his take on the UUP with that in mind.

So, if he's not having a laugh what responses are appropriate to his claims about the main party of unionism? One set of possible responses commends itself if we assume that the UUP is entitled to dispute McCartney's attack. We might wonder whether the UUP – on the assumption that his tale is simply preposterous – should ignore it completely on the grounds that it'll quickly be forgotten because it is nothing more than a concoction of a febrile imagination.

Or, if there is something to the tale but not quite what he infers, we might think it advisable for the UUP to try taking the sting out his attack by offering whichever of the following potential lines of retort is suitable: by admitting the existence of a document but denying authorship of it; by admitting authorship but confessing to having shifted position since 1992; by admitting authorship but disputing the spin put on those bits of the document singled out for special attention; or by admitting authorship but claiming that the document was exploratory or unrepresentative of the UUP's likely final position and never intended to be authoritative in the manner McCartney implies. Not of course that any of these responses is likely to cut much ice with McCartney; introducing doubts about the authorship of *Democratic Realism*, disavowing an earlier position, or quibbling over textual interpretation and intention are unlikely to distract him since conceding ground on any one of them threatens to unsettle the conspiratorial mode of thinking from which he seems to derive comfort.

What, however, if he's right about the UUP? We could then be encountering a discovery capable of bringing a smile to every non-unionist face. More than that, a discovery that should prompt raucous celebrations among republicans. If only Sinn Féin would catch on. The hero of Drumcree, the leader of the largest political party in Northern Ireland is apparently a bit watery on the Union and a potential push-over. Equipped with this knowledge, Gerry Adams should have little trouble in arranging a reinstalment of an IRA ceasefire – and an irrevocable one at that – by tomorrow morning at the latest. Alas, this seems too much to believe. Unionist perfidy is one thing, but the self-defeating perfidy McCartney suggests is quite another – why would being complicit in achieving a united Ireland suit the UUP's interests? Besides, if the Framework Documents are at root a UUP creation why have its representatives railed against them since they were published? McCartney's only answer seems to be because they are untrustworthy. But why would they choose to be untrustworthy on a matter such as this? He doesn't tell us. Moreover, why have other parties to the 1992 talks not informed us about the UUP's role long ago? Why hasn't John Hume – whom one supposes must have known whatever there was to know about the UUP's (alleged) capitulation to a nationalist agenda – briefed Gerry Adams more adequately ("no need for Canary Wharf explosions and the like to concentrate British minds big lad, the game's already in the bag")? And other fairy tales, including the one about a secret pact on decommissioning designed to give republicans a free pass.

So once more it's difficult not to conclude that McCartney's narrative is close to unbelievable. And yet it remains capable of causing mischief. It evidently does appeal to certain unionist mind sets, including some found within the UUP. But one sign of hope is that the UUP is sufficiently alert to recognise the snares in McCartney's attempts to forge unionist unity on his terms alone. Trimble has resisted the claim that working within the procedures of multi-party talks implies acceptance of the Framework Documents. Even so, he does seem inclined to believe that negotiating on the basis of *Frameworks for the Future* involves proceeding down a slippery slope all the way to a united Ireland. Here he appears susceptible to a crucial element in McCartney's (and Paisley's) analysis. A curious scenario thus emerges: McCartney's invective against the UUP is brushed aside as empty prattle at one level but accepted as potentially wounding at another. In a sense the gauntlet has been thrown down: is unionism's best bet for avoiding a united Ireland found in refusing to engage on the current terms stipulated by the British government and others – and so risk decisions being made without its input – or in consenting to engage in the belief that only by doing so can it realistically hope to impress its design on affairs and check tendencies with potentially deleterious consequences?

My preferred response is to say that the latter option is the only responsible choice, but to add that unionists *per se* (excepting the handful of noble souls who identify with what I've called in my book "civic unionism"!) have lost the run of themselves. It is a mistake to make such a bogey man out of the Framework Documents; there is no need to concede anything to McCartney and Paisley here. To the contrary, the virtue of *Frameworks for the Future* is that they raise most of the issues that must be raised if we're ever to agree on how to live together in Northern Ireland. It's not that their treatment of these issues has to be accepted as impeccable in every respect. What counts is being willing to engage one another about those things that matter to us, even if they have been sources of division.

Pragmatic Unionists

Of course, I would say that especially since I'm barely troubled by anything in the Framework Documents (see Chapter one for some minor quibbles), and don't read them as necessarily involving a slippery slope to anywhere. What's more interesting, however, is trying to make sense of those unionist politicians who are prepared to participate in multi-party talks but are nervous about *Frameworks for the Future*, who think it's foolhardy to withdraw from government sponsored talks about Northern Ireland's destiny even as they worry about being forced into acceding to arrangements that they find undesirable. Another intriguing line obtrudes here. Such unionists are presumably open to pragmatic exhortations from the British government (and perhaps others). Level-headed stuff is going on we might think; a steady resolve, without histrionics, giving promise of a positive and clear direction for unionism and of vastly improved relations between unionists and nationalists. And yet there is room to doubt whether this is all there is to it. Given that there's now intense pressure within unionism to prove that involvement with non-unionists doesn't immediately signify a sell-out, it's perhaps to be expected that pragmatically disposed unionists think they have to project a tough image to match that of Paisley's and McCartney's. Here a temptation is to turn the tables on unionism's prominent nay-sayers by contending that only a strong unionist presence at talks will safeguard Northern Ireland's integrity; that opting out is the soft choice; and that, consequently, it is McCartney and Paisley, despite their uncompromising rhetoric, who imperil unionism's best interests.

Well, maybe. But let's think about what's entailed in succumbing to this temptation. In pressing such a hard-line rationale for participating in talks, Trimble and his team give the impression that their most urgent task is not so much to reach tolerable agreement with their political rivals as it is to refine their calculative skills in the hope of outwitting republicans certainly and other nationalists possibly. If they must play in a political game not really of their choosing, the dominant attitude seems to be that of ensuring only minimal losses are incurred and at least some significant victories recorded. But, of course, this means they are forever nervously looking over their shoulders at critics from within the unionist fold, ever conscious of being accused of betraying unionism. Playing the game McCartney and Paisley currently disown is risky because there's no guarantee that Trimble's bravado will be rewarded with victories sufficient to vindicate involvement. And so, the UUP remains vulnerable to the taunts of other unionists; its leaders stay haunted by McCartney and Paisley whose invective, for all its overblown silliness at times, still hurts and appeals to a sizeable section of the party. Far from breaking free from the negative pull of this invective, pro-talks unionists continually feel the need to justify their actions in its light and are thereby deprived of much scope for compromises with nationalists. Which helps explain why at times they give the impression of being delicately balanced on the edge of a precipice without any assurance against a loss of footing that could easily loosen their calculative grip on pragmatism and tilt them backwards into the waiting arms of their atavistic brethren (and for the most part it is brethren we are talking about). We might wonder, then, whether unionists of any sort are going to be able to agree terms acceptable to other parties to the talks.

We don't have to look far into the recent past to find evidence capable of supporting suspicion that it wouldn't take much for the UUP to relapse back into the comfort zone of its unionist critics. Images of a red-faced David Trimble storming out of television studios or of his exuberant, triumphal march along Garvaghy Road with Ian Paisley (which was arguably calculative in another sense in which flamboyant display was reckoned to be the most adroit means of appealing to those who mattered most in this case, namely unionist hard-liners) give flavour of what I'm getting at. Even when pragmatic "realism" appears the order of the day, a lot of unionist politics continues to be played on turf occupied by McCartney and his new fundamentalist friends. A tendency to excitability, rarely associated with conciliatory gestures towards nationalists and never towards republicans, is seldom far away. Therefore, even for "pragmatic" unionists the appeal of recalcitrance occasionally seems irresistible; and what looked like McCartney's political ineptitude in another context may appear as anything but within the closet of unionism – where compromise means weakness and unionist unity is of the essence when potential threats to Northern Ireland's constitutional status within the UK are regularly deciphered. And so, it remains an open question now just what ultimate difference it'll make for some unionists to engage in talks while others don't. A question that may sharpen in intensity if Sinn Féin is eventually permitted to assume a role as one of unionism's dialogical partners.

On Unionist Reactions to the Blair-Adams Meeting

Leaping ahead a few months, the moment of Sinn Féin's political rehabilitation has arrived and is creating unease among unionists. As anticipated, PIRA restored its ceasefire in late July and in mid-September multi-party talks resumed with Sinn Féin attending the first plenary session. No unionist or loyalist parties were present. Two days later, however, David Trimble and his negotiating team turned up, arriving ostentatiously by marching (part of the distance) there alongside leaders of the loyalist PUP and UDP, David Ervine and Gary McMichael. Tough talk was on the agenda. A little later, giving flavour of what to expect from unionists, UUP MP, Ken Maginnis (oddly regarded by some as a bit of a liberal) announced that by allowing Sinn Féin into the talks, the British government had "elevated an evil Mafia to a status that would shame any other country in Western Europe" (*BBC News* 23 September 1997). Undeterred, the British government ploughed on and, as an extension of republicans' reintegration into official political processes, Tony Blair invited Gerry Adams and Martin McGuinness to a meeting at 10 Downing Street on 11 December 1997. Prior to the meeting, Trimble advised the British Prime Minister to change his mind suggesting that to proceed as planned would be "an embarrassment" with negative consequences for the peace process; and pontificating that by persisting with his intention Blair would be "damaging himself in the eyes of right-thinking people" (*BBC News* 30 September 1997). Following the meeting UUP spokesperson Jeffrey Donaldson added that the British government had pandered to republicans due to "the violence and threats of the IRA", and in doing so had revived "ideas which...are totally unacceptable to unionists". As a consequence, "prospects for a talks agreement were fading" *(BBC News* 12 December 1997).

Let's take stock here. On the back of the PIRA ceasefire,

Sinn Féin accepted the Mitchell principles eschewing violence as a legitimate means of political advancement, and thereby removed the barrier blocking its access to the talks-process. In response, unionism, to stick to the language I've been using, rediscovered its unifying potential by flexing its recalcitrant muscle. This display of unionist machismo was exacerbated by (what I'll now refer to for convenience as) the Blair-Adams meeting in Downing Street. The last time a meeting between these parties had taken place at this venue was in 1921 when David Lloyd George – British Prime Minister at the time – had met a Sinn Féin delegation led by Michael Collins. Unionists were outraged, and, as I've indicated, not only those opposed to the current talks process. Now in one sense, what we're dealing with here is pretty trivial and not much hangs on it. In another sense, however, it offers a further fascinating insight into unionist perceptions, reasoning and ways of doing politics. What sort of considerations informed unionists' cantankerous reaction to this particular Blair-Adams encounter? And is there anything to say for them? Three considerations stand out. One I'll call historical-political; a second practical-political; and a third moral-political.

Historical-Political

The historical-political consideration is that there's something deeply unnerving about seeing Sinn Féin being granted the type of recognition and legitimacy – which a meeting at 10 Downing Street symbolises – that British governments have denied it since Lloyd George met Michael Collins. But if we unpack this reason, what does it amount to? Does it suggest some fateful sense of historical replay which unionism has good cause to fear? Hardly, as Adams scarcely carries the clout that Collins did since he wasn't there to represent the Irish people (only a small percentage of them). Moreover, unlike Collins, he wasn't there to negotiate a deal with the British government. And before we get carried away by the historical significance of Adams being the first Sinn Féin leader since Collins to make it to Downing Street, we should consider that he is the first such leader since Collins to be in a position to do so: *the history of IRA militarism and political abstentionism* precluded this possibility for earlier republican leaders; it's only comparatively recently that Sinn Féin has sought a democratic mandate; and it's only more recently still that such a mandate has contributed to its signing up to the Mitchell Principles. So, it's a bit misleading to overplay the historical significance of the meeting to unionism (it's significance to republicanism is another matter): it doesn't have the same connotations that Collins' meeting with Lloyd George had, and the circumstances that make possible a meeting between a British Prime Minister and Sinn Féin in Downing Street have only recently been created.

Unionism's historical-political objection is therefore quite weak. It boils down to an unease at watching those traditionally regarded as Ulster's enemies being treated in a way most unionists had only read about in history books but didn't anticipate witnessing with their own eyes.

Practical-Political

The source of unease informing unionism's historical objection to the meeting is found in its other two considerations for objecting. Take the practical-political reason which says something like this: Blair shouldn't have met Adams because the real political task, at least as David Trimble understands it, is for unionism to cut a deal with the SDLP and the two governments to the exclusion of Sinn Féin. Realpolitik dictates squeezing Sinn Féin out not inviting it in, as Tony Blair did in the most symbolically provocative way possible.

The huge problem with this reason is that it flies in the face of the entire rationale of the talks process. Let's put it simply: (1) all parties to the talks are subject to the same conditions of entry; (2) having satisfied those conditions all parties become entitled to equal treatment and, if the point of the process is to reach political agreement, this means that all parties are entitled to speak and be listened to by all other parties, to engage with and be engaged by all other parties; (3) therefore, there can be no justification for differential treatment of parties, which is what Tony Blair may have been accused of if he hadn't met with Sinn Féin in Downing Street. Within the structure of the talks process, unionism can't fault Blair for meeting Adams without destroying the deepest rationale of the process itself. In conspicuously refusing to engage directly with Sinn Féin, it's unionists who're violating both the spirit and principles upon which the process has been established. The bottom line of course is that unionists make their objection here precisely because they think the rules don't apply equally to Sinn Féin, because they want Sinn Féin thrown out of the talks-process. Whether that makes the pragmatic sense they imagine is doubtful; certainly, it's not a view shared by the two governments, the SDLP and some other smaller parties. But at root it's a view driven by unionism's moral-political consideration.

Moral-Political

And the moral-political reason is of course the one that's been dominating the airwaves: Sinn Féin is comprised of unreformed terrorists with whom no democratic government worth its salt should have any truck. And so on. This makes Tony Blair (and many others) morally culpable and very gullible. Indeed, it implies that unionists alone have sufficient moral fibre and nous not to be taken in by the consummate confidence-tricksters which republicans must be.

There are two obvious problems with this form of reasoning.

First, it's not clear why anyone should accept that unionists alone are equipped to discern the true nature of Sinn Féin, since they've had no contact with republicans and given that they refuse to acknowledge the sometimes subtle and other times more pronounced reformulations of Sinn Féin's political position that have been occurring over the past few years. Second, it's not clear how unionism can claim moral consistency here, given the UUP's willingness to work with loyalist parties. A rather feeble counter is to suggest that there may be acceptance of some unionist-republican negotiations in the future, but that it's too soon to expect these now. This is feeble not only because it's unclear how much time would be required before Sinn Féin qualified as acceptable interlocutors; but also, because no similar restrictions were placed on loyalists after the UVF and UDA ceasefires. Within weeks of the latter, prominent unionist politicians from the UUP and the DUP shared public platforms with loyalists and engaged them openly.

So, we're forced to account for a selective use of the moral-political argument. It may mean one of two things, if not both. One is that dead Protestants are to be mourned more than dead Catholics (though no constitutional politician is ever going to say so in such blatant sectarian terms), and therefore that republicans are more unforgivable than loyalists. Or the practice of unionist selectivity may indicate that different standards are deemed acceptable because republican violence was directed against the state, whereas loyalist violence (however mistakenly) was directed in its defence (as UDA wall murals claim of loyalist prisoners: "Their only crime was loyalty"). And those unionists (worryingly) enamoured by Carl Schmitt might like to tell us that loyalists are political friends and republicans are political enemies, and that more is due to friends than to enemies.

An irony here is that unionists in supposing that they are occupying the moral-political high ground in their opposition to

Sinn Féin's presence in negotiations are, on the contrary, slouching towards a moral-political quagmire. From whichever angle we approach their stance it seems to risk sinking deeper into moral and/or political sludge. Take a moral angle. It's hard to imagine an argument capable of showing that loyalist paramilitarism was ethically superior to republican paramilitarism and therefore deserving of better (political) treatment. Surely, then, it's advisable not to be exposed to charges of hypocrisy by implying there's a moral justification for selectivity on the topic of paramilitarism when there patently isn't. But how would that work out? Given how prominently the weapon of moral denunciation features in unionist attacks on republicanism to drop it from the arsenal would require a massive shift in unionist practice. One that most unionists would undoubtedly cavil at not least because they'd fear that their criticisms of Sinn Féin would thereby be rendered anaemic. An alternative is to retain moral language but apply it indiscriminately against paramilitaries on all sides. Presumably, given the pattern of unionist reasoning against Sinn Féin, that would entail advocating the removal of loyalists and republicans from talks while their paramilitary organisations remained intact. McCartney and Paisley would approve. But, even restricting attention to strictly ethical considerations there are complications. Without going into details, I'd strenuously argue that neither the UUP nor the DUP can plausibly claim non-entanglement with paramilitarism in their histories; and so, they too may appear ethically compromised. And once we start to factor in the moral dubiousness of various of constitutional unionism's relationships with shadowy organisations (the DUP and the "Third Force" for instance), and the moral irresponsibility of much of its language of incitement the ethical case for political exclusions starts to vanish.

Even so, it'd be naïve to underestimate unionist shamelessness in adopting double standards in their dealings with paramilitarily associated political actors. Accordingly, let's consider matters from an angle which prioritises politics and blatantly treats ethics as its handmaiden. This would allow unionists to feel morally unchallenged by playing the type of card Schmitt provides to justify their use of selective standards in shunning Sinn Féin. Here, as the weight falls on political justification of their treatment of republicans, it may seem possible to avoid any inconveniences of moral scruple by reasoning as follows: naturally we're going to treat our "own" more sympathetically than we do those "others" who threaten our way of life; and, sure, we might be guilty of a selective use of morally condemnatory language, but that's only to be expected when we're playing politics based on a friend/enemy division. Thus, any moral inconsistencies are more than compensated for by the overriding primacy of the political point: in matters of supreme consequence concerning the integrity of Northern Ireland, we have to be alert to the threat posed by opponents with a history of ruthlessness who have not abandoned their goal of eliminating British rule in the North; accordingly, they must be denied encouragement – such as equal partnership in talks – precisely because not losing politically is what matters most. And so we could go on.

But down this path a political quagmire beckons. The talks process isn't built on Schmittian principles. The point of it is to transcend zero-sum politics by exploring ways in which traditional opponents may agree on political arrangements with which all citizens can live. To subvert this minimalist rationale of reconciliation by advocating Sinn Féin's exclusion from discussions is to set unionists apart from their other negotiating partners and almost certainly guarantee a return to political stalemate. In trying to banish from politics those on the republican side who have historical associations with guns also risks precipitating a return to paramilitary violence which would almost certainly prompt more paramilitary retaliation in response. This is to envisage a return to very dark days when the prospect of political activity improving our lot in Northern society seemed dim indeed. The only coherent sense I can make of unionist reasoning which throws up this possibility is to conclude that what's being undermined is the peace process itself; it's almost as if unionists are really proposing that the military demise of PIRA is a pre-requisite to republicanism's political normalisation. To which a prolonged gasp of incredulity may be the most appropriate response. Following that, it may be worth remarking that unionists here typically overlook the abnormality of Northern Ireland and seem to have difficulty understanding that it just isn't feasible to apply unproblematically principles that pertain to more settled forms of liberal-democratic experience, that is, forms which aren't beset by threats of sectarian violence engendered by disputes over territorial legitimacy and (seemingly) incompatible political identities. And it's hard not to add that this is at least partly because unionists excel at glossing over how Northern Ireland came into existence - something republicans have never forgotten – and the roles played by such legally questionable events as the formation of the original UVF, Larne gun-running, mutiny at the Curragh and so on.

Reminders of events leading to Northern Ireland's contested existence aren't merely awkward for unionists keen to affirm their superiority over rebellious republicans; they also suggest the arbitrariness of isolating politically favourable outcomes from moral scrutiny, however convenient it is to do so. This point may be made even more forcefully when we reflect that it was by allowing politics to trump ethics that a blind eye was turned by unionists to the many bad practices of discrimination in Northern Ireland under the old Stormont regime which eventually led to the years of overt conflict from 1969-1994. To persist with this kind of fateful allowance – as sticking with the logic of friend/enemy politics requires – is to have learned nothing. In teasing out the entailments of unionism's opposition to the rather routine occasion of Tony Blair's meeting with Gerry Adams, it transpires that unionists are in something of a pickle. If pursued, the logic underpinning their opposition yields ethically messy equivocations and an ill-equipped defence against potential political turmoil. The tragedy is that precisely the sort of moral and political quagmire that ceasefires and talks-processes give promise of saving us from is what unionists appear to be inviting. Cavalier politics indeed. We may hope that enough of them change their minds.

To sum up, frequent use of florid language combined with recalcitrant refusal to deal on equal terms with Sinn Féin brings the UUP's political behaviour closer to McCartney's and Paisley's than it does to that of its talks-partners. In the wider context of inter-party and inter-governmental politics, it may be deemed inept: it won't persuade Irish nationalists and it hasn't moved the British or Irish governments to change course. The UUP's behaviour has protest value only within the claustrophobic world of unionist politics, but even here its efficacy isn't guaranteed; and it is susceptible to being considered inept by other unionists too, albeit for very different reasons. The impression remains that it is within this world that the UUP's main playing field is located; it is here that it is always competing and having to prove itself in severely restricted space. So, even if it's encouraging that some unionists are prepared to engage more widely than others, it's hard to become too optimistic about the future given prevailing modes of unionist behaviour and terms of unionist thought. One potential solace is that – strange as it may seem to most unionists – it doesn't have to be like this.

8

Unionist Degenerations and Beyond

This chapter is unusual in that it is comprised of two quite distinct sections which, unlike the previous chapter, I haven't tried too assiduously to join. Each section is based on an oral presentation delivered to non-unionist audiences in different parts of Ireland. I hope that the inclusion of both under one chapter heading isn't too jarring. For what it's worth, the first deals more with the theme of "unionist degenerations" and the second more with going beyond them, even though the second's delivery preceded that of the first by some months. In presenting them in the order I have, I'm ignoring chronological niceties and privileging (what I trust is a semblance of) thematic continuity: having pointed to problems (in the first section) I suggest some ways of overcoming them, albeit not always directly (in the second). If this continuity fails, or isn't obvious, the sections may be read as discrete pieces; an option made easier by my retention of the original versions of the respective presentations.

Whither Unionism?

Another quick word of explanation may be helpful. What follows immediately below is the text of a talk I gave to the Workers' Party in West Belfast in the latter half of 1997. The organisers suggested the title. In trying to characterise my response to the question it poses, I think that the theme of unionist degenerations comes close to capturing what I'm getting at, including why, despite efforts to correct these by some unionists and loyalists, an overall picture of political deterioration is the product (unwittingly) painted by unionism. As already indicated, I've decided to leave the text unedited.

Introduction

Thanks for the invitation to speak here tonight. The topic – "whither unionism?" – is an important one which needs addressing. Although I think this is the case and although I'm grateful for the opportunity to give my thoughts on it, I must confess that the more I mused over what angle to take, the more irritated I became with John Lowry (a prominent Workers' Party organiser who issued the invitation) for having put me in this position. This is no reflection on John I hasten to add; it's more a reflection of my unease with the style, content and direction of unionist politics. In other words, the more I think about unionism the worse it becomes for my health, for my liver certainly and for my mental well-being. This is a little surprising given that I've already written a book on unionism in which I laid out my criticisms of much unionist thought and practice and suggested an alternative way in which unionists and others might go about the business of politics in Northern Ireland. It's not that I now think that what I wrote in the book is redundant, and it's not that I've changed my mind on the central themes I dealt with. It's more that since finishing the book I've become even more disconcerted by unionism's priorities and ways of doing politics.

So, I'm tempted to give an exceptionally frank and critical response to the question – whither unionism? One saying that in the final analysis, unionism as defined by its major defenders is confused, tribal, hypocritical, mean and misdirected; a response that concludes that, given such degenerations, if the future of this society were ever left to unionists alone to decide, the case for mass emigration would be compelling. Of course, in saying this much I've already succumbed in part to the temptation. And I daresay I'll succumb to it even further as I proceed. But to do nothing more than this would smack too much of sour grapes, and it'd give a somewhat imbalanced impression. Unionism has to be understood within the larger circumstances of political life of Northern Ireland and it's against these that its political modes should be evaluated. Therefore, let me try to characterise the circumstances in which unionism finds itself, mention a couple of positive aspects of its attempts to respond to these circumstances, and then indicate a little more fully why I think unionism is in a threateningly degenerative state which helps explain the inadequacies of its handling of the political challenges that we all face today.

Circumstances

I'd like to start with three admittedly sweeping and impressionistic observations about our current political circumstances.

First, the British and Irish governments share a determination to see a political settlement reached quickly in Northern Ireland. And, whatever the occasional strains in Anglo-Irish relations and whatever their differences of nuance, there's a fair amount of agreement between the two governments about what shape such a settlement should take. Its contours are outlined in the Framework Documents and, barring a minor miracle, it's some variation of *Frameworks for the Future* that they'll be pressing for – unless of course the parties at the present talks can come up with some new alternative among themselves (in which case we'll have witnessed such a miracle). So, one way of describing our current circumstances is to say that they're being shaped significantly by a reasonably unified Anglo-Irish resolve, purpose and plan.

A second way of describing them is to say that we're living through a period of upbeat nationalism. There is a danger of exaggerating the significance of this: relations between the SDLP and Sinn Féin can be pretty frosty, the so-called "pan-nationalist" front sometimes looks fragile upon inspection, and much of the rhetoric about history being on nationalism's side is little more than hot air. Nevertheless, it is true to say that Northern nationalism has never been as politically organised and effective as it is now, that nationalists exude a confidence in themselves and their cause that's probably unrivalled in Northern Ireland's history, and that no political deal can be done without at least the approval of the SDLP.

If upbeat nationalism is a second way of describing our circumstances, downbeat unionism is probably a third way. During the past generation unionism, by its own reckoning, has lost considerably more than it has gained; there are widespread perceptions among unionists that the Britishness of Northern Ireland is continually being eroded; and unionist disunity has almost reached crisis proportions – or so some unionists tell us.

And so, we live amid circumstances that appear quite depressing to certain unionist eyes. For Paisley, McCartney and sections of the UUP, the only response is to hold the line against the two governments and nationalism; to refuse to engage on the terms agreed by the other parties at the Stormont talks; and, in short, to keep insisting that their view of obdurate unionism remains canonical for 'genuine' unionists. For David Trimble and the loyalist parties, the response is to defend the Union through political engagement (if that's what the actions of the UUP can be called); to attempt to cut a deal that will (ostensibly) satisfy unionist sentiment and yet also be acceptable to others. The fact that such differences of approach exist within the unionist fold is sufficient evidence of my earlier point about contemporary unionism being in a state of confusion and disarray.

Positive Aspects

But it could be said with some justification that the fact of such unionist confusion and disunity contains positive aspects. Let me mention two.

First, there is something encouraging about the fact that the UUP especially has held out against the scaremongering tactics of Paisley and McCartney and taken its place at the talks table. This implies, on a generous reading, that the largest unionist party now recognises that unionism must leave behind its renowned "siege mentality", resist the lure of its ancestral voices, and, for the sake of the future of this society, get down to serious political negotiations with non-unionists of various descriptions. On a slightly less generous reading, the UUP's participation in the talks process still admits of a positive gloss: that like it, or not political realities dictate that the cause of unionism, to which after all a clear majority of citizens in Northern Ireland subscribe, will not be served well by abstentionist politics. Either way, at a pinch we might conceivably say that we are currently witnessing something heartening: the major political party in the North apparently showing rare willingness to try its hand at constructive politics instead of merely reacting against circumstances of which it disapproves.

A second positive aspect of unionist disunity in the face of challenges from the two governments and Irish nationalism is the fact that the loyalist parties and their paramilitary friends are no longer at the beck and call of their ("respectable") traditional manipulators. Indeed, it's probably fair to suggest that the PUP and the UDP are currently showing more signs of independent, creative political thinking than is obvious at present among other unionist groupings. It's within the ranks of the loyalist parties that we're most likely to find unionists who believe that there's considerably more to politics than constitutional issues, and (especially within elements of the PUP) who even suggest that when going beyond matters constitutional we should be thinking in socialist categories. Given the rather dismal fate of socialism within the constituencies represented by loyalism we might wonder how sustainable this suggestion will prove to be; but that it's even being made under current conditions is an encouraging sign.

Criticisms

Thus, all may not be as gloomy within unionist circles as my opening remarks suggested. Why then am I discontent? Does being so amount to anything more than nursing a curmudgeonly spirit? I think it does. To summarise wildly, my appreciation of those positive attempts by unionists to respond, against certain of their primordial instincts, to circumstances not of their choosing is tempered by at least the following considerations.

Tribalism

Unionism, including that of the UUP and the loyalist parties, remains tribal. Since it was first mooted that the UUP was considering redefining its link with the Orange Order around 1994, we've witnessed little short of a reaffirmation of unionism's Orange credentials. True, one doesn't have to be a member of a loyal institution to belong to the UUP, but it helps if one wants to make it through the ranks. More to the point, however, is the fact that it would now be considered an act of unionist heresy if a commitment to Orangemen's right to dander where and when they please weren't crucial to a UUP member's political agenda. Support of Orangemen is once more a badge of unionist orthodoxy; and those few unionists who may dissent tend to keep their own counsel. Back to the future seems the order of the day.

This may not quite be the case within the loyalist parties, but tribalism is very much to the fore with them in other respects. We need only think of the painting spree undertaken by the PUP during the summer in order to mark out its territory in Protestant areas of Belfast to see that this is the case, and of course to recall the close relationship between both loyalist parties and Protestant flute bands.

The upshot is that unionism in all its main varieties underwrites a tribal definition of Britishness in Northern Ireland. And a lingering suspicion is that the panic evident in various unionist circles over Britishness being eroded in the North reflects in part fear of any moves to de-tribalise our politics. This isn't terribly encouraging.

Hypocrisy

Then we have the small matter of hypocrisy, which is particularly pronounced in mainstream unionism's refusal to engage with Sinn Féin even with the restoration of the PIRA ceasefire. I don't particularly want to harp on about this, but it's worth remarking that any so-called constitutional politicians (including prominent representatives in the DUP) who can share a platform with a notorious gentleman from Portadown (a ruthless former leader of the UVF in mid-Ulster and more lately the major figure in the breakaway Loyalist Volunteer Force (LVF)) should be capable of having a cup of tea with the devil himself, yes even you Dessie (Dessie O'Hagan a member of the audience was nicknamed "the Devil" due to his anti-clerical stances as a leading figure in Official Republicanism in the late 1960s and 1970s – and, contrary to what many of his detractors thought, retained a sense of humour)! Whilst members of the UUP who can effortlessly enter arrangements with a man responsible for one of the most brutal sectarian murders of the entire Troubles (formerly a significant player in the UDA and currently a member of the UDP's negotiating team) should at least be up to a bit of political rough and tumble with members of Sinn Féin. My only point in raising these instances of hypocrisy is that they seem to indicate the presence of underlying sectarian sentiments within mainstream unionism; sentiments that in turn reduce politics to farce, antics and various forms of grandstanding.

Meanness

I also suggest that unionist politics continues to be characterised by a deep-seated meanness which blinds unionists to their responsibility for the political mess we've experienced for as long as anyone cares to remember. I'll put this point starkly: from issues of civil rights onwards can we think of any concession that unionists have made to non-unionists or, more pointedly, to non-Protestants that haven't been forced out of them? I'm struggling to think of one. And if we broadened the compass of the point to include the entire history of Northern Ireland, I'm not sure the answer would be different. That what I'm (rather charitably) calling meanness is seemingly viewed as untroubling within unionist circles is an indictment of the political practice of unionism; that it's not recognised as anything of the sort suggests the presence of a moral malaise, which all the self-righteous fulminations against the bad actions and subversive intentions of republicans cannot camouflage.

Priorities

These criticisms could possibly be dismissed as relatively petty asides of no real significance to the crunch issues of our politics, if they didn't impinge upon the priorities unionism espouses. But, in my view, they do impinge. Quite simply, unionist politics across the board is organised in terms of one overriding priority: upholding "the Union, the whole Union, and nothing but the Union". Disputes within unionism are in essence about how this priority is best maintained. Paisley and McCartney's attacks on Trimble focus precisely on this point: unionists can only be losers within the talks process since it's structured to compromise the Union. To which Trimble, in company with Ervine and McMichael, replies: the only way to safeguard the Union is to confront the two governments and nationalists within the talks process; only then can unionists exercise a veto that prevents shifty deals being agreed over their heads or dirty deeds being done behind their backs.

Notice for a moment how my other criticisms of unionism fit in here. Unionism can justify, to itself, what I've called tribalism because defending the Union has predominantly been a Protestant concern. Therefore, any diminution of so-called defining aspects of the Protestant/British way of life in Northern Ireland is construed as an attack on the Union. The charge of hypocrisy can be swept aside here too: if what counts is defending the Union then we obviously are partial to those loyalists who resorted to violence in defence of the Crown. That doesn't mean we approve of their actions, but they belong in an entirely different category from the violence of Provos which was hell-bent on destroying or smashing the Union. And as for meanness, well that's easily accommodated: what I call meanness is better described as vigilance against the devious machinations of those non-unionists whose ultimate aim isn't to create a better

Northern Ireland, but to weaken the Union – bit by bit. So, don't imagine that the crafty ploys of the Stickies (a nickname of the former Official IRA from which the Workers' Party emerged) have escaped attention!

I regard all this as rather less than convincing. And I have tried elsewhere to say why I do at much more length than I've been able to do here. At root the cause of my dissatisfaction with unionism lies with its prioritisation of the Union, which, in my view, cramps the way it does politics, constrains its vision and cripples its dealings with political rivals. Whither unionism? Left to its own resources, unionism (at least in its dominant forms) is afflicted by degenerations it often confuses for virtues and doesn't seem up to crafting a future worth having for all citizens. One hope is that it will never be left to its own resources again; that against its basic instincts the UUP at least will be dragged into making an agreement with other parties at the talks, principally through pressure from the British government; and that through such agreement (some forms of) degeneration may be halted. Another, much less likely hope, is that it'll take my advice and shift its priority from upholding the Union to that of making Northern Ireland work; that is, by prioritising the quality of social and political life of this society in a fashion that respects our complex Irish-British condition and puts a premium on discovering more edifying and beneficial forms of doing politics. A more comprehensive fix for degeneration lies down this path. Unlikely to be followed, as I say, but there's still a place for dreaming.

Thoughts on Northern Ireland (in Clare)

Dreaming continues in this second piece in which the focus shifts from criticisms of unionism to my alternative way of thinking about Northern Ireland, which, although not expressed in such language, is the more comprehensive cure for unionism's degenerations that I've just hinted at above. Even though a critical component continues to be present, it is briefer and is directed as much at nationalism as at dominant forms of unionism. And it is set in a wider context of a Summer School in County Clare during August 1997 which was devoted to the theme of "Ireland after 75 years of Independence". What follows below is another short offering that provides only a cursory outline of arguments I have developed in much more detail in my book "Rethinking Unionism" and in other chapters in this volume. I include it here if only to indicate something of my endeavour to introduce another approach to reflecting on unionism and Northern Ireland to wider audiences. As with the first piece in this chapter, the second is an unedited version.

Introduction

I'd like to thank the committee of the Merriman School for this opportunity to share a few thoughts about Northern Ireland. And, although it may sound strange coming from someone from a Northern unionist background, I'm particularly pleased for the chance to be reacquainted with County Clare. I vividly recall my last visit to Clare in 1986 when, somehow or another, I ended up in Milltown Malbay for the Willie Clancy week. And now I find myself in Ennistymon for the Merriman Summer School. Is there, I wonder, any kind of deeper sense to be made of this? From Milltown Malbay to Ennistymon, from Clancy to Merriman, from music to poetry: is there some subtle progression here that I haven't yet grasped? Or is it simply that I'm a sucker for good company and plentiful refreshments? Or is Clare just destined to haunt my imagination?

Who knows, who cares and whatever the case may be, I'm delighted to be here. Now let me turn to the matter at hand: thinking about Northern Ireland. I gather that the overall theme of the Summer School has been that of thinking about Ireland after seventy-five years of independence. Obviously, thinking about Northern Ireland impinges upon that general theme, although exactly how it does is no doubt a controversial question.

At one pole, there are those for whom the very notion of an independent Ireland that excludes six counties of the island is radically inadequate – not least because it implies a deficient grasp of what precisely Ireland is; a deficient grasp of which self-understandings should be taken as constitutive of an Irish state. Quite clearly, for those of this persuasion, the question of Northern Ireland – or, as they'd prefer, "the North of Ireland" or the "six counties" – is inherently subversive. It has the capacity to disturb any number of complacent Southern attitudes to the North, and to undermine some stock Southern definitions of Irishness.

At another pole, there are those for whom Irish independence is quite appropriately discussed without much reference to the North. Those who've long since accommodated themselves to the reality of partition; those who, for principled or pragmatic reasons, are reconciled to recognising Northern Ireland's status within the UK. And those who, for the most part, are relatively indifferent to life in the North and whose one fervent wish is that the North's problems aren't transported South. (Taking the liberty to adjust slightly a line of a very famous song from around these parts, "It's a long, long way from Clare to *Harryville*" – and *"long may it so remain"*, they might quip). For those of this persuasion, then, the question of Northern Ireland is quite tangential to reflections on seventy-five years of Irish independence. In between these two poles, of course, lie any number of other stances, including, I suspect, those of recent Irish governments.

Having flagged up the potential importance of Northern Ireland for Southern understandings of seventy-five years of Irish independence, I now wish to change tack. What I intend saying does bear indirectly on such understandings; but I now wish to take as my explicit focus the question of Northern Ireland from a Northern, unionist perspective. But I should immediately qualify what I mean when I say that. I don't mean that I'm about to reiterate a standard, mainstream unionist line which merely insists upon the undiluted Britishness of Northern Ireland and demands that the Republic adopt a "hands off" attitude to the North. I find that line altogether too simplistic. I mean, rather, a personal reflection on Northern Ireland from someone from a unionist background. And here it may be helpful to know in advance that one of my guiding principles is simply that if charity is meant to begin at home, then so too is criticism. In my case, the outworking of this principle can be intimated by saying something like this: although it'd be an extravagant exaggeration to say that I'm as representative of mainstream unionism as Mao Zedong was of the girl-guides, it'd be an exaggeration with a point to it.

Northern Ireland: Mischaracterisations and Skewed Priorities

Let me start with a simple question: what is Northern Ireland? For most unionists the answer is straightforward: Northern Ireland is a site of the Union. For traditional nationalists the answer is also straightforward: the North is the fourth green field awaiting return to its proper owner. Most nationalist thinking, including, I believe, that of Sinn Féin, has ditched this traditional way of putting things – "an agreed Ireland" which involves the consent of both traditions is now the favoured mode of expression. The rub remains that Northern Ireland can't be defined independently of the rest of Ireland. And rightly or wrongly (and in many instances I do think wrongly) many unionists suspect that the ideology of the lost green field lurks just beneath the surface of the new political language of nationalism.

Anyway, the main point I'm anxious to underscore is that these conflicting definitions of what Northern Ireland is, unsurprisingly issued in quite incompatible political priorities: "the Union, the whole Union, and nothing but the Union" on one hand; and a united Ireland, if not tomorrow then eventually, on the other. Two further points are worth making here.

First, these priorities have been singularly unhelpful: in their name, people have been murdered, sectarian divisions have deepened, mistrust has escalated, and political stalemate has come to seem part of the natural order of things. Of course, at this moment of time, there's a whiff of optimism in the air: the IRA has restored its ceasefire, the British government now appears determined to see a settlement reached sooner rather than later, multi-party talks are about to resume. The optimism is, nonetheless, qualified: unionists are by and large disaffected and are even at odds with each other about how to proceed, and questions linger about the true intentions of Sinn Féin.

The only prediction I'd make with any confidence in such uncertain circumstances is that durable agreement about how Northern Ireland should be governed will remain elusive, whatever the upbeat rhetoric of the British and Irish governments, so long as the political priorities of unionism and nationalism remain unaltered. And if they remain unaltered then I'm tempted to say that this is sufficient proof that we in the North are all bonkers and collectively certifiable. I do of course exaggerate, if only a little.

But, as we know, changing political priorities is easier said than done, especially in Northern Ireland. This is because, second, the priorities in question reflect the underlying differences I've alluded to about how Northern Ireland should be understood. Accordingly, the problem is deeper: it's not just one of inappropriate political priorities, but one of inappropriate answers to the question of what Northern Ireland is. Or, put another way, my argument is this: standard unionist and nationalist definitions of Northern Ireland distort the reality of our collective Northern condition. And it's precisely these distortions that need correcting.

Re-characterising and Fresh Priorities

My attempt at a corrective could be put very simply, albeit vulgarly: we're all mongrels and being a mongrel should be a matter of pride. In slightly more detail, what I mean is something like this. Northern Ireland isn't as Irish as Clare or as British as Finchley; and those who suppose otherwise are indulging first-class fictions. Thus, the North shouldn't just be seen as a site of the Union or as the lost green field. It is, in a sense a place apart; and should, rather, be seen as a site where British and Irish factors intermingle and clash and exert influences that nobody escapes. Accordingly, as Edna Longley suggests through her helpful metaphor, Northern Ireland should be considered as a *cultural corridor* open at both ends to the rest of Ireland and the rest of Britain. Therein resides its strangeness: Northern society's difference from the rest of Ireland and the rest of Britain is properly understood as a product of such openness. And the development of political arrangements in six counties of Ulster – which are unique on the two islands – is one crucial way of giving adequate expression to the North's peculiarity.

Those who would close off either end of the Northern corridor are, then, in my view politically irresponsible; but, possibly worse, they are denying what we collectively are: people who are shaped and influenced by a distinctive mix of Britishness and Irishness. The trick is to appropriate this view of ourselves, rather than continue to define Britishness and Irishness in oppositional terms. And, as I say, we should proceed to allow our politics to reflect this appropriation of who we are together.

New Priorities

So, thinking of Northern Ireland in this manner creates different political priorities which may be captured under the general heading of making the North work, that is, concentrating on improving the quality of social and political life here rather than simply focusing on maintaining the Union or on aspiring to a united Ireland. At the very least, and given the peculiar conditions prevailing in Northern society, this involves recognising Northern Ireland as part of the UK, given its status in international law, and given that the consent of its citizens is required before it can legitimately be thought of otherwise. It also involves recognising, however, that partition was a tragedy, badly handled North and South; and that by virtue of being an open-ended corridor, Northern Ireland requires the accommodation of an "Irish dimension" – through various North/South bodies, say, and a continuation of some low-level role for Dublin in Northern affairs; as well as, most importantly, through an intermix of Britishness and Irishness in Northern Ireland's public institutions.

What is required, furthermore, are priorities that cohere in pursuit of the goal of common citizenship. The most pressing political task in Northern Ireland is precisely developing a sense of citizenship shared by everyone, a sense that cuts through and across traditional identities and sectarian allegiances. At least four main requirements are entailed in pursuit of such a goal of common citizenship:

- First, there's what I've called in my book, *Rethinking Unionism*, the liberal requirement: namely, that all members of a polity should be treated as "free and equal citizens"; that is, where all are granted the same rights and entitlements and where

nobody is discriminated against on grounds of race, religion, gender, and so forth.
- Second, there's what I've called the (classical) republican requirement: where it's acknowledged that to be viable a polity must be characterised by institutions and practices capable of commanding the allegiance of all citizens; that is, institutions and practices which we regard as "ours". This requirement has never come close to being satisfied in Northern society much to the chagrin of unionism. And yet the absence of its satisfaction puts any society in a precarious position. Little wonder, then, that Northern Ireland's history has been so troubled and that its politicians frequently continue to operate at cross-purposes. Prioritising the classical republican requirement enables us to cut through lots of the prevailing political cackle by specifying why a quest for common citizenship in the North is so important. Conversely, to marginalise or ignore the creation of inclusive institutions is to minimise the importance of citizenship; and in the case of Northern Ireland, it's to allow tribalism, traditionalism and sectarianism to dominate the political landscape.
- Third, there's what I've called the "democratic requirement", which stipulates that a democratic mode of politics properly privileges the practice of dialogue. Here the big idea is that it's only as we engage one another, listen to one another, challenge one another, address one another's concerns, put up arguments, amend arguments, retract arguments – in short deliberate together – that we can expect to reach durable political agreements. Agreements capable of winning our consent or even reflecting a consensus (I'm allowing myself moments of optimism!). In the absence of dialogue, maybe it's possible to envisage stop-gap compromises, tactical alignments, transactional alliances and the like; and maybe enough

of us would be prepared to settle for any of these out of convenience or weariness or whatever. But I think it's close to delusional to imagine that any such non-dialogically based solutions would be other than temporary; it's hard to see how, lacking dialogue, we'll ever begin to overcome properly the divisions that contaminate our politics or develop lasting bonds of trust and understanding with those who are different from us.

- Fourth, there's what I've called the interpretive requirement: namely, that we (as individuals or as members of a cultural/political tradition) have to admit that our understandings of ourselves or of our society at any given moment are always open to revision. Implicitly or explicitly, we interpret and re-interpret what counts for us and why. And here, I suggest, the whole business of interpretation/reinterpretation, evaluation/re-evaluation finds its locus in dialogue. It's through testing, say, the plausibility of our own views against others and being exposed to theirs that we may arrive at deeper, richer understandings of what matters to us and why. This interpretative requirement also makes dialogue central, then. In doing so, it calls into question the operative assumption of so many in Northern Ireland, namely that "our" tradition has an exclusive grasp of truth, goodness, beauty, and rightness; or, if that's too hyperbolic (and it is) that "our" tradition is culturally and politically superior; and, crucially, that "we" have nothing to learn from another tradition, especially "the" other tradition. On my terms, such an assumption encapsulates self-deluding nonsense, and is dangerous to boot. As should be obvious, with its emphasis on dialogue, the interpretative requirement reinforces the democratic requirement: dialogue is good for us politically and more generally as human beings.

To conclude, I am submitting that a type of politics based on these requirements of citizenship and reflecting the complex British-Irish condition of Northern Ireland is altogether more conducive than are the standard politics of unionism and nationalism to achieving a decent future for all of us, a future beyond sectarianism, division and stalemate.

9

Expanding the Unionist Imagination: Appropriating 1798

This chapter is a slight extension of a paper delivered at a conference in the Mansion House, Dublin, on the theme "1798: Memory and Meaning" in November 1997. It's possibly accurate to say that I am here pushing unionism to its limits by proposing that it embrace a tradition (in significant measure, even if not fully) to which it has historically been hostile. The reasons I give are controversial and no doubt need more development. Needless to say, I think they have promising persuasive potential. I doubt if many will agree, but there are still grounds for remaining hopeful.

A Question

What meaning should 1798 have for us now and more especially for unionists? This may seem a pointless question to some. Others may concede its point but decide that its only plausible answer is "none". And yet others may agree on it having a point but think that its best answer is "quite a lot". I want to argue for a version of this last response. Doing so will involve going against the grain of conventional unionist wisdom and against that of entrenched forms of Irish nationalism/republicanism. I begin by briefly saying why the other responses to the question don't appeal.

A Pointless Question?

The question may seem pointless in the sense that it invites the wrong approach to history. If our concern is to discover the truth about the events of 1798, then to introduce concerns of contemporary unionism into the picture is simply to add confusion. Or so certain historians would tell us. Here the idea is that only those whose vision is undistorted by political perceptions can deliver the authentic story of 1798. So, on these terms, to take my question seriously is to indulge bad history. To allow present commitments to influence our orientation to the past, says Brian Walker, is to suppose that history is appropriately "used to supply role models or simple answers" (Walker, 1996: 60). Not only is this bad, he thinks, but reckless too. Or at least it is in an Irish context, where such an attitude to history frequently underpins sectarianism. Perhaps, then, the rub is this: my question should be treated as pointless, since if it isn't it becomes potentially very dangerous.

Walker and those who reason like him are on to something. To reduce the complexities of the past to models and answers that simply underwrite current political prejudices produces bad history. And such bad history frequently does have dangerous implications. But that's about as much as can be conceded. What can't be admitted is the possibility of "neutral" history, not least because the very language in which history is written or told is the language of some tradition or another. Here even professional or "non-political" historians can't ultimately prevent prejudices acquired from their present circumstances affecting their explanations of past events.

But the real issue at stake isn't how we go about writing faithful accounts of 1798. The question I've posed has a much broader compass, one which imagines a continuing interrelation of past and present. It supposes that the meaning of 1798 is disclosed through a variety of forms, not to mention through the conflicts between them. It is revealed, for example, not just through the experiences of the United Irishmen, but also through subsequent experiences inspired by theirs, not only through their original ideas, but also through later extensions and even transformations of these ideas. In short, the question I am focusing on only makes sense if 1798 is thought of in terms of a tradition that is ongoing and open-ended. And it's precisely such a way of thinking that is missed by mutterings about questions of this sort being either pointless or dangerous.

Negative Meaning

This is not what is missed by those unionists and republicans who value working within a tradition. Both would see the point of the question but would typically think it allows a negative reply only. Their problem is a different one. Nonetheless it's not hard to understand the logic of their thinking.

Consider for a moment a standard unionist line. 1798, far from ranking with such definitive dates in the collective unionist memory as 1690 or 1912, seems to carry negative connotations of two sorts. First, it recalls a past which almost deprived unionism of a future. Second, it anticipates a future in which unionism will be rendered redundant anyway. On this reading, 1798 refers to a set of subversive goals that had the very real potential to destroy unionism. Had the '98 Rebellion succeeded in ending British rule in Ireland, there would not have been an Act of Union and unionism as we know it would probably never have developed. To celebrate the memory of the United Irishmen, then, seems simultaneously to lament unionism's continuing presence in Ireland. And since such a lament can scarcely be expected of unionists, neither, it appears, can such celebration.

The explicit anti-unionist overtones of 1798 are not just matters of historical curiosity, however. They appear integral to the republican tradition inspired by the United Irishmen. Many of those who trace their ideological origins to Wolfe Tone and make annual pilgrimages to Bodenstown dream, quite simply, of an Ireland united and independent. This is, of course, an Ireland in which unionism as such can have no political purchase. And it is, needless to say, just such an Ireland that unionists fear. Accordingly, 1798 can have no significance for unionists today, except as a symbol of their fears. It represents a hostile tradition. Or so it seems.

Seeming so is, however, somewhat misleading. On the foregoing reading, the significance of 1798 is reduced to the issue of British rule in Ireland, and thus to the fundamental constitutional dispute between unionism and nationalism. Sure, certain narrowly conceived unionist and republican interests may be suited by this reading. But the reductionism it entails makes for thin history and unimaginative politics. It suggests a closed tradition.

Positive Meaning

An open tradition permits a much broader interpretation of 1798's significance. And it's such an interpretation I now wish to press for. I want to suggest that 1798 contains considerable meaning for all of us in Ireland today, North and South, unionist and nationalist. This meaning is communicated through three specific challenges which don't so much threaten unionism's existence, as ask searching questions of what it stands for.

Challenges

Recapturing Anti-Sectarianism

One challenge is that of recapturing the progressive, anti-sectarian ideals of 1798. No doubt this is a challenge for all political persuasions in Ireland today, but it is a particularly poignant one for unionism. To see why requires posing stark questions about the dissenting tradition which championed the ideals of 1798, and which subsequently became unionism's main constituency. These are questions reflecting an ongoing puzzle I've had about causes of the shifts in political outlook within dissenting/Protestant ranks over time. How was it that ideas associated with that date seemed to vanish so speedily from large tracts of Irish affairs? Or why was it that ideas central to the American and French revolutions, and, more generally, to the Enlightenment – ideas which clearly inspired a generation of dissenters/Protestants, especially in Belfast – proved to have such a short tenure? Why did they become marginalised so effortlessly within dissenting/Protestant circles?

Historians have of course come up with various answers here:

- Dissenters' grievances were quickly settled by the English and so the source of their rebellion against English rule, especially in Antrim and Down, was removed.
- Catholic sectarianism motivated certain of the United Irishmen and as this became increasingly obvious, it became progressively harder for Protestants/dissenters to associate with the cause of rebellion.

- Contradictions ran through the agendas of the United Irishmen – the radical ideas of Tone and the Belfast leadership weren't shared by the Father Murphy's of the world.
- 'Revolutionary' ideas thrived in Belfast at a time when Catholics there comprised a tiny minority of the population and this fact helped disguise a latent Protestant sectarianism which didn't take long to surface under new social and political circumstances.
- Beyond the educated circles of the United Irishmen's leadership in Belfast, radical ideas took little root in wider Protestant/dissenter culture.

Now all of these explanations may be more or less true – though what we've already heard today about circumstances in Wexford should prompt a little revision of some of them – but none of them has ever quite satisfied my puzzle. A puzzle which only grows in its perplexity. Unless we're prepared to buy some form of religious or economic reductionism, the apparently easy marginalisation of memory of 1798 continues to bother.

Sure, we can admit that sectarian tendencies were present among the United Irishmen, and that these ran counter to the ideals for which they stood. We can also concede that there were serious divisions among dissenters and Protestants about what the United Irishmen represented – divisions which continued to be played out in smaller, less dramatic, and modified ways during the nineteenth century, through disputes between "Old Light" and "New Light" factions within Presbyterianism for example. And we can allow further that the English moved more energetically to mollify dissenters than they did Catholics (to understate matters radically), and that after the Act of Union "disloyalty to the Crown" took on an increasingly Catholic hue.

But acknowledging all of the above doesn't resolve the

conundrum. After the explanations of historians (not to mention the rationalisations of unionist apologists) have been factored in, I remain unsettled by precisely this thought: the ideas that turned much of Europe upside down and drove a generation of Irish dissenters to take enormous risks seem subsequently to have been cast aside too cheaply for comfort. Worse still, there is the shocking truth that ideas that were (at the very least) anti-sectarian in nature, were generally swapped within Protestant/dissenting circles for ideas that fitted within a sectarian mould. This seems to me the crucial and truly disturbing point.

Even if we can find reasons why by the time of Gladstone's First Home Rule Bill most Protestants identified with the cause of unionism, these reasons don't tell us all we need to know. They don't tell us why so many dissenters complied, either meekly or enthusiastically, with the Orange and Tory prescriptions with which the unionist cause (to its great discredit in my less than orthodox opinion) has for so long been lumbered. It's not enough here to blame Catholicism's attempted hijacking of all things Irish. For this implies that one kind of sectarianism can only be met by another. We are confronted, rather, with a very discomfiting loss of political and moral orientation within the dissenting tradition. One which I don't claim fully to understand.

Thus, the puzzle and predicament for people like me. For the sake of the Union, dissenters were for the most part willing to forfeit the radical, anti-sectarian ideals that had earlier fired the imaginations of their forbears and had given brief promise of a better future for all of us on this island. This is part of the tragedy with which we've all had to live. The challenge now is for unionism to rediscover what it lost as memory of 1798 receded in the dissenter consciousness and was replaced by memories of a different kind. This is to appropriate 1798 for unionism. It is to prioritise anti-sectarianism in a way that effectively dislodges the privileged place Orangeism continues to enjoy within unionist ranks. Facing up to the challenge of 1798 demands nothing less unless we are resigned to associating unionism only with forces of reaction.

Retrieving and Re-articulating Citizen-Centred Politics

In truth the challenge demands a good deal more. To capture and sustain the anti-sectarian legacy of 1798 involves taking up another challenge, namely that of retrieving and re-articulating a citizen-centred politics which was emerging within radical factions of the United Irishmen. And, for those who may be interested in such matters, responding to the challenge involves addressing (at least tacitly) whether events or ideas retain their original force and validity 200 years on and simply need fresh translations into our very different circumstances, or whether the original ideas themselves need reworking in order to continue speaking to us in compelling ways. I want to argue that a bit of both is true regarding the contemporary meaning of 1798. I do so by drawing on the guiding ideas of the French revolution – equality, liberty and fraternity – which (at least most of the leadership of) the United Irishmen freely appropriated, and by relating these (very briefly) to Tone's vision of the "unity of Protestant, Catholic and Dissenter".

A late-eighteenth century rendering of the ideas of equality, liberty and fraternity emphasises their potential to undermine and replace the *ancien régime*. Thus, in the name of equality, hierarchical systems of privilege and socio-political organisation are called to judgement and found wanting. In the name of liberty, individuals are declared free from those patterns of domination that have prevented them from taking charge of their own affairs, and that have tried to restrict them from thinking and expressing their own thoughts (especially in public). In the name of fraternity, it is affirmed that the bonds that matter are not those acquired through (supposedly noble) birth lines or status, but those enjoyed through our participation in a common humanness.

What is also going on through the advocacy of these ideas is a claim that political power is properly the preserve of "the people" and not of a monarch. Moreover, such power is taken to require for its organisation a republican form of government, where the people are defined as citizens and not as subjects. In the eighteenth-century Irish case, this requirement acquires an additional rub: the achievement of republican goals is seen to demand breaking loose from the domination of English rule.

It is pretty clear that various of these eighteenth-century meanings of equality, liberty and fraternity remain relevant to us. No doubt, they comprise part of the taken-for-granted background against which much of our political thought and action occurs. Given that the demise of the *ancien régime*, not to mention the lessons of the French revolution, are well behind us, eighteenth century meanings are of course relevant in different ways now – ways that remain open to fresh translations. The thorny question, needless to say, is whether we must continue to underwrite the United Irishmen's conviction that pursuit of republican goals in Ireland requires independence from Britain. I'll return to this question shortly.

I want to suggest, first, that the guiding ideas of the French revolution can be extended in their meaning for us by being reworked beyond their eighteenth-century formulations. I can only gesture here at what this suggestion might amount to. Its key is relating ideas of equality, liberty and fraternity to a central republican conception of politics, namely that it is integral to the purpose of politics to create social and political conditions conducive to the flourishing of citizens.

For example, once we prioritise citizens' flourishing, it quickly becomes evident that more than formal equality is necessary. Of course, it's important to insist upon the political and legal equality of citizens, as it is also to press for a principle of equal opportunity. But, unless we believe the fiction that capitalism makes everyone a winner, that the market economy and its mythical "hidden hand" deliver just shares of the social cake, then much more is due to citizens in the name of equality. Across the board of economic and social life – from employment to wages, from health to pensions, from education to social benefits – an equality geared to giving all citizens decent prospects of flourishing demands more than a market economy is capable of delivering. It demands that a properly republican society doesn't do what the market cannot but do, namely reward the arbitrariness of fortune by turning a blind eye to the social and natural disadvantages some citizens suffer from through no fault of their own.

However loathe they are to admit it, apologists of unbridled capitalism prescribe a deeply inegalitarian society which can't take seriously the implications of citizenship. Which is why citizens can only have reasonable hope of flourishing under certain conditions: when a substantive social equality – which is impossible to achieve without government playing a strongly active role in economic affairs – is seen as a necessary accompaniment to the formal equality so rightly valued by eighteenth century reformers and revolutionaries.

To prioritise the good of citizens is also to admit that liberty is about more than citizens being permitted to choose what they want. Sure, it's vital that citizens are allowed to think their own thoughts and are as far as possible free from external forces of domination that would squeeze them into oppressive forms of life. But liberty has a political meaning too, which is captured in the republican idea of government as the self-rule of citizens. This idea was familiar enough in the eighteenth century and lay behind French, American and Irish quests to acquire independence from aristocratic, colonial and imperial forms of rule.

To recapture the force of this idea now, however, requires a more expansive imagination than eighteenth century examples provide. The belief that citizens are entitled to have a say in matters affecting their well-being has to be worked out beyond formal tiers of government to include the life of civil society. What's at stake here is an attempt to give substance to the republican insight that flourishing citizens are active citizens and not passive consumers. And enjoying political liberty crucially hangs on precisely this insight. Unfortunately, powerful trends in Western culture and politics – from hyper-individualism to managerial and ultra-bureaucratic models of government – combine to deprive the republican notion of political liberty of much of its meaning. Which is why republican commitment to liberty, in conjunction with republican commitment to equality, entails a searching critique of prevailing modes of politics. A critique inspired by the example of our eighteenth-century forbears but one that, for us, must dig deeper and reach wider.

The idea of fraternity fits in here too. Without doubt, we need to think of this idea in an international sense: it serves as a reminder of our common humanity. A reminder which ought to give pause to those parochial inclinations which too often excuse the brutalisation of ("foreign") others. But, in a more local sense, fraternity is properly linked to the bonds we share with fellow citizens - those we work and deliberate with in order to shape a decent social and political life for us all. And, as with its international dimension, this rendering of its local dimension in terms of citizenship helps correct those tendencies in our own society which reduce (and bastardise) fraternity by restricting it to relations with members of one tribe, tradition, religion or whatever. It is fraternal citizens who are devoted to making society work as a whole; it is they who most keenly recognise their interdependence, who grasp most clearly that their flourishing is something we win together.

To summarise, the guiding ideas of the French revolution were radical in their day but due to their incorporation into the Western mainstream, seem unremarkable – though still important – to many of us now. However, a more stringent republican reworking of these ideas, along the lines I've briefly suggested, reveals that their radical bite may yet be felt. And there are few places of which this is truer than contemporary Ireland, North and South. Not only does the republican privileging of citizenship have profound ramifications for our general understanding of how ideas of equality, liberty and fraternity ought to bear upon practices we share in common with other European states; it also subverts in the strongest possible way the peculiar and odious sectarian practices that continue to blight our social and political lives.

And here the republican emphasis on citizenship links up with Tone's vision of the unity of Protestant, Catholic and Dissenter. It is only in terms of this emphasis, I'd submit, that we can entertain the expectation of realising some version of Tone's vision in our time. Only a common sense of citizenship seems to me capable of putting our confessional/denominational differences into proper perspective and of preventing them from continuing to wreak the sort of political havoc that they have during the last generation. And to state what I think is the obvious, there is considerably more to valuing the dignity of citizens by developing a common sense of citizenship than unionism typically allows. For unionists, it's enough that all citizens in Northern Ireland are in principle granted the same procedural entitlements. But, even if, despite cultural unionist resistance we thought that that was within reach, it wouldn't be enough at all. Running through my brief remarks on the central ideas of the French revolution is the claim that what's required in addition is the creation and cultivation of a shared civic identity. In the divided society that is Northern Ireland, this is only possible through concerted standing against religiously based segregation in areas of housing, education and the like. Also required is the creation of public institutions capable of commanding the allegiance of all citizens, and not just members of one tradition. This is to anticipate a future for the North that unionists have difficulty grasping, but it is one that memory of 1798 opens up. And as should be obvious given the language I've been using, it is a future in which it's not considered oxymoronic to join (at least a civic understanding of) the terms unionism and republicanism.

Affirming Irishness

It is of course naïve to suppose that such a future is possible without unionism facing a third challenge from 1798, that of affirming Irishness. Part of the difficulty here, however, is knowing what this should involve.

For some it involves nothing less than strict adherence to the United Irishmen's convictions that British rule in Ireland must be ended, and that religious divisions can be transcended through an affirmation of our common nationality. There is, let me be clear, nothing wrong in principle with aspiring to Irish unity on such grounds and perhaps doing so may even seem compelling in the future. At present, however, the trouble with this rendering is that it fails to account for three things: (1) that there is a difference in kind between a British government (now) that declares it has no selfish strategic or economic interest in Northern Ireland and one (then) that imposed its rule in arbitrary, corrupt and despotic ways; (2) that, unfortunately, Irishness stopped being a cure for sectarianism the moment it was colonised by Catholicism; and (3) that it is far-fetched to expect unionists to consent to their own extinction. So simply to leap from the experience of 1798 to the present, to imagine that there is an unbroken line leading from that expression of Irish republicanism to the one that grabs the headlines in our time, and to proceed as though the same arguments hold now as then is not terribly convincing. In addition, given the reality of partition, it seems to me that a republican agenda that prioritises national unity risks diminishing, if not losing track of, the deeper republican goal of attaining the type of citizenship, North and South, that's able to go beyond sectarianism. A terrible plight of republicanism now (at least in the North) is that it's dismissed outright by many contemporary Protestants as merely a password for violent sectarianism. This is a cruel irony. The memory and meaning of 1798 have been travestied and tarnished beyond recognition.

A more realistic rendering of the challenge of affirming Irishness might go something like this. It is implausible to regard the North simply as a site of the Union. It should be regarded, rather, as a site where British and Irish factors intermingle and clash and demand mutual recognition. Accordingly, unionism should stop defining Britishness and Irishness in oppositional terms. Irishness (like Britishness) should be accommodated within Northern Ireland and within North-South bodies. Although more modest, this rendering still challenges two dominant tendencies within unionism: the Ulster Protestant particularism exemplified by Ian Paisley and various loyalist paramilitaries, and mainstream unionism's demeaning craving for recognition by the British establishment. A re-appropriation of the Irishness of all of us on this island and a determination to give it its due would help ease unionism out of the defensive mindset in which it has been stuck for too long.

I realise that my so-called realistic gloss on the third challenge is guaranteed to provoke intense disagreement. My pitch amounts to this: yes Irishness needs proper recognition in the North, but to recapture the genuinely anti-sectarian memory and meaning of 1798 in our time and given our circumstances requires, I think, making a republican conception of politics and citizenship primary and the issue of partition secondary. Otherwise our prospects of overcoming the sectarian madness that thrives in our midst seem dim indeed. That may change sometime in the future, of course, if among other things it becomes clear that only reunification offers a long-term solution to sectarianism. But that is to project too far into the unknown. The immediate point is that the fact that we can even now hope to transcend such sectarian madness in the name of republicanism is in no small measure due to the example set by the United Irishmen 200 years ago. And, even if we aren't obliged to follow them to the letter, those of us who want to think of our politics as (civic) republican to the core remain very much indebted to them in spirit.

To conclude, a unionism prepared to take leave of its Orange and conservative affiliations and respond positively to the challenges of the United Irishmen by moving beyond sectarianism, prioritising citizenship and accommodating Irishness would offer rare hope to us all, North and South. That it's even possible to speculate on its doing so attests to the lasting power of the legacy of 1798, which still proves capable of appealing to certain types of optimists among us and warrants appropriation by unionists.

PART FOUR

THINKING MORE BROADLY

In the next three chapters the focus shifts to broader themes in Northern Irish politics. Unionism is no longer the preoccupation, even if it continues to warrant mention. All three began as oral presentations; one to a primarily religious audience in Belfast (Chapter ten) and the others to academic audiences in Dublin and Melbourne respectively. Two were composed prior to the Good Friday or Belfast Agreement of 10 April 1998 – one in 1996 and another in 1997 – and a third in the Agreement's wake in September 1998. Substantial portions of the academic presentations (Chapters eleven and twelve) were eventually incorporated into my book on reconciliation in Northern Ireland, *The Elusive Quest. Reconciliation in Northern Ireland*.

10

Politics: Blessing and Bane?

The following is an expanded and slightly modified version of a talk delivered in February 1996 to a Forum on Christian Citizenship organised by ECONI (Evangelical Contribution on Northern Ireland). The talk's title was chosen by the organisers.

It may be advisable to signal something about its content in advance: it advocates a line on Northern Ireland's politics consistent with that articulated in previous chapters but does so by drawing on Christian theology as well as on other modes of reflection. And this may strike some readers as quite strange granted that in my previous writings on Northern Ireland I haven't given much indication of religious attachments, let alone engaged in any form of religious advocacy. On the latter point, my resistance to such advocacy has been shaped by the conviction that much of it has been implicated in the politics of division and vilification and should be avoided like the plague. I thought it prudent, therefore, to underplay a religious dimension of my thinking. And this was largely an untroubling thing to do because the political analyses I offer on Northern politics do not depend upon the acceptance of any particular religious commitments.

They don't require subscription to the doctrine of the Trinity or belief in the resurrection. But metaphysics aside, they do appeal tacitly to an ethical background that is, in my view, most coherently understood in Christian terms, even if one doesn't have to share Christian sympathies to be shaped by it and, more pointedly, even if nonbelievers often exhibit more of its virtues than do believers. I haven't argued for any of this here or elsewhere; at best the odd hint appears, especially in this chapter.

Another reason for my reticence to invoke religious considerations when advocating political change in Northern Ireland is that I didn't wish to encourage further commentary on the differences between my views and those of my late father's. Briefly explained, my father, with whom I share the same name, had for a time been a prominent public figure in Northern Ireland. He was renowned for his identification of the cause of unionism with the cause of evangelical Protestantism. It was clear that my agenda diverged from his, politically and theologically. But whereas the political divergences were transparent, the theological ones weren't quite so much. And I think I was happy enough about that not least because I was uncomfortable with contrasts, whether positive or negative, being drawn between my father and me – so better not to add more grist to that particular mill. It's only now that I have (minor) regrets about not expressly articulating a different theological route to the politics of Northern Ireland. As I say, it's implicit in my various reflections in this volume and other books. And, for what it's worth, I developed my alternative understanding of theology and its relation to politics in the 1980s but only made it publicly available recently (Porter, 2020). I intend eventually to write more fully on the personal aspects of my relationship with my religious and political background. For the moment, it's enough to indicate the presence of a significant influence on my thinking which may have escaped notice, but which may cast light on what follows now.

Introduction

I'd like to start by thanking David Porter (no relation) and others from ECONI for this opportunity to lay out a few thoughts on the topic of politics. But I have, I must confess, some strangely mixed feelings about being here tonight and about addressing this topic. Being here evokes mixed feelings, principally because the venue – the YMCA – brings back a flood of memories from what now seems like a bygone era, and whose power I have to resist if my appearing here tonight isn't to seem (to me at least) overwhelmingly distracting. To appreciate why I say this, why memories of the YMCA are so strong, it should be borne in mind that I've spent the greater part of my adult life in Australia: I left Belfast when I was eighteen in 1970 and only returned in July 1994. So, when I think of the YMCA, I automatically think of it as it was then rather than as it is now. And the "old" YMCA has such a hold in my memory because I vividly recall it as a venue of significance in two very different ways.

First, I recall its billiard room or snooker hall as a place of daily retreat where I wilfully, and quite chirpily, frittered away several of my teenage years and where I witnessed an event of (what I took to be) momentous importance, namely, a young – then amateur – Alex Higgins registering a maximum 147 break in around 4 minutes. But the billiard room is no more and the less said now about poor Alex (or "Higgy" as I knew him) the better.

Second, I recall the major hall of the old YMCA – the Wellington Hall – as a place where I was reluctantly dragged by my father to attend monster rallies which invariably extolled the virtues of evangelical Protestantism and warned of the perils of Romanism, especially, Brian Lennon (a congenial Jesuit priest who was one of the respondents to this talk), a Romanism dressed up in the beguiling garb of Jesuitism. But, as with the billiard room, the Wellington Hall is no more, and I haven't attended a comparable Protestant rally since. Although I should add here that the only ECONI meeting I've previously attended had a touch of *déjà vu* about it inasmuch as the major topic under discussion was that of Orange marches. At times during the debate, I detected ever so faint echoes of the old Wellington Hall days.

Anyway, the point is that to think clearly about tonight's topic, I have to cast aside haunting memories of the old YMCA and resist the temptations they invite: to reach for a snooker cue or lapse into a fiery denunciation of the wily ways of Rome. For the record, the temptation to reach for a cue is infinitely the stronger of the two and any denunciation of Rome would be entirely tongue-in-cheek.

Turning to the topic under consideration tonight, "politics – blessing and bane?" I experience mixed feelings: it poses a challenging question worthy of deliberation, but I'm not overconfident that my deliberations will be worthy of it. It's the kind of question that makes me look askance, that raises the suspicion that there's a clue to finding *the* answer, a political clue maybe but more likely a theological clue. If the question had been "politics – blessing *or* bane?" I perhaps wouldn't have felt the same sense of suspicion or consternation. But it's worded "blessing *and* bane?" Sure, this wording doesn't preclude the possibility of answering that politics is entirely a blessing or entirely a bane, but it does seem to load the dice in such a way as to suggest that it's neither entirely but a bit of both. And if it is a bit of both, are we talking equal or disproportionate bits? How are we to work this out? Maybe, as I say, there's some clue which once discovered reveals all. Well, if there is, I'm pretty sure I haven't located it.

So, in the absence of any magical clue which would enable me to deliver a definitive and utterly compelling response to the question before us, I'd like to suggest two possible ways of fashioning an answer. These are ways which try to make sense of the question in relation to the peculiar politics of Northern Ireland but do so by employing rather different interpretations of the concept of the kingdom of God and of the nature and purpose of politics. As I hope to show, such different interpretations here yield different appraisals of the requirements of politics in Northern Ireland and put different emphases on the senses in which politics may be a blessing and a bane. This doesn't mean that they hold nothing in common. And to reinforce this point, I want to start with a brief ground-clearing exercise which offers a preliminary statement of the relationship between politics and the kingdom of God that both positions (or at least dominant versions of each) would, I think, sign up to, followed by an extremely terse overview of meanings associated with the concept of the kingdom of God. Then, with these in mind, I'll embark upon a quick exploration of the principal differences between the two positions I'm bringing to attention and try to sell you one of them.

Preliminaries

In offering a preliminary clarification of the relationship between politics and the kingdom of God, I'll defer to what I take to be a principal part of the rationale of ECONI. I'll put it like this: *the kingdom of God commands our ultimate allegiance* and it's in the light of the priorities and perspectives it makes available that the claims of political ideologies, movements and parties are to be judged.

It is of the essence here to refuse to allow the demands of the kingdom to be trimmed in such a way that they are easily accommodated to the interests of any parochial political position. Or, more sharply, any attempt to identify the kingdom of God with any political cause must be approached sceptically and almost certainly opposed. Throughout Western history, there has been little more damaging to the reputation of Christianity, not to mention to the lives of countless human beings, than the *delusion that God is on our (political)* side and therefore against our opponents. This is a delusion that we in Northern Ireland know well. For example, the slogan, "For God and Ulster", ranks, I'd suggest, as one of the more unfortunate to have been adopted by Protestants and unionists and has had fateful consequences in this part of the world, not least because of the rationalisation it affords to those who are inclined to "demonise" Catholics, nationalists, or republicans. This isn't to overlook that an equivalent "For God and Ireland" sentiment – which typically relegates Protestants to the status of heretics – has been present too and is also culpable in distorting relations between our main communities. And perhaps it's best not to become distracted by the unfortunate consequences that have often attended the USA's sense of exceptionalism and belief in its "manifest destiny". And thus, we could go on.

An appreciation of the ultimacy of the kingdom of God, of its pointing to a mode of existence which is "not yet" and so forth, helps to place the contingent political aspirations of this group or that group in some kind of perspective. But this appreciation still leaves a lot unsettled. To return to our question, it perhaps permits us to say that a politics which collapses the distinction between the kingdom of God and a particular political movement, that assumes that the cause of God can conveniently be domesticated to underwrite some local political cause, is more likely to be a bane than a blessing. But it doesn't permit us to say much more than this. In particular, it leaves open such questions as the following. Does a preoccupation with the kingdom of God properly make us indifferent to politics of any kind? Or does such a preoccupation impel us to certain kinds of political action? And, if it does, what kinds of political thought and action are warranted? Or, put another way, what is it legitimate to expect of politics without losing sight of the ultimate claims of the kingdom of God?

To tackle questions such as these we need to work with four

factors: (1) a clearer sense of what we mean by the kingdom of God; (2) a notion of what politics is about, of what purposes it properly tries to achieve, and of where these purposes figure in our conceptions of what matters to us; (3) another notion of how political purposes relate to the priorities of the kingdom of God; and (4) an indication of how such notions of politics and of the kingdom of God translate in specific political circumstances, in this case those prevailing in Northern Ireland. And, I'd suggest, the sorts of answers we give to our central question, "politics – blessing and bane?" depends on the kind of packaging of these factors which we're prepared to buy. After offering some further clarifying comments about the concept of the kingdom of God, I'll quickly sketch two different kinds of packaging and, as I've indicated, try to persuade you to buy the second.

The Kingdom of God

I've already alluded to ways in which I understand the kingdom of God and its bearing on our affairs; ones which I hope aren't too controversial (at least in this company!). But a little more needs to be clarified if we're to get a firm grip on the different packages I want to introduce and the disputes between them. The concept of the kingdom of God has a range of meanings. It brings into focus the idea and nature of God's rule, the realm over which the rule is exercised and how this realm may be accessed, the extent of the rule's reach, and questions about its presence and its completeness. Big topics which I can hardly hope to address other than fleetingly. To compound difficulties of dealing intelligibly with crucial aspects of the concept, another challenging realisation emerges: these aspects admit of expressions often in tension with one another. For example, we might be told that God is sovereign and love (and, indeed, absent sovereignty couldn't be God) but that forces of evil are still abroad in defiance of his sovereign will; that God's rule is not dominating but gracious and enabling and yet that we should expect to be judged harshly if we're guilty of resisting it; that God's kingdom is spiritual ("not of this world") and that it is accessed through personal *metánoia* ("Repent the kingdom of God is at hand") and yet that his will is to be "done on earth as it is in heaven", and that entrance to the kingdom seems to extend to those who may not have repented ("Today you will be with me in paradise"); that the kingdom's reach is concentrated on the life of the church and yet that it may expand to the life of society; and that the kingdom is now and is among us, and yet that we await its completion, that it is a present reality and that it is also an eschatological expectation.

Unsurprisingly, important differences between the packages I now wish to discuss reflect diverging emphases on these tensions, or at least some of them.

A Minimalist Package

A Spiritual Kingdom

In relation to the *kingdom of God*, one package, which I'll call "minimalist," tends to stress that the exercise of God's sovereignty is inscrutable, but that for several reasons – ranging from severe notions of "double predestination" through to respect of humans' freedom to choose evil with all the risks that entails – isn't impugned by forms of human (or even demonic) contrariness which will eventually receive their definitive come-uppance. The problem of theodicy, in other words, isn't decisive. It's not uncommon either, to be informed here that torment is the lot we deserve as humans due to our being mired in original sin, that divine judgement is unavoidable, and that those who are spared divine wrath only evade it because they are recipients of divine grace, which demonstrates God's unswerving love (to the elect if to nobody else). Initially, the realm in which God's rule is encountered is that of the heart; it is a spiritual domain that we gain full access to via a type of repentance which transforms our spiritual world by effecting our spiritual rebirth and granting us (a grace-conferring) eternal life. This is a life shared now with others who have similarly experienced the transformative work of divine grace and with whom we constitute the church; and it is the church that serves as the locus of the kingdom of God on earth and through its sacraments (or symbols as Protestants prefer) allows us to participate in the life of the spirit, which is different in kind from the life of the "flesh" (to use Pauline language). Through the church and our private spiritual practices, we have, then, foretastes of God's kingdom, but live in anticipation of its completion (for believers) at the end of time, with the prospect of a cataclysmic drama shortly prior to then (at least according to those with fertile prophetic imaginations).

Politics as Limited

It isn't difficult to appreciate that anyone entertaining a conception of the kingdom of God with these emphases is likely to think of politics serving only very restricted purposes. Which is what I mean by a "minimalist" package. So, given the theological backdrop I've just sketched, to accept a minimal package is to think that even at its best politics exists only for the sake of something else; a something which isn't political in kind but a something of far superior value. This is to think of *politics as inherently limited.* The fact that we have politics, that we have to structure our life in society, that we require governments and so on is a testimony to our human frailties. Politics *per se* is not part of the human good. Theologically expressed, politics here appears as a product of original sin and the future of human perfection we anticipate through the complete dawning of God's kingdom is decidedly apolitical in kind.

Politics, accordingly, can merely be expected to achieve narrow purposes, and perhaps one purpose in particular, namely that of creating a peaceful and orderly society in which we're *protected from* the worst excesses of human nature. Why is this such a good purpose? Granting the foregoing take on the kingdom of God, we might say that it commends itself from a theological perspective because it enables us to concentrate on what matters most – preparing for our eternal destiny, attending to our spiritual duties, preaching the gospel, living according to the rule of God, and so on.

I should note in passing that it's possible to espouse similar sentiments on non-theological grounds. To those of a more secular disposition who prefer not to think in theological terms, and thus are (understandably) squeamish about the mention of original sin, it's enough to say that we need politics to curb the worst effects of human selfishness and competitiveness. Here too, politics appears as necessary only to compensate for the most horrible extravagances of human nature. And one of the compensations politics may afford is the beneficial purpose of leaving us free to pursue our individual inclinations, to satisfy our desires by living a life of relatively unhindered consumption, and so forth. In our time, it's typical of those who express their political minimalism in secular terms to add that a peaceful and orderly society properly conduces to the benefit of individuals when it is accompanied by a state's recognition and protection of individuals' rights. Theologically inclined minimalists tend to agree, even if some appear not to care.

Minimalist Politics and the Kingdom of God

The big point is that however we describe what matters to us, on the terms of this minimalist package politics has worth only because of the external goods it makes available; it is useful or necessary not for its own sake but for the sake of things that are essentially apolitical. Given a minimalist package, then, I think we are likely to draw one of two possible conclusions regarding the *relationship between politics and the kingdom of God* and, by implication, one of two on the question of whether politics is in principle a blessing and a bane.

One is a thoroughly *apolitical conclusion* which regards *politics utterly as a bane*; and which may be held so tenaciously that there is no guarantee that the merest whimper would be raised in defence of entitlements under jeopardy. It might go like this. Since what truly matters to humans is apolitical in nature, and since politics is steeped in original sin (or some secular equivalent), we should simply accept that politics is unavoidably a bane. Politics is best left to those who are deluded enough to chase impossible dreams or corrupt enough to covet the trappings of power. But for those of us who are not so deluded or so corrupt, it is more profitable to devote our lives to what really counts. And, from a Christian viewpoint, what really counts is the kingdom of God and the imperatives it places on our lives. To seek first the kingdom of God here requires us to eschew the shady world of political power and its false temptations. For a preoccupation with the concerns of the kingdom of God does properly make us indifferent to politics, especially since politics is of no ultimate consequence.

There are plenty of examples of Christian expressions of such a conclusion: at individual levels we may cite contemplative escapes from social entanglements or pietistic retreats from involvement in "worldly" affairs; at collective levels, we might mention the appeal of monastic orders for some, or of strange sects such as the Exclusive Brethren for others, or for still others, of alternative communities purportedly based on a "kingdom ethos" which contrasts sharply with the ethos of secular societies. One anomaly here is that represented by a group of otherwise apolitical Christians who are vocal in their support of the stance of Israel in the politics of the Middle East. This exception to apoliticism is justified on the grounds of biblical prophecy where war in the Middle East is deemed to be part of the eschatological unfolding of things precipitating the final realisation of God's kingdom (there are supposedly steps to such an unfolding which I have no interest in rehearsing).

Leaving aside this anomalous exception, another possible conclusion doesn't go quite as far in writing off the importance of politics to matters pertaining to the kingdom of God. I'll call this the *qualified conclusion* which views politics definitely as a bane but also as a (potential and limited) means of delivering blessings of sorts; or, otherwise put, thinks of politics as in principle *a bane and a mixed blessing*. Politics is a bane for the types of reasons mentioned in the apolitical conclusion: it's a sign of our fallenness, it's perpetually open to corruptions and eventually, with the fulfilment of the kingdom of God, we'll be well rid of it. Nevertheless, institutions of government and law are necessary given the deeply impaired state of the human condition and are ordained by God for our benefit. And there is little denying that there are distinctions to be drawn between better and worse forms of government and between better and worse forms of law. The better sorts give us peace and order and perhaps also respect our individual rights, including our right to worship according to the dictates of our consciences. And these are blessings inasmuch as they provide conditions which enable us to attend to those things that matter most – worshipping God or preaching the gospel, say, or attending to the various needs of our families and friends, and so on.

The greatest Christian expression of such a qualified conclusion runs along Augustinian lines where a distinction is drawn between two cities – the heavenly and the earthly – which Luther took up in his own way through a notion of two kingdoms, and which for my very limited purposes now we may think of as a distinction between the church and society/state. Augustine's point was that the ultimate divorce between the two would occur at the end of time, but that meanwhile many of us find ourselves inhabiting both "cities", even though only one is of full and enduring value. Prior to the *eschaton* there is an unavoidable intermingling of the two and, accordingly, modest expectations of politics are appropriately entertained; it is only immodest expectations that aren't.

Evidently, in terms of this kind of conclusion, it isn't sufficient to say that concern for the kingdom of God makes us indifferent to politics. Politics may not rate highly among the things that we esteem, but as soon as we concede that politics of a certain kind may yield benefits or blessings then to turn our backs on it almost amounts to a failure of duty. Thus, modest expectations may be recommended. Indeed, it seems we have a duty to do all that we can to enhance the development of the kingdom of God; a duty that involves estimating how politics (though feeble in the final analysis to prevent the triumph of God's kingdom) may in the present indirectly affect the development of its prospects, negatively or positively. If specific political conditions are inimical to such development, then it's up to us to stand against them. So, in a sense, preoccupation with the kingdom of God does impel political actions of some type: to advocate, say, that peace is pursued, that the law is upheld, that rights and liberties are protected, and so forth.

Minimalism and Northern Ireland

How do these minimalist considerations translate into the *politics of Northern Ireland*? On *apolitical minimalist* terms the answer is easy: by offering individuals deliverance from, rather than promising society a possible transformation of, these politics. On the terms of what I'm awkwardly calling *qualified political minimalism* the answer is more complex and merits a little more attention. There are at least three aspects to it.

First, there is probably a lament about the fact that much of what passes for political practice in Northern Ireland reveals more of the *bane of politics* than it does its blessing. There is disagreement with the "For God and Ulster" merchants and the spirit of intransigence they foster. There is probably a degree of consternation with how slowly the peace-process is progressing, with how fear and loathing stand as obstacles to consolidating a situation that remains inherently fragile. If peace and order and the rights of individuals are the blessings politics is designed to deliver, it is regrettable that political practice in Northern Ireland makes them uncertain achievements.

Second, for those who take seriously the notion that politics is capable of yielding these kinds of blessings, there is probably an impetus to see *political practice in Northern Ireland changed*. And it is possible that the changes advocated may include recommendation of a Bill of Rights to secure the entitlements of individuals. Beyond that, a call for change is likely to include encouraging unionists to be prepared to take bigger risks in the interests of peace and advising those holding weapons to consider handing them up for the sake of peace and lasting order. Opinions probably differ here, however, on the sorts of concessions that unionists, for example, should be willing to give in the absence of compliance from the IRA.

Third, and in addition to these particular issues, there is at work an *overriding vision* of the future of Northern Ireland which sees it as a place where everyone is accorded equal rights and entitlements and where respect of government and the law is reinforced and maintained. For, at the last, this is all that matters politically, since this is all that's needed from politics to allow us to attend to the more important issues of life unhindered by political unrest and violent upheaval.

A Few Criticisms

The extent of my disagreement with both forms of minimalism becomes apparent through my presentation of a maximalist package. To give a quick foretaste, I have difficulty accepting the theological rationale which limits the kingdom of God to the spiritual experiences of believers or to the life of the church; a difficulty exacerbated when these limitations trace back to a line on divine sovereignty involving predestinarian distinctions between the elect and the reprobate which are expected to receive a stamp of eschatological finality; and a difficulty that is accompanied by a sense of farce when encountering the (anomalous) case of premillenarian support of Israel in the name of (dare I say fanciful, but nevertheless potentially dangerous) prophetic conviction. Moreover, the thoroughgoing apolitical conclusion – which reduces politics to a bane – hardly commends itself by effectively abandoning the political realm to forces of conservatism and powerful interests, and in so doing showing indifference to the negative impact these forces typically have on the lives of the least well-off members of society. It is very peculiar to be told in effect that the realm outside of private spirituality and the church in which most of human existence is concentrated is simply of no consequence to Christians. Why so peculiar? Well, given the universal connotations integral to a Christian conception of God how can it be that the circumstances in which most of us spend our lives are at best tangential to this God? It makes little sense. And neither does the irresponsibility it implies in the context of Northern Irish politics, where for the sake of protecting our spiritual purity, it seems unimportant to apply a brake to sectarian practices and attitudes. I can't help but suggest that only a perverse reading of the Gospels could tally such irresponsibility with the picture we are given of Jesus of Nazareth and his preoccupations.

Unsurprisingly, it doesn't take much to aver here that the more qualified (Augustinian-type) of conclusion – where blessings of a restricted kind are allowed of politics – has more going for it. But even its less austere version of a minimalist package provides insufficient incentives for political engagement. To think of politics as at best a kind of necessary evil, or at least as a distraction from the more important matters of life to be engaged in only for their sake, means that political advocacy or involvement is undertaken in a spirit of sacrifice that too easily becomes begrudging. And there's always the temptation to rationalise that someone else is better equipped or situated to make that sacrifice. Or, to revert to the situation in Northern Ireland, there's a lingering doubt about the adequacy of this form of thinking to shake up complacencies and entrenched prejudices that ought to stand more explicitly under Christian scrutiny. In short, a minimalist package short-changes us at general theological and political levels, as well as at the more particular level of Northern politics. We need an alternative.

A Maximalist Package

The alternative I'll now attempt to convince you of is what I'm calling a maximalist package; one in which politics is taken to serve larger purposes and to create internal goods. Although not strictly necessary, an impetus for this more positive interpretation of politics may come from a different reading of the *kingdom of God* and its meaning for us.

A Universal Kingdom

The major theme of (my version of) this reading is the universality of the kingdom. This is intimated in Jesus' announcement that the kingdom of God is at hand, which in effect is to say that God is not only Creator (who may have nipped off and left creatures to their own devices) but also King of the world (indicating that he has done no such thing). It's an announcement whose universal implications are reinforced by the revelatory significance subsequently attributed by Christians to Jesus Christ as the Incarnation of the *Logos* and so to the deeper meaning of his life, death and resurrection; a revelatory significance facilitating anticipation of nothing short of the eschatological transformation and consummation of the world as the Kingdom of God. To tune into this way of thinking is to allow everything to be turned on its head. So, when Jesus teaches his disciples to pray for God's will being "done on earth as it is in heaven", part of what he's driving at is that the realm beyond human manipulation (heaven) is now invading the world seemingly within human control (earth) with the intention of utterly remaking it. This is the message of the kingdom of God, which (assuming God is who Christians say he is) cannot but be universal in its scope.

Now, in reference to the sorts of tensions raised by talk of the kingdom, does it make much difference to favour a universal reading over a spiritual one? On the tension involved in the problem of theodicy I'm not sure if it does. But let me clarify what my angle on it is: the problem of theodicy remains a genuine mystery which only admits of an eschatological resolution when God is "all in all" (1Cor. 15: 28) – and so the question becomes whether (what I'll call for convenience) the *Christ-event* gives sufficient grounds for believing such a resolution is possible (and clearly, I think that it does, although I'll have to leave you guessing as to why). On other tensions differences are more apparent. Take that between God's grace and divine punishment which bears upon the question of who qualifies as a kingdom member. According to my reading, there is no predilection to predestinarian favouring of the few (elect) over the many (reprobate); an agnostic shrug may commend itself instead on the issue of membership, as may (a probably more compelling) universalist objection to the very idea of an eternally condemned reprobate class of persons – an objection which projects that the logic of a universal kingdom eventually purged of evil suggests that distinctions between the few and the many are ultimately dissolved, and that grace and love, in short, prevail.

Then we have tensions between spirituality and social life, and between the church and society. A spiritual reading clearly privileges private spirituality and the practices of the church. My universal reading is more nuanced and expansive. Sure, private spirituality is not to be sneezed at, and neither is the significance of the church as the pre-eminent sign of the kingdom of God in our midst. Paying proper dues to both entails acknowledging that spiritual practices nourish experience of living, even incompletely, with a sense of God's rule, not least with gratitude that life isn't merely a (brute) given, but a (graciously bestowed divine) gift; and appreciating that the church uniquely embodies the eschatological character of the Christian faith in its awareness of a distinction – underscored though its sacramental/symbolic functions - between the provisional and the ultimate. What is to be contested, however, is that the kingdom's proper reach ends with these, since it's the entire social texture of human life, not least in its political manifestations, that's given the promise of eschatological fulfilment in the advent of the kingdom of God. Thus, Jesus indicates that the coming reign of God offers "good news to the poor", "release to the captives," "recovering of sight to the blind", "liberty to those who are oppressed" (*Luke* 4: 18-19); and it involves blessing peacemakers, justice-seekers, the merciful, those persecuted for doing right (*Matt* 5: 3-10), and so on. Such news and blessings are devalued if not applied to the life of society and government. They are political, even if their being so doesn't exhaust all that they are. Or to press further, and to pick up on the tension between the "now" and the "then" of the kingdom, we may say that the church currently symbolises that which shall eventually transcend it, namely the eschatological community of a new humankind in the kingdom of God. At the last, indeed, the divine kingdom surpasses Christianity; it is universal and fulfils that which the church hints at and gives promise of. Christians act as custodians of the kingdom "now" but "then" their role becomes redundant. The mistake is when Christianity loses sight of its provisional status by assuming forms of permanence which detract from its proleptic role of keeping attention focused on the future; a mistake that may be remedied by allowing the eschatological and universal meaning of the kingdom to occupy centre-stage; and through such an allowance by recognising that the kingdom's implications impinge on our present social and political concerns as well as on our religious ones.

Politics and Human Flourishing

A theological door opens here for reception of a maximalist package and its *expansive understanding of politics* (a version of which is, of course, available without going through any theological entrance – but that is neither here nor there for now). Something like the following rationale is involved. Undoubtedly, we might concur, there's more to life than politics and politics may indeed be useful in creating the conditions under which we enjoy what's more. Peace and order are good things, as are having individuals' rights protected and having the space and liberty to attend to contemplative or devotional concerns. But to insist that politics exists only for the sake of such things, to reduce it to a purely instrumental role and to think of it merely as a compensation for human defects is to make a terrible mistake. It is to overlook the fact that *politics is part of the human good*; that there are benefits to human beings that are intrinsic to politics; that a decent notion of human flourishing accords a crucial place to politics. Openness to an interpretation of the kingdom of God which highlights its universality at least means we don't need to grimace at such talk; on the contrary, our flourishing as humans seems pivotal to precisely such an interpretation, since the kingdom's promise of an eventual fulfilment of our humanness is what our flourishing is oriented towards. We may obtain further insight into what's being claimed here by considering a possible maximalist rendering of the purposes of politics.

Generally stated, I want to claim, *the chief purpose of politics is to create, protect and sustain a way of life worth having*. Such a way of life concentrates on the dignity of citizens and on the various institutions and practices required for their flourishing. And from these a set of subsidiary purposes emerge. Before expanding on what I'm gesturing at, let me state very rapidly my rationale for bundling together citizens' dignity, flourishing and a life worth having (or a good life). For a start, why am I emphasising the dignity of citizens rather than just human dignity? My answer is that I'm echoing the spirit of Hannah Arendt's argument that the "right to have rights" (Arendt, 1968: 296) presupposes political membership without which talk of rights remains an abstraction; so too I'm suggesting, a basic dignity which humans *qua* humans enjoy – let's say, by virtue of bearing a divine image (as Christians would claim) or of possessing rational agency (as some philosophers might insist) – frequently needs to be linked to citizenship to be efficacious, since frankly neither the rights nor dignity of "stateless" refugees can be guaranteed recognition. Sure, Christians, for example, could console themselves that as members of the kingdom of God their ultimate well-being is guaranteed regardless of their legal and political status, but (though tremendously inspiring) the adequacy of such consolation is difficult to accept indefinitely and, more to the point, it is unnecessary to settle for – we work at being faithful kingdom members not in some abstract space but in the particular spaces made available by the social and political circumstances in which our lives are situated. Belonging somewhere, being acknowledged as a citizen of a specific polity, is vital for our sense of ourselves and crucial to having our rights and dignity affirmed. Accordingly, we need to operate not only with a rudimentary conception of human dignity, but also with some notion of citizen dignity.

On the issue of citizen dignity, perhaps its most crucial feature – and the one I'm highlighting now – resides in a capability of practical reason which, in principle, indicates an inherent ability to organise, arrange, evaluate, discern, judge, et cetera things that matter to humans and how they live in society. And what I'm calling flourishing relates to the exercise of this capability in its multifaceted dimensions, with the emphasis falling decisively on courses of action reflecting not so much choices based on strength of desire as those discerned (evaluated, judged) as appropriate (enhancing, edifying, joyful, ethical, and so on). Moreover, the political sense of a worthy or good life that I'm invoking is one that accommodates citizens' dignity and flourishing by creating, protecting and sustaining the conditions that make them possible – which it can't do independently of the input of those citizens for whose sake it exists. Citizen dignity, flourishing and a worthwhile life are interdependent, which is why I've bundled them together.

We may see this interdependence and indicate the sorts of institutions and practices – not to mention some subsidiary purposes – associated with it by picking out individual, cultural and civic indications of its presence. At the level of the individual, a worthwhile life entails institutional recognition of our status as *free and equal citizens* in two major ways: (1) through a set of protective measures

– safeguarding our equal rights and legal standing, maintaining our various liberties, and so forth – which pronounce that we bear a common dignity as citizens; and (2) through creating conditions promoting our flourishing (which go beyond the formal protections political minimalism is satisfied with) by provisions of adequate health care, social benefits and educational opportunities, by assurances of non-degrading work and of adequate remuneration, by encouragement of economic growth and of just distributions of its rewards, and by similar initiatives designed to ensure that (other than in extreme cases of disability) nobody's opportunity to flourish is impaired by unfortunate natural or social disadvantages for which they cannot be held responsible.

At a cultural level, a way of life worth having entails accepting that *citizens are also cultural agents* whose sense of dignity often can't be dissociated from their cultural attachments; it is one that is aware that citizens' flourishing at this level may hang on valued cultural attachments being granted public expression and representation. Otherwise, there is a very real prospect of citizens becoming alienated from the public life of their society, mainly because they perceive that their cultural dignity is being traduced and that their cultural avenues of flourishing are being blocked. In culturally homogeneous societies this problem of alienation is rarely encountered as major institutions reflect a culture everyone shares. In increasingly multi-cultural societies, as well as in societies with major cultural divisions, things are not so simple. And sensitivity to historical particularities suggests that there's no formulaic means of defusing the worry of social and political discord, which may attend complaints of the exclusion of this or that cultural identity from official statements of *who we are* as a society or as a nation, or whatever. Here symbolism becomes important. For instance, take legal and security institutions. With respect to these, it's not enough (though it is important) that they are open to applicants of sufficient merit, whatever their background, or that they are widely regarded as impartial in their implementation of the law, or even that they are exemplary in their protection of individuals' rights and liberties; it is also that through their symbolic nomenclature and so on they are seen as culturally inclusive and not merely as an extension of a dominant cultural-political form. The hope is that via the genius of practical reason, citizens in diverse situations with often troubled histories may figure out how best to facilitate their cultural complexities in forms that fit with their peculiarities; and, in so doing, define a worthwhile way of life that respects the dignity at stake in citizens' cultural affiliations and enables their flourishing through cultural expressions that resonate with their self-definitions.

Finally, at a civic level, a way of life worth having is one in which *citizens identify with the institutions of (democratic) self-government (as theirs) and view themselves as participants in a common public life.* The focus here is on citizens *qua* citizens who, whatever their cultural differences, work at achieving enough cohesiveness to enable a society to function in ways that underwrite their dignity and give hope of their flourishing. This is to allow for the possible emergence of a shared civic identity developing alongside the various cultural identities exhibited among citizens; it is also to intimate that another instance of citizens' dignity is in play, one tied to allegiance to society's major self-governing institutions and practices. On this latter point, if citizens are cut off from such institutions and practices (assuming that we live in a society that operates according to them) then it's probable that their dignity as citizens is undermined precisely because being cut off implies being denied a voice in how society organises its affairs, and in being so denied citizens are effectively being dominated, controlled, dictated to. Alienation and powerlessness are not the stuff of citizens' dignity. On a positive note, where there is, on the contrary, an embrace of the institutional life of a self-governing society, then not only is citizens' dignity made more secure, but prospects of citizens' flourishing are enhanced. This is to say that at a civic level flourishing is bound up with being participants in the business of deciding the shape and future of society, with developing bonds with other citizens (even with those who are culturally different), with helping to shape a new shared civic identity, and, in the process, with cultivating a range of character traits or civic virtues which potentially introduce fresh and fulfilling forms of self-understanding. Once again, then, we may see how concerns of dignity, flourishing and a worthwhile life fit together – this time at a civic level where the central consideration is how to capture a viable sense of what may be held in common.

So, I'm submitting that the chief purpose of politics is to create, protect and sustain a way of life worth having, and that from this at least the following subsidiary purposes follow: to treat all members of society as free and equal citizens; to respect and accommodate the cultural allegiances of citizens; and to promote forms of self-government with which citizens identify and in which they participate. This submission and its ramifications envisage politics playing a much larger role in human affairs than the minimalist package can allow. In a nutshell, what I'm calling here a maximalist package distinguishes itself by viewing politics not just as a corrective for human blemishes but as partly constitutive of human good.

Maximalist Politics and the Kingdom of God

In turning now to the question of how this view of politics relates to my (universal) interpretation of the kingdom of God, I hope the answer is sufficiently obvious to warrant only a very brief reply. Three points I trust will suffice.

First, I'd argue that something like this notion is entailed in the *basic rationale of the concept of the kingdom of God* once its universality is properly acknowledged. To explain, and in line with my reading of the kingdom's meaning, the rationale in question consists of at least these claims: that God's rule extends over the whole of life; that recognising this rule is conducive to our discovering liberating and fulfilling expressions of our humanness; and that the full realisation of the kingdom lies in the future as does the complete realisation of our humanness. Now accepting these claims commits us, again in harmony with what I've already maintained, to conceding that God's rule must therefore include the realm of politics, not bypass or sideline it; that human liberation and fulfilment affect us as social and political beings who live in communities; and that part of our hope of the future includes expecting a more thorough expression of what we are as social and political animals, of what it means to share our lives with others in community. In short, I'm saying that recognising politics as partly constitutive of human good is involved in a certain way of thinking through what it means to be human and that it is entailed in the logic of the concept of the kingdom of God (at least as I interpret it).

This first point is reinforced by a second. The concerns integral to my presentation of a maximalist view of politics – for the creation of institutions with which people may identify, for practices of social and political inclusion, and for legal and social justice, and so forth – fit with the type of concerns that are expressed in the name of the kingdom of God, or its equivalent, in much of the writings of the Old Testament prophets and in the gospels. In a sense, I'm trying to give contemporary social and political form to these biblical concerns because it is in doing so that a Christian tradition is kept alive. What a theologically informed angle adds, however, is a sense of the provisionality of all efforts to accommodate these concerns, since even our best efforts are invariably incomplete and susceptible to premature ossification in a world as frail as ours is bound to be prior to the *eschaton*. That's why big things may be expected of politics now, but not impossible things.

An unavoidable conclusion of this line of argument is the third point I wish to make here: *politics is in principle a blessing*. It is a blessing because it has the capacity to enrich our humanness as well as our understanding of what God requires of us. There are goals of human life which can be achieved through politics and politics alone. To create a just and democratic society (which we might reasonably think of as an important priority in the late twentieth century West) is not a one-off achievement, but something that we must strive to sustain through ongoing political activity. And (to reiterate the gist of my second point) because this creation is never sufficient, because it's always only an approximation, the tasks of politics appear endless. To tackle such tasks, in whatever ways we can, is not, in my opinion, an optional extra. It is, rather, part of our vocation as human beings and it is of monumental significance (for Christians at any rate) that it figures as such in our anticipation of our eschatological destiny as members of a new community living under God's unrestricted reign. Or so it seems to me.

Maximalism and Northern Ireland

Of course, to say that politics is in principle a blessing is not to say that it is never in practice a bane. And, in turning to consider some implications of a maximalist package for the politics of Northern Ireland it is perhaps the *bane of political practice* that is most striking. That is to say, the achievement of anything approaching what I described as a way of life worth having seems distant to the preoccupations of many of Northern Ireland's politicians who, with a few notable exceptions, have arguably succeeded in turning politics into one of the most baneful arts imaginable. Nevertheless, we do not need to take our bearings from them; a maximalist view does have positive ramifications for Northern Irish politics.

On a constructive note, maximalism offers a way of life with important socio-economic, legal, and political consequences; it touches us at individual, cultural and civic levels and may serve as a vision of the sort of society Northern Ireland could become. This is a vision that is intended to appeal to those of any persuasion – unionist, nationalist or neither – even if its acceptance (if at all imaginable) would likely come in differing degrees. Within the context of Northern Ireland its point is this: if efforts were concentrated on creating, protecting, and sustaining such a way of life or vision new possibilities of co-operation would open up and old hostilities would be put under severe pressure. Common ground would be discovered by citizens devoted to making (an inclusive) Northern Ireland work; new forms of citizen attachment and identity might appear alongside traditional ones. New divisions would also undoubtedly surface, but at least they wouldn't necessarily cut along predictable sectarian lines.

To be frank, what I'm effectively calling for here is a *shift of political priorities* away from a politics of constitutional stand-off towards a politics that privileges democracy and justice. I'm maintaining that what counts most in the search for durable peace and reconciliation in Northern Ireland is an unswerving commitment to build a just and democratic society capable of commanding the allegiance of all citizens. It's in terms of this commitment that I think the interests and recommendations of the British and Irish governments should be judged, as should those expressions of unionism and nationalism which effectively make democracy and justice secondary considerations. And by this commitment, especially that bit of it which refers to democracy, I'm referring to much more than a means of deciding our constitutional future. I'm also talking about the implementation of forms of government and practice which give power back to the people who live here; forms which are inclusive of the full range of (democratic) political parties and (at different levels) of diverse community voices. And I'm gesturing emphatically at a type of political engagement in which practices of dialogue and deliberation are central.

The call for such a shift of political priorities should also, in my opinion, be accompanied by a genuine attempt to face up to the sources of division in Northern Ireland. And one of the important things this means is being receptive to the idea that *institutional life in the North must somehow accommodate expressions of Irishness as well as of Britishness*. In the absence of this, there is little hope of effecting any shift of political priorities since nationalist alienation from the Northern "state" will remain intact. In this case, I think it's a duty of unionists to try to recognise, in ways they haven't done before, that a Northern Ireland whose integrity is respected has to be one in which nationalists have a sense of belonging.

Conclusion

Much more needs to be said about all this and a good deal else. But to conclude, I'd simply reaffirm two points. First, politics is in principle a blessing even if in practice it may appear a bane. And secondly, by buying what I've called a maximalist package (with or without the theological rationale I've tried to provide for it) we may detect fresh possibilities for the politics of Northern Ireland – possibilities which I think carry responsibilities that are too serious for any of us legitimately to duck.

11

Reconsidering Reconciliation

This chapter is based on the 1997 John Whyte Memorial Lecture delivered at University College Dublin in November 1997. I have barely changed a word. A good deal of the lecture's content was incorporated into my subsequent book, "The Elusive Quest. Reconciliation in Northern Ireland" (2003).

Introduction

I should emphasise from the outset how honoured I am to be invited to deliver the 1997 John Henry Whyte Memorial Lecture. I only hope that the thoughts I propose to lay before you will be (at least in some small measure) faithful to the spirit of John Whyte's exemplary work.

My thoughts this evening take the form of reflections on the theme of reconciliation. In particular, I want to reconsider what we mean when we speak of reconciliation in the context of Northern Ireland. Or, more accurately, I want to reconsider some of the things we mean by reconciliation in this context. Other things that we might mean – reconciliation's theological ramifications, for example, or its implications for North-South relations – won't feature very prominently here, even if I do nod in their direction from time to time. This isn't to dismiss as of no consequence questions of theology or questions of relations between the two parts of the island (and I hasten to assure those with highly trained noses, who fancy that here they catch a whiff of the rat known as a purely internalist/unionist approach to the North, that their sense of smell has got the better of them, since there's no such rat on the loose); rather, I am simply indicating that my principal interest tonight is in reconciliation's cultural and political meanings, especially as they bear upon the Northern situation.

Having declared my principal interest, let me also declare the two major tasks which I think reconsidering reconciliation entails. First, there is the task of ascertaining whether reconciliation is the good thing many of us presume it is and, if it is, then, second, there is the task of inquiring what an adequate conception of it should consist of. Most of my attention is devoted to the first of these tasks. Here I sketch a rather gloomy picture of reconciliation's fate in Northern Ireland which leads me to ask hard questions of its viability. I take up two of these questions and, in doing so, engage with serious challenges to any intelligible notion of reconciliation. I defend reconciliation against its detractors and towards the end touch upon the second task, by gesturing at a conception of reconciliation which I think has most going for it, but which others might find too strong to be either welcome or plausible. But I'll be trying hard to leave the fight about that for another occasion. My main concern is to clear a space within which it becomes possible to conceive of the sort of strong idea of reconciliation I find attractive, which is why I concentrate on the critical task of defending reconciliation as in principle, a good thing.

Reconciliation's Absence and its Puzzles

The prompt to reconsider reconciliation comes from the reality of its continuing absence from so much of the life of Northern society. Perhaps for most of us here – who're all too familiar with the North and its problems – this reality has lost its power to shock. More likely it's simply a fact of life we've all become accustomed to, and, as such, something we merely shrug at as typical of the status quo in Northern Ireland. Maybe it's only in moments of intense piety that some of us even imagine how it could be otherwise. And, yet, observed from a certain angle, the reality of reconciliation's continuing absence ought to shock; or, if not shock, at least disconcert and puzzle.

Disconcerting Puzzles

It is, I suggest, a disconcerting and puzzling reality given the sheer number of attempts that have been made to foster reconciliation between unionists and nationalists, or between Protestants and Catholics. Consider the nature and scope of these attempts. They may be informal or very formal in character; they range from personal contacts to government-sponsored initiatives; they include low-budget, locally run, cross-community social and cultural events as well as high-budget, officially backed economic and political partnerships. Promoting reconciliation consumes the energies of many community organisations, voluntary associations and church groups. The cause of reconciliation commands the attention and financial support of governments and their agencies in Britain and Ireland.

Reconciliation in Northern Ireland is also an international affair, economically and politically. Projects designed to enhance its prospects may receive funding from European Union and United States sources. And, we are assured, the more signs of progress it shows the greater the chances are of securing job-creating, inward investments from international companies. Unprecedented political initiatives to encourage reconciliation run alongside international economic inducements. The historic visit to Northern Ireland by U.S. President Bill Clinton, for example, and the pivotal role played by George Mitchell in chairing political talks at Stormont attest to the type of commitments major international political players are prepared to make for the sake of reconciliation in the North.

And yet reconciliation continues to elude us. Its success manifestly cannot depend only on the time and effort spent on its behalf by local community, voluntary and religious activists, or on programmes devised by those employed in various capacities to promote it in Northern Ireland, or on intergovernmental initiatives and sponsorships, or on international concern, economic incentives and political commitments. If any, or some combination, of these factors were decisive, Northern Ireland would be by now a model of reconciliation. But it isn't. It's a deeply divided, segregated society. Gains for reconciliation no doubt have been chalked up at community, religious and economic levels. The reconciliation industry's time, energy and money haven't all been a waste. Nonetheless, in terms of cultivating an ethos of tolerance and respect that extends beyond certain sectors of civil society their results are pretty meagre. The issue of marches in particular vividly illustrates the depth of cultural-political divisions in Northern Ireland – divisions exacerbated by segregated housing areas and the paucity of integrated educational opportunities.

And then, of course, there is the conspicuous lack of reconciliation at the political level, notwithstanding the current talks process. Without denigrating its prospects – which in truth is about the last thing I wish to do – optimism about the talks process is severely tempered by two considerations: first, by the fact that a significant number of unionists want no part of it, and second, by the fact that some participants in the process appear more determined to defend their corner than to contribute to an inclusively won agreement which most of us could be persuaded to buy. Political reconciliation continues to be hampered by extremely deep-seated suspicions and hostilities.

Hard Questions

Such a disturbing state of affairs calls for analysis and questioning. We might want to ask, for instance, whether the reconciliation industry's priorities and targets have been the most appropriate of those available; whether time, effort and money could not have been better directed elsewhere and to greater effect. Or we might wish to ask questions of the strategies for political reconciliation pursued by the British and Irish governments: why they've delivered so little; whether more could have been done to treat the sources of disaffection obvious in certain political circles; whether, indeed, Anglo-Irish strategies betray a serious misunderstanding of the nature of political conflict in Northern Ireland. We might also wish to put local political parties in the dock and insist that they face some stiff interrogation: whether they have shown sufficient inclination to place the interests of all Northern Ireland's citizens above party (some might say sectarian) interests; whether they have genuinely tried to find common ground with their political adversaries; whether they have been prepared to show qualities of leadership aimed at breaking down barriers of mistrust between unionists and nationalists, between Protestants and Catholics. And so on.

Pursuing questions such as these may make the absence of reconciliation in Northern Ireland less puzzling than it initially appears. But to focus on these alone may not force us to pose questions that disconcert even more. For example, perhaps we in the North have to ask of ourselves, and not only of our politicians and bureaucrats, just how significant the commitment to reconciliation really is. And perhaps we have to entertain the possibility that those things that ultimately separate and divide us are too deep and profound to be reconciled. It is these issues I'd now like to turn to.

Peace without Reconciliation?

Reconciliation is a word with strong connotations which demand a lot of give from us all if our cultural and political divisions are to be healed; perhaps they demand too much. Perhaps reconciliation is the wrong word to describe what many of us think is either desirable or feasible in Northern society today. Perhaps many would settle for peace (defined minimally as an absence of violent conflict) and take their chances on reconciliation; perhaps, that is, uncoupling the terms "peace" and "reconciliation" would reveal a less edifying but truer picture of Northern sentiment: we can have (minimalist) peace without reconciliation and peace is what we really crave. Perhaps, then, since the quest for peace is hard enough and apparently can't be won without concessions from all sides, the more exacting requirements of reconciliation should be set aside for another time, if not dropped altogether; perhaps to insist upon them is unduly to burden the peace process.

Perhaps. I suspect that what I'll call "peace without reconciliation" is a position that resonates in parts of Northern society, even when it's not articulated in such terms. And, arguably, one explanation why political reconciliation is in such scarce supply is because "peace without reconciliation" is the implicit position of more people in Northern Ireland than many of us care to admit. Maybe it's this position that feeds the political intransigence evident in various political parties and that is, in turn, reinforced by such intransigence. Whatever the case, it's a position that may derive from several sources, including those of indifference, fear and bitterness.

Indifference

Of the three sources of the "peace without reconciliation" formula I've just picked out, indifference – though perhaps interesting enough sociologically – is the least defensible. Indifference is most likely to be found among those whose lives have been relatively unaffected by the "Troubles"; those who are most seriously devoted to a life of conspicuous consumption; those who have opted out of politics in any sense. The "contented classes", as Colin Coulter refers to them, obviously fit into this category: that is, those who've enjoyed the economic benefits of direct rule, without having had to incur any of the political costs (Coulter, 1996: 174-6). The indifference frequently exhibited among such classes underwrites the "peace without reconciliation" formula by tacitly saying something like this: peace (minimally defined) is to be valued if for no other reason than that violence and the security measures necessary to counteract it are irritating inconveniences; but reconciliation has no comparable value since, if taken seriously, it promises only unwelcome intrusions into more or less settled lifestyles.

Now even if we assume, as this line on indifference implicitly does, that the value of reconciliation is to be measured according to some cost-benefit calculus, it's not evident that the calculations being relied upon amount to much more than risky short-term gambles. On one scenario, for example, the political and economic conditions conducive to indifference may prove very transient: where, say, political agreement is reached, direct rule ends, and Westminster's subvention is reduced substantially. Or, on a quite different scenario, the "immunity from conflict" conditions conducive to indifference may prove exceptionally precarious: where, say, current attempts at political reconciliation fail miserably, republican and loyalist ceasefires collapse, paramilitaries on both sides lay part of the blame for breakdown at the door of the contented classes, and decide to unsettle their complacency through inflicting upon them a bit of sharp suffering – suffering which is designed, ultimately, to put them in a better mood for reconciliation. Of course, if we don't assume – and I certainly don't – that the value of reconciliation is reducible to the vagaries of cost-benefit calculations, then there's little more to say about indifference than that it's morally and politically irresponsible.

Fear

Fear as a source of the "peace without reconciliation" formula is a little trickier to evaluate. Unlike indifference, it may be rooted in deep commitments to ways of life that are perceived to be under threat; and, rather than encourage political apathy, it may impel political action of a certain sort – invariably a defensive sort that stresses protecting one's patch as the principal rationale of political engagement. It's hard not to think of much of the North's politics as in part a reflection of fear: fear of the "other", fear of losing one's identity through too many concessions being granted to one's opponents, perhaps fear of losing power, influence and a position of dominance which "our" kind consider their due. For those in the grip of such fears, peace (again minimally understood) has obvious attractions, but reconciliation demands too much: its request for compromise is little more than a polite demand for surrender; its request for the recognition of both traditional identities typically overreaches itself politically and becomes, in effect, a demand for a diminution of "our" identity and its political entitlements; and its request that we empathise with the "other" tradition in order to reach a mutually acceptable accommodation is, in truth, a demand that is existentially impossible to meet.

Such a fearful opposition to reconciliation is hard to ignore, given its prevalence in the politics of Northern Ireland. And it perhaps deserves sympathetic treatment inasmuch as it points to an acute edginess at the prospect – which many unionists claim to dread – of familiar practices being disrupted to the point where radical disorientation becomes a common experience. In other words, in certain circumstances it may be prudent to proceed cautiously rather than brashly when trying to implement some programme of reconciliation. It'd be counterproductive if the promotion of reconciliation simply exacerbated the type of radical disorientation that made social and political instability more probable than not.

Being sympathetically alert to such a possibility shouldn't mean, however, capitulating to the perceptions and analyses of the politics of fear. In the nature of things, these perceptions and analyses, though sincerely held, would be expected to involve seriously defective elements – as I think is unquestionably the case in Northern Ireland, even though I haven't time to demonstrate it. If pressed, I'd certainly be prepared to defend the claims that Northern politics of fear (whether unionist or nationalist) typically entail jaundiced views of the British and Irish states, and of the intentions and nature of the "other" tradition. To put matters sharply, to allow one's attitude to reconciliation to be dictated either by the apparent intractability of the politics of fear or by sensitivity to its existential plight of disorientation is ultimately to pay costs that should be too great to contemplate: it is to downplay the fact that distortions of others and their motives are unacceptable, and then to affect obliviousness of the consequences of such distortions for the rest of society; it is to turn a blind eye to the advocacy of differential treatment to the point of virtually tolerating the intolerable; it is to invite atavism and to close off responsible thinking about an alternative future. There is a danger, in other words, of allowing prudent caution to mask a lack of moral and political courage.

Bitterness

Bitterness as a source of the "peace without reconciliation" formula is in some respects the most difficult to deal with. This is because bitterness may frequently be a product of extremely traumatising experiences: of having been subjected to acts of injustice, humiliation or brutalisation that offend against our most basic moral sensibilities. And in Northern Ireland too many such acts have been committed for the grossest sectarian reasons. A few victims of particularly horrendous crimes may be so damaged that they find acceptance even of minimalist peace difficult, such is their desire for revenge. But for many more it is reconciliation that is the problem and, in particular, its requirement of forgiveness. Forgiveness seems to some too exacting a request and too naïve a remedy. Too exacting because it demands more than the emotional and moral resources of many victims are capable of mustering, because it seems to set an impossibly high standard of virtue. And too naïve because forgiveness, even if forthcoming, wouldn't be the panacea some imagine; it wouldn't constitute an adequate assault on the cultural-political conditions which cast some in the role of oppressors and others in the role of victims.

I have three comments to make. First, the request for forgiveness at the level of the individual has to be handled with the utmost sensitivity, but not relinquished altogether. Here it may seem heartless, if not downright callous, to impose such a request on those individuals who've endured tragedies the rest of us have escaped. This is indeed delicate territory upon which to tread. What's easier for some to entertain is harder for others; and different people deal differently with their hurt, grief and pain. At the very least, it's obvious that the request that victims forgive their oppressors (often enough without their oppressors asking for it or expressing remorse, let alone repentance) can't be made in any homogeneous way: there isn't some formula that all victims should be expected to adhere to. But does that mean it's unreasonable to request forgiveness at all? I don't think so. To explain why, I'll introduce my nod in the direction of theology, by allowing the Croatian theologian Miroslav Volf to lay out the basic answer. Modifying his wording slightly, he reasons as follows:

For a victim to [forgive] means not to allow the oppressors to determine the terms under which social conflict is carried out, the values around which the conflict is raging and the means by which it is fought. [Forgiveness] thus empowers victims and disempowers oppressors. It 'humanizes' the victims precisely by protecting them from either mimicking or dehumanizing the oppressors (Volf, 1996: 116).

Accordingly, those who can't find it within themselves to forgive, however understandable their predicament, risk becoming like their oppressors – if not in deed then in thought. They risk being warped by a twisted intent that succumbs to a dreadful logic of "dehumanization" which is ultimately why the request for forgiveness remains indispensable to reconciliation, however harrowing its granting may seem.

Second, if it is true to say that the request for forgiveness holds at an individual level, it is true to say with even greater force that it holds at a political level. This isn't to advocate any cavalier dismissal of the political grounds on which both unionists and nationalists consider themselves victims. There is a point to unionist perceptions of themselves as victims of a sustained IRA campaign to rob them of their Britishness, as there is also to nationalist perceptions of themselves as victims of a type of state-sponsored violence and a regime of discrimination that have deprived them of a sufficiently meaningful expression of their Irishness.

But there are exaggerations and blind spots in both sets of perceptions, which are particularly evident in the tendency of both to lay the bulk of blame for our woes on the "other" side. And it's precisely this tendency that inhibits acknowledgement of any shared responsibility for our difficulties in the North. Here one of our most poignant quandaries arises: how are we to break out of the (often vicious) cycle of mutually accusing definitions of political victimhood? Forgiveness seems to me a key to any adequate answer. That's why it's important to treat forgiveness as a political virtue and not merely as a private one. Hannah Arendt's remarks have a salience in this context, when she writes of forgiveness as a "genuinely free act which does not merely re-act", as an act which "breaks the power of the remembered past and transcends the claims of the affirmed justice, and so makes the spiral of vengeance grind to a halt" (Arendt, 1959: 216).

Forgiveness, then, has the capacity to relieve us from the often-onerous burden of our history; it has the capacity to break the cycle of perpetual victimhood (and its debilitating practice of "whataboutery"), by not insisting that justice (as we conceive of it) be done first. And that's why, again, forgiveness deserves to be thought of politically.

Third, to stress the centrality of forgiveness to reconciliation is not to sideline investigation of the cultural and political circumstances which make the quest for reconciliation so arduous. If forgiveness is regarded as a panacea, then it's rightly to be ridiculed.

But Arendt's points about forgiveness breaking "the power of the remembered past" and transcending "the claims of affirmed justice" aren't meant to imply some form of political acquiescence. They aren't pious ruses for abandoning concerns of history or of justice. Forgiveness, rather, enables us to address these concerns in a less precious or self-righteous way. This is a way that opens up space for types of political exploration and interchange that would otherwise be closed off. Put simply, forgiveness is a necessary but not sufficient condition of reconciliation. And the hope isn't some absurd one that in embracing forgiveness the political and cultural obstacles to reconciliation will be instantly transformed (as if by magic), but that these obstacles can be tackled with a little more magnanimity and a little less obsessive rancour.

To summarise, "peace without reconciliation", whether deriving from indifference, fear or bitterness, is a radically inadequate position, even if there are occasions when its claims need to be treated gently. In addition to the reasons I've already raised against it, I'd like to add two others of a more general nature. As a guide to political practice, it isn't up to scratch, first, because its achievement would undoubtedly prove too fragile to work for long, and those who suppose otherwise – namely, that lasting peace is possible without reconciliation – seem to me to be in flight from political realities in the North; and as a guide, it isn't up to scratch, second, because it entails a very miserly view of politics and of what's required to create and sustain a decent society for all citizens. To operate within its boundaries, in short, is to court escapism and to entertain a very narrow notion of political responsibility.

Difference and Reconciliation

Now it is one thing to maintain that the terms "peace" and

"reconciliation" shouldn't be uncoupled, that refusing to yield to indifference, fear or bitterness opens us up to creative explorations of our differences, and that, being so unshackled as it were, we may anticipate the development of a more generous and inclusive mode of politics; but it is another thing entirely to suppose that maintaining any of these amounts to a sufficient guarantee that our differences are in fact reconcilable or that our politics can be transformed. Quite frankly, it doesn't. And as soon as we admit this, we see that the idea of reconciliation confronts another set of challenges of a quite formidable kind.

Differences

For example, how are we to bridge our rudimentary constitutional divisions, especially if they are reinforced by a whole series of binary oppositions that bring into play cultural-political differences of ethnicity, religion, history, and so on? How is it possible realistically to imagine unionists and nationalists in the North reaching some mutually acceptable agreement when so many of them plug into quite exclusive self-definitions which are shaped by such different historical memories and heritages? How is it possible even to imagine unionists and nationalists engaging in the sort of dialogue that gives promise of a reasonable outcome when they seem to have such utterly different understandings of what it means to conduct political talks, understandings which may, in turn, reflect underlying disagreements about language itself - whether words should always admit of strict literal meanings, for instance, or how much ambiguity and fudge should be allowed to our formulations? (and to complicate matters further, these are disagreements which, according to Padraig O'Malley (O'Malley, 1990), trace back to different views of the world which are rooted in disputes between Calvinism and Thomism). Or how can we envisage breaking out of the ethical impasse that creates such barriers between, say, the republican movement and mainstream unionism: where apparently different moral vocabularies are drawn upon and where the moral outrage expressed by one side has no effect whatsoever on the other? (Am I being sufficiently depressing?)

Against Reconciliation

One response to questions of this sort is simply to ignore the challenges they imply by saying in effect that reconciliation means assimilation, and if assimilation isn't forthcoming then too bad for reconciliation. This farcical approach to reconciliation, which just thunders through the field of difference, amounts to advocating either that unionists should catch themselves on and realise they were always only confused Irish nationalists, or that nationalists should "wise up" and realise the sufficiency of a British political identity for everyone in Northern Ireland. To adopt Levi-Strauss' terminology here, this response boils down to saying: we will refrain from vomiting you out if you let us swallow you up.

Another response is to play up our differences either because they are taken to matter more than any desire for reconciliation, or because concentrating on them is regarded as necessary preparation for reconciliation. Let me take this latter formulation which, at first glance, sounds odd, but which points to an increasingly common approach in the North. Something like it, for instance, is found in community relations funding of "single identity" projects where the rationale seems to be that only communities strong enough in their own sense of themselves can embark upon a path of reconciliation without fearing the consequences. We can see perhaps the most spectacular manifestation of the approach in the development of the now "quasi-independent republic of West Belfast", especially during its annual festival where we witness increasingly vibrant and self-confident expressions of an Irish republican identity that are utterly out of kilter with the self-understandings and mores of unionist parts of the city. During the last summer in particular we have seen Protestant East Belfast playing catch up here, especially through the painting spree conducted by loyalists to mark out their territory in a way designed to engender self-pride and confidence in their Protestant/British cultural identity. Or so we're told.

Now there's no doubting that community relations' workers regard single identity projects as fitting into the bigger picture of reconciliation between the "two communities"; and there's no doubt too that the political parties most closely associated with community developments in West and East Belfast – Sinn Féin and the PUP respectively – claim to be keenly interested in reconciliation. But even though I've no wish to doubt anyone's sincerity here, I've two main worries with this approach. First, I wonder why having lived together for 300-400 years we still need coaching with our own before engaging properly with the "other". I'm tempted to retort that when considering how, when, where or if we should dabble in cross community exercises, there is no better advice than that offered by the Nike ad – *just do it*. Second, it's not clear to me that affirmations of our separate identities are making the business of reconciliation easier to conduct; rather, they appear to accentuate our differences in sometimes unhelpful ways. Splattering East Belfast with red, white and blue paint, loyalist graffiti and symbols, and seeing their equivalents replicated in West Belfast may make (some) people in those areas feel better about themselves, but it doesn't necessarily make them feel better about each other. Or more to the point, the better republicans feel about themselves, the worse they are regarded by unionists/loyalists who are decidedly unnerved by shows of republican self-confidence (and perhaps vice versa). At any rate, not too many Protestants/unionists are keen to participate in the West Belfast festival, even when invited. And republicans needn't even expect to be invited to comparable events in East Belfast.

The strong temptation here is to conclude that, given our differences, we'd be better off, and certainly much less prone to self-delusions, by trimming our expectations of reconciliation. Sure, let community relations, the voluntary sector, the ecumenical movement and, as far as she's able, the President of Ireland try to build whatever little bridges they can. But don't expect to make much impression in the opposing cultural heartlands of the North, and, in particular, don't expect much political purchase.

"No high-wire political acts are going to work," said Jim Molyneaux. Not only do most unionist politicians seem to agree, but so do a number of academics. Richard English, for example, advises the two governments to stop trying to find a solution to the problem of Northern Ireland they expect unionists and nationalists to agree on - in particular one that engages the "extremes". Instead, they should concentrate more realistically on "managing" the problem. And the best hope English can find for anything approximating reconciliation is the following speculation: "within a generation [the problem] will be essentially over". "The end will not result", he conjectures, "from well-meaning initiatives but rather from demographic, economic and wider political changes that are not programmed with a view to peace, but which change the nature of the questions people ask" (English, 1997: 275). Or there is the line Arthur Aughey began to develop in last year's John Whyte Memorial Lecture (Aughey, 1997: 1-12) when he invoked Carl Schmitt's distinction between friends and enemies as a more analytically useful tool than anything available in what he elsewhere referred to as "the banal but corrosive jargon of the peace process" (Aughey, 1995: 12). The idea here is that, by virtue of their opposing constitutional positions, unionists and nationalists necessarily regard each other as enemies and their own as friends. And, politically speaking, that's just the way it is. Thus there's no point in becoming carried away by impossible dreams of reconciliation.

Without discussing thoroughly particular problems with the details of English's and Aughey's "pessimistic-realist" views of the impossibility of reconciliation between unionists and nationalists (for much more on Aughey see Chapter six and the Afterword), it is worth mentioning that they both paint a picture of a present in which a debilitating fatalism looms large. Their implicit – and sometimes explicit – message is: unionists are what they are, nationalists are what they are, and both like it that way. So: don't expect changes to come from within these mutually exclusive communities; don't challenge or ask hard questions of their self-understandings; and keep believing that not doing so will deliver a workable society, albeit a deeply unreconciled one. This, I suggest, isn't pragmatic realism but the stuff of fantasy; it's politics built on castles of illusion.

For example, since the plantations of Ulster in the seventeenth century, our history has been plagued by some variant of the friend/enemy distinction, so (1) Aughey didn't need to go scuttling off to give it some pseudo-justification by drawing on a source that inspired German fascism, (2) it's deeply worrying that he supposes we still require a distinction that has underpinned Irish hostilities for close on four centuries (and has been employed to rationalise every sectarian brutality in the book), and (3) it's intellectually and politically perplexing that he avers that it's precisely this distinction that enables us to think clearly about our political future, since it guarantees only stalemate at best and risks considerable unrest if not worse. Moreover, as we await the realisation of English's vision of modernity's eventual triumph in the North (through the withering away of traditional allegiances), it's not obvious (1) what we're supposed to do in the meantime (besides not engage in political reconciliation work), or (2) what he imagines the organisation we were once assured "hadn't gone away" is going to do (not to mention its equivalents on the other side) as its political representatives are told there's no place for them in politics (as presumably they must be if the "extremes" are to be excluded). At the last, the "reconciliation as impossible" thesis advanced by certain unionist politicians and academics is susceptible to the general criticisms I raised against the "peace without reconciliation" thesis (of which it's probably a variant anyway): it amounts to a flight from political realities in Northern Ireland, and it works with a miserly view of politics which justifies an abrogation of our most compelling political responsibility – creating a society for all citizens (not just for friends), and trying to create it now.

For Reconciliation

I'm unconvinced, then, of either the worthiness or the practicability of any of the anti-reconciliation approaches to difference I've briefly touched upon and want to remain "bullish" about reconciliation's indispensability in the North. But, as I intimated at the start, I can only gesture at the "strong" conception of reconciliation which I think permits us to deal more adequately with those things that divide us. Very schematically, this is a conception with the following (general) emphases:

- It recognises that cultural-political identities aren't static and are rarely homogeneous, but that they shift and crosscut.
- It appreciates that identities are open to internal probing/ questioning.
- It insists that cultural interactions are a good thing in that they open us up and broaden our horizons, and that the onus is on those who disagree to defend the proposition that being opened up and broadened out – and thereby coming to richer, deeper understandings of ourselves, not least when

we're forced to see ourselves as others see us – is a bad thing (I concede that fundamentalists of various persuasions possibly think that it is, but that's another matter).
- It hopes that in terms of, say, our traditional historical differences, or our differences over language and morality it's possible that through genuine dialogical encounters we may find more common ground among ourselves than we imagined, and that we may all discover reasons to change here or modify there – but the point is we'll never find out without engaging one another.
- It acknowledges that, in sum, questions of who/what we are, especially posed in a world as rapidly changing as ours, rarely admit of final, definitive answers, and that the challenge is to articulate and re-articulate our self-definitions in an ongoing way that doesn't obliterate our differences, but that allows us to see them in larger perspective – in relation to others and in relation to what's good for our society as a whole.

Pursuing such an approach to difference – which doesn't block off any possibility of reconciliation – presupposes the achievement of a tolerant and pluralist civil society. It impinges not only on how we do politics, but also on our political priorities, on what we value most and why. Reconciliation implies changing certain of our dominant priorities. At the very least, this involves acknowledging that whatever constitutional package we prefer, we require the establishment of institutions reflecting our complex (minimally, British and Irish) condition; that such institutional arrangements are indispensable to overcoming perhaps our most acute political problem – alienation – which has plagued Northern Ireland since its inception, as nationalists/republicans have typically felt cut off from its public institutions, just as unionists have always felt alienated from institutions in the South; that it's only when all of us can give allegiance to our major institutions that we can begin to develop a sense of common citizenship capable of putting other of our differences into proper perspective and preventing them from destroying society; and that there are tasks and challenges here which take us beyond traditional formulations of unionism and nationalism and have the liberating potential to break through the dreary politics of constitutional stand-off to which we've all become accustomed, and to which various of our politicians and academics want to keep us tied.

Teasing out the implications of the foregoing sketch is a task for another occasion. My only hope is that I've provided sufficient reasons to create a space that enables us to entertain the approach to reconciliation they suggest. Whether such an approach proves plausible can't be decided in advance. But two things can be decided now: (1) that the grounds for scuppering such an approach from the outset aren't convincing; and (2) that concerns of reconciliation confront us with our most intellectually and politically demanding challenges. If this lecture has helped establish these two things, it has succeeded. And if it has succeeded, then at the very least we can see that the strong conception of reconciliation I'm gesturing at, and wish elsewhere to develop and defend, is a world removed from the "touchy-feely" circles to which its critics cynically consign it. And to see this is a bonus.

12

Political Change in Northern Ireland

This chapter first took the form of a paper delivered in Australia at the Tenth Irish-Australian Conference, La Trobe University, Melbourne, September 1998. Like the previous chapter, a lot of its content appears in my book, "The Elusive Quest."

Introduction

The simple argument of this paper is that the overdue and significant change in Northern Irish politics, of which recent events give promise, is confronted by problems which *may* be resolved in practice, but which certainly *can* be resolved in principle. As I present it, this argument consists of four claims which may be summarised as follows. First, the sort of political change Northern Ireland currently faces is historic and welcome. Second, such change is threatened by what I'll call *the problem of overt opposition*: a problem which, though important, fortunately isn't in itself sufficient to block change. But change is also threatened, third, by what I'll refer to as *the problem of clashing interpretations*: a problem that's potentially very serious because it's located among change's supporters and not just its opponents. Fourth, the threat posed by this problem may be averted either by a form of pragmatic muddling through or, preferably, by the adoption of an alternative and more convincing interpretation of change, that is, an interpretation that's better equipped than its clashing rivals to make sense of the new practices change implies.

Let me now take up each of these claims in turn. As I do so, I should add a note of caution. The lines of inquiry I pursue in explicating the four claims won't be developed either fully or tightly enough to clinch the paper's central argument. My ambition is therefore quite modest: it is to *gesture at* the types of reasoning and evidence that the argument requires in order to become compelling.

Political Change as Historic and Welcome: The Good Friday/Belfast Agreement

The sort of political change I refer to in this paper is that intimated in the multi-party agreement – typically referred to as the Good Friday or Belfast Agreement (henceforth the Agreement) – that was delivered after two years of negotiations on April 10, 1998. So, when I claim that the political change presently on offer in Northern Ireland is historic and welcome, I'm simultaneously claiming that the Agreement is historic and welcome. This isn't to say that all suggestions of reform contained in this document are unproblematic; it isn't to say that the Agreement's every detail should be uncritically endorsed. But it is to say that, whatever the difficulties likely to be encountered by certain of its proposals, the terms of the Agreement are generally appropriate to the circumstances prevailing in

Northern Ireland today: not only is the spirit of the Agreement admirable, but its fundamental thrust is sound, and the basic institutions and practices it recommends are worthy of support. Perhaps above all else, the Agreement is commendable because it opens up fresh political space within which appear unique and promising opportunities to make Northern Ireland work in ways that have been previously impossible.

This is a large claim. Three considerations help to vindicate it. For a start, there's a *prima facie* case for supposing that the Agreement – by virtue of being a product of *multi-party* negotiations – signifies an improvement in the politics of Northern Ireland. Simply put, a political world in which the Agreement is present is better than the world from which it was absent. Let's call the consideration I'm invoking here that of *an historical appreciation of what the Agreement represents change from*. There are countless ways of describing what it might constitute a change from, but given that its principal concern is to devise new arrangements of government, it is particularly apt to depict it in these ways: as a change from the partiality that characterised Northern Ireland's previous experience of self-government; as a change from the relative unaccountability that has characterised its most recent experience of government in the form of direct rule from Westminster; and as a change from a sterile politics of constitutional standoff that has characterised debate within the North, has stymied earlier attempts at a political breakthrough, and has created a vacuum too easily filled by violence.

The historical appreciation these depictions presuppose is crudely as follows. For fifty years from the partition of Ireland until 1972, Northern Ireland experienced a form of devolved, self-government unavailable to any other constituent member of the United Kingdom. This government was partial in the weak sense that through the auspices of majority rule it was controlled by one party – the Unionist Party. It was also partial in the strong sense that unionist rule was seldom even-handed, and, indeed, rarely succeeded in making the parliament at Stormont much more than a "Protestant parliament for a Protestant people", as Northern Ireland's first prime minister so succinctly and honestly put it (albeit in response to Eamon de Valera's claim that Ireland was a "Catholic country for a Catholic people"). It has to be added that unionist partiality was considerably aided, and perhaps permitted to persist for as long as it did, by the absence of a politically effective opposition. Northern nationalists and Catholics, feeling betrayed by Ireland's partition in the first place, largely abstained from formal political involvement.

The awakening of nationalist political consciousness – principally through the Civil Rights campaign of the mid-late 1960s and early '70s – precipitated a unionist backlash of such proportions that in 1969 the British government was forced to intervene in the affairs of Northern Ireland and in 1972 to prorogue Stormont. In place of unionist rule, Northern Ireland was ruled directly from Westminster. It is perfectly true to say that direct rule had certain obvious benefits in hastening the processes of social reform in Northern society, but it represented a relatively unaccountable form of political authority: Northern Irish citizens were governed by political parties that they couldn't vote for or against, and much of the day-to-day administration of society was undertaken by quangos whose members were appointed by the British government rather than elected by citizens. Such undemocratic practices were justified on the grounds of being merely stop-gap measures necessary in the short-term to prevent a total collapse of order in Northern Ireland. Direct rule was nobody's preferred option, least of all the British government's. But it continued much longer than was ever anticipated because agreement on its alternative proved elusive.

There have been various initiatives introduced to replace direct rule and it is against the backdrop of these that the Agreement finally emerged. Any account of the most important initiatives would include at least the following. Pride of place probably still belongs to the initiative that came early on and for a few brief months appeared to have a slender chance of succeeding, namely the Sunningdale Agreement of 1974. Sunningdale proposed, and for a short time worked, a power-sharing executive and proposed the establishment of a Council of Ireland. But it was opposed by the IRA and, much more significantly, by a majority of unionists who succeeded in destroying it principally through the agency of the Loyalist Workers' strike. It's worth remarking here that the present Agreement bears such traces of Sunningdale that Seamus Mallon, deputy leader of the SDLP, has called it "Sunningdale for slow learners". The Anglo-Irish Agreement signed in 1985 by the British and Irish prime ministers was easily the most crucial government initiative to follow Sunningdale. It not only signalled a new development in British-Irish relations, but also a rupture in the relationship unionists imagined they enjoyed with *their* government (especially one headed by the supposedly arch-unionist, Margaret Thatcher). The Anglo-Irish Agreement was worked out between the two governments without unionist input, and it allowed the Irish government a consultative role in Northern Irish affairs. In the face of intense unionist opposition, it was built upon through the '90s. Unionists' inability to have what they perceived as its most objectionable features removed partly contributed to the collapse of the Brooke-Mayhew talks, involving constitutional unionist and nationalist parties, in 1992. But despite unionist opposition and loyalist and republican paramilitary activity, the Downing Street Declaration drafted by the British and Irish prime ministers in December 1992 and, more especially, the Framework Documents published by the British and Irish governments in 1995 revealed both governments' determination to develop a common approach to the question of Northern Ireland, and to put pressure on local parties to think of compromise as a political good rather than as an evil to be avoided like the plague.

The fact remained, however, that none of these initiatives proved capable of commanding enough support within the main political factions in Northern Ireland. Nationalists refused to accept a purely internal solution – that is, a solution involving internal reform of the North without an Irish dimension – and unionists balked at admitting anything more than an internal solution. Various aspects of the initiatives I've mentioned reappeared in different packaging in the Agreement, but prior to April 10, 1998, it seemed that fundamental constitutional divisions between unionists and nationalists defied reconciliation. And in the absence of constitutional agreement, movement on other issues was halted on the principle that "nothing is agreed until everything is agreed". Political stalemate became taken for granted, posturing and grandstanding on apparent trivia appeared normal, and paramilitaries – certainly prior to 1994 and more definitively 1997 – continued to exploit the political gridlock, very often to barbarous effect.

Pitched against such a backdrop, the Agreement at once intrudes as a historic and welcome achievement inasmuch as it suggests change from a situation where basic constitutional agreement seemed impossible, and where progress on a raft of other issues was thereby hindered.

A second consideration which prompts thinking of the Agreement as historic and welcome arises here, namely *the range of support it has attracted*. The Agreement owes much to the industry and ingenuity of the British and Irish governments, with the particular help of the current American administration and the more general goodwill of international opinion. And there's probably something historic and welcome about this current Anglo-Irish accord which, unlike the original agreement to partition Ireland, is not saddled with colonial connotations, and doesn't involve any Collins-De

Valera type split within the Irish ranks. But it is historic and welcome in more obvious senses still. In addition to input from the two governments, the Agreement was negotiated by eight local parties which were specifically elected for the purpose of reaching an agreement: on the unionist side there was the Ulster Unionist Party (UUP), the Progressive Unionist Party (PUP) and the Ulster Democratic Party (UDP); on the nationalist/republican side there was the Social Democratic and Labour Party (SDLP) and Sinn Féin; and in between there was the Alliance Party of Northern Ireland, the Northern Ireland Women's Coalition and the Labour Coalition. Two unionist parties – the Democratic Unionist Party (DUP) and the UKUP – were elected as participants in negotiations but withdrew upon the arrival of Sinn Féin. What is historic about this range of party support within Northern Ireland, despite the withdrawal of two parties, is that not only have constitutional unionist and nationalist parties reached an agreement that previously seemed beyond them, but so too have the major unionist party (UUP) and Sinn Féin. This latter fact is close to staggering.

Just as staggering is the fact that unlike any previous initiative, the negotiations that produced the Agreement included political representatives of the main paramilitary organisations. And from the actions of Sinn Féin, the PUP and the UDP we can conclude that the Agreement has the backing of the Provisional IRA, the Ulster Volunteer Force and the Ulster Defence Association. To those with other than extraordinarily short memories, this range of paramilitary support almost beggars belief.

To add to the list of historic moments occasioned by the Agreement, we must also include the fact that it was overwhelmingly endorsed by the people of Ireland in separate referenda, North and South (with the North registering 71.8 percent support and the South a massive 94 percent). This was the first time since partition that citizens North and South had been given the opportunity to vote on a common proposal affecting the constitutional future of the island of Ireland (and let's not forget that the Irish people weren't granted the opportunity to vote on partition in the first place).

There are, then, several undeniable historic features about the Agreement when we look closely at its support. What's welcoming about these features is that they suggest that at last the people and politicians most closely involved in and affected by the troubles that have afflicted Northern society are indicating through their support of the Agreement a willingness to chart a new political future, a future which they are determining themselves rather than one they're having imposed upon them.

A final consideration which lends weight to the claim that the Agreement is historic and welcome concerns what it represents *change to*. In a nutshell, it represents change to a political situation in which, to use a buzz phrase, "the totality of relationships" within the North are arguably given their due for the first time. Institutional facilitation of "the totality of relationships" in turn reflects recognition of the complex condition of Northern Ireland. Such recognition was essential to a deal being struck between unionists and nationalists; it was indispensable to movement beyond zero-sum politics. And through its incorporation of this sort of recognition, we discern the truly historic and hugely welcome *substantive* achievement of the Agreement: its re-imagining of political life in a way that is true to our collective condition in Northern Ireland.

Political re-imagining here involves three dimensions which are taken to reflect "the totality of relationships" within the North: an internal Northern Irish dimension, a North-South dimension, and an East-West dimension. Very briefly, the salient features of each dimension are these. Regarding its internal government, Northern Ireland will maintain its representation at Westminster, but will also be granted a significant measure of self-government. Various powers, in areas such as health, employment, education and the like, will be removed from the domain of quangos and devolved to a new assembly operating not on a principle of majority rule but on a principle of power-sharing. The exclusivity of the old unionist domination at Stormont will be replaced by inclusive arrangements whereby unionists and nationalists will share governmental responsibilities in accordance with their party strengths. Strikingly, the Agreement here makes probable the almost unthinkable: Sinn Féin's membership of a Northern Ireland executive. The power-sharing assembly will also be supplemented by a consultative civic forum comprising representatives from business, the unions, and the community and voluntary sectors. Protection of individual and group rights will be formalised by the incorporation into Northern Ireland law of the European Convention of Human Rights. Interestingly, this means that Northern Ireland will have a Bill of Rights before either the Republic of Ireland or the rest of the UK. Leading explicit measures of reform of Northern society is that of the RUC, and a Commission to propose changes in policing has already been established under the chair of Chris Patten. Among the more controversial recommendations of the Agreement which affect the life of Northern society is the release within two years of those paramilitary prisoners whose organisations maintain their ceasefires. In terms of the North-South dimension, a new set of institutions is to be created to deal initially with twelve areas of common interest and mutual benefit, including agriculture, tourism, social security and education. A North-South ministerial council, comprised of ministers from the Northern assembly and Dáil Éireann, will oversee these institutions. Significantly, the Republic of Ireland is to alter its constitution to drop its territorial claim to the whole island of Ireland, and to acknowledge instead that Irish unity is an aspiration whose realisation requires the consent of a majority of Northern citizens. On the East-West front, a new British-Irish Council is to be set up, involving representatives from Scotland, Wales, Northern

Ireland, the Republic of Ireland, Westminster and perhaps the Isle of Man. A new British-Irish Intergovernmental Council is also to be established in place of the existing intergovernmental council established under the terms of the Anglo-Irish Agreement of 1985. The Agreement replaces that, and all other, previous agreements between Britain and Ireland.

These, then, are the new structures to be brought into being by the Agreement. As a safeguard, they are intended to be mutually reinforcing. For example, the Northern assembly will not be allowed to operate in the absence of North-South bodies. But the general point is the one I wish to emphasise: in its attempt to address the "totality of relationships" the Agreement's proposed structures open up an exciting new political space which gives Northern Ireland the sort of chance of working it hasn't had before. This is historic and welcome.

The Problem of Overt Opposition

It is hard to deny that it is historic, but not everyone agrees that it is welcome. The obvious problem the Agreement confronts is that of overt opposition from certain republican and unionist factions. This problem is serious, but not serious enough to wreck the Agreement. Let me explain.

The rationale of *republican opposition* to the Agreement is simple: it doesn't deliver a united Ireland, and it doesn't respect Irish republicanism's fundamental principle, namely that of the Irish nation's right to self-determination. It is undoubtedly true that a united Ireland isn't what's immediately on offer in the Agreement, but it's less clear that the principle of self-determination has been violated by an Agreement endorsed so overwhelmingly by all the people of Ireland, albeit in separate referenda. Strictly speaking, the Agreement's legitimacy probably rests on a principle of co-determination rather than on one of national self-determination. In other words, although everyone entitled to vote on the island of Ireland was given the opportunity to do so on the same day and on the same issue, voters weren't deciding their collective fate as one national unit but as two. Thus, the republican objection. But in the face of the resounding support it received, especially among non-unionists throughout Ireland, it requires a mentality of the most unbending fundamentalist sort to believe that the Agreement should carry no moral or political authority whatsoever for those who think that it is the entitlement of Ireland's people alone to decide their constitutional future.

Fortunately, republicans who do believe this, or, more correctly, who believe it to the point of actively opposing the Agreement, are few in number. Unfortunately, they happen to be dangerous and have clear paramilitary connections. They include the Irish National Liberation Army (an early '70s splinter group from the Official IRA), Continuity IRA (an outgrowth of a 1986 split in the Provisional IRA), and the so-called Real IRA (a very recent splinter group from the Provisional IRA). On their own, these groups do not have either the numbers or the might to destroy the Agreement. The only fear is that they may grow in strength as more republicans come to see the Agreement as a sell-out. Their versions of republican purity, however, are destined to have very much a minority appeal only.

Unionist opposition to the agreement is more significant. The core rationale of such opposition has two forms: either it's a protest against the fact that the Agreement signals the final constitutional death-knell of Protestant domination in Ulster (though that's rarely how it's articulated), or it's a complaint against the fact that the Agreement abandons the prospect of Northern Ireland's citizens ever being treated as equal British citizens. What is common to both forms is a refusal to accept the dilution of British sovereignty in Northern Ireland which the Agreement surely suggests, not least through its proposed implementation of North-South bodies which can only work effectively by a pooling of sovereignty. Other aspects of the Belfast Agreement irk too, especially those bearing on internal matters. Proposed reform of the RUC, for example, is seen as an unnecessary capitulation to nationalist propaganda, and the proposed release of paramilitary prisoners is viewed as an appeasement of terrorism which plays fast and loose with democratic conventions. The suggestion that unionists should share power with Sinn Féin is just unthinkable.

Prominent among anti-Agreement unionists are Ian Paisley and his DUP, Robert McCartney and his UKUP, the Orange Order (whose leadership for the first time publicly broke ranks with the UUP during the referendum campaign), and the Loyalist Volunteer Force (LVF) - a small but lethal loyalist paramilitary group which a couple of years ago split from the larger UVF (on the grounds that the UVF's political representatives, the PUP, were swapping Protestant fundamentalism for socialism, and that the UVF's ceasefire was a bad thing). But that's not all. Recent referendum and election results suggest that anti-Agreement unionists, although clearly in a minority in overall electoral terms, enjoy the support of close to 50 percent of the unionist electorate. And the largest unionist party, David Trimble's UUP, although officially for the Agreement is in truth split down the middle over it – six of its nine Westminster MPs, for example, openly campaigned against it.

If anti-Agreement republicans pine for a world that has never existed except in their imaginations, anti-Agreement unionists lament the loss of a world that is gone forever. Neither have alternatives to the Agreement that are remotely likely to win enough cross-community support to be workable, or that will be permitted to see the light of day by the British and Irish governments. That's why we shouldn't be over-worried by their opposition to the Agreement.

But neither should we be complacent. The potential exists for anti-Agreement forces to wreck the Agreement, even if they can't hope to replace it with their preferred options. As things currently stand, with three unionist parties, the two main nationalist/republican parties, all non-aligned parties, the British and Irish governments, international opinion, and a substantial majority of citizens North and South backing it, there are solid grounds for thinking this won't happen. But that doesn't mean that the Agreement's success is a foregone conclusion. The uncomfortable fact remains that there's a precarious balance of support for the Agreement on the unionist side, and there's still a chance that this balance might shift. And it would be premature to suppose that Sinn Féin is utterly invulnerable to sniping from other republicans. A lot depends on the strategies pursued by anti-Agreement factions and on how successful they are in exposing chinks in the pro-Agreement armour.

On both republican and unionist sides the oppositional strategies are two-fold: to precipitate crises which make new political arrangements hard to operate, and to maintain the battle for republican and unionist hearts and minds. How these strategies pan out is a matter of conjecture. But we know enough to suggest something like this. Given its concentration in organisations which retain belief in the efficacy of armed struggle, a republican attempt to create a crisis in Northern society will primarily be violent in kind. Part of the hope will be to provoke the main loyalist paramilitary organisations to retaliate and break their ceasefires and, with luck and enough carnage, to draw the Provisional IRA back into the fray. This hope, like the violent strategy that sustains it, now looks pretty forlorn following the massive reaction within republican circles against the Real IRA's bombing of Omagh in August 1998. Indeed, at the time of writing, it is the Continuity IRA alone that has not called a ceasefire. The only strategy left, then, is that of applying continual pressure on republican activists to desert Sinn Féin and the Provisional IRA in the name of republican orthodoxy.

Unionist attempts to provoke a crisis will probably be a little more complex. With the LVF in the picture, there is the chance that a violent card matching the republican one will be played, although this organisation too has belatedly called a ceasefire. But paramilitary violence won't feature very prominently among anti-Agreement unionists. More emphasis will be placed on emotive issues capable of drawing on the support of pro-Agreement unionists. Orange marches are the best example of these. Here the aim will be to create a form of unionist unity – based, say, on a defence of Orangemen's right to march along their traditional routes regardless of any other consideration – which polarises Northern society to the point of putting unbearable strain on power-sharing government. Arguably, Drumcree 1998 came perilously close to doing just that. There will also undoubtedly be attempts to subvert the new assembly from within by any number of blocking tactics. And because of the assembly's complicated voting procedures – which require a motion to acquire the support of a majority of unionists and a majority of nationalists – this could be possible. All the while, there will be an ongoing appeal to pro-Agreement unionists to change their minds. And this is an appeal which remains very powerful particularly because it has the capacity to exacerbate the difficulties which exist among the Agreement's supporters. Let me now turn to the problem these difficulties cause.

The Problem of Clashing Interpretations

More serious than overt opposition to the Agreement is the fact that its support appears fragile. And it appears fragile because there's anything but unanimity among certain of the key parties to the Agreement. To get the point here we need only recall that Agreement was attained without the UUP exchanging so much as a pleasantry with Sinn Féin, let alone entering into political discussions with its representatives. Obviously, in the absence of the sort of communication required to reach a common mind, both parties saw some tactical advantage in signing up to the same deal. But, just as obviously, what one party perceives as an advantage, the other typically perceives as a disadvantage, and very often a threatening one. The Agreement appears fragile, then, because its success virtually depends upon a fine and ongoing balancing act where perceived gains and losses for unionists and nationalists keep relative pace with each other, and where all parties appreciate the foolhardiness of overplaying their hands. What's immediately worrying about such a situation is that it presupposes the presence of some deft and well-honed political skills, and, unfortunately, it's precisely such skills that Northern Ireland's politicians are hardly famous for having perfected. What's more deeply worrying about it is the realisation that the Agreement hangs on understandings among its various supporters which may not differ simply in terms of nuance and pedantic detail, but in terms of fundamentals. And here we are pointed to the Agreement's most acute problem: that of clashing interpretations.

To illustrate the extent of the problem posed by clashing interpretations, I'll stick to the examples of Sinn Féin and the UUP. Doing so risks giving a slightly distorted picture of Northern Irish politics, especially since it leaves out any discussion of the SDLP, the constitutional nationalist party whose role in brokering the present political deal was crucial. But focusing on these examples has the advantage of highlighting the difficulties the Agreement faces. There are two major issues I want to focus upon here: the manifest differences of interpretation, and the difficulty of reconciling these because of each interpretation's vulnerability to charges of ideological sell-out from anti-Agreement factions.

Republican and unionist interpretations of the Agreement clash most obviously on the constitutional question. For Sinn Féin, the Agreement signals a further step on the road to a united Ireland, for the UUP it guarantees the Union. For one it is a means to another end, for the other it is the end. North-South bodies represent for Sinn Féin a blurring of the Irish border and a taste of things to come. For unionists they represent an institutional expression of cordial relations between friendly, neighbouring states which makes good political and economic sense. The East-West dimension of the Agreement is emphasised by unionists as strengthening the British tie, whereas Sinn Féin sees it as merely a toothless concession to unionism the only virtue of which is that it enabled unionists to accept the much more important North-South dimension. In terms of the internal Northern dimension, Sinn Féin stresses the importance of substantial reform: of the RUC certainly, and of the implementation of its so-called equality agenda which envisages Northern society being stripped of its vestiges of British dominance and "parity of esteem" being granted to an Irish identity; it also interprets the Agreement as ensuring Sinn Féin's immediate and effective participation in the government of the North. The UUP balks at all of this: RUC reform should be minimal, Northern Ireland's British character should be maintained, and Sinn Féin's role in government should be prohibited until the IRA has given sufficient proof that it has gone permanently out of business.

Given that Sinn Féin and the UUP are supposed to be cooperating in order to make the Agreement work, we are dealing here with interpretive differences of considerable consequence. What makes matters worse is that the scope for political fudge of such differences appears very limited in view of each party's vulnerability to attack from the anti-Agreement factions I mentioned previously.

And here's the real sting of the problem of overt opposition to the Agreement: while not in itself enough to impede change, it is capable of doing a wrecking job by circumscribing the room for manoeuvre available to certain of the Agreement's supporters. This poses particular difficulties for the UUP, but it also poses difficulties of sorts for Sinn Fein.

With regard to the latter, Sinn Féin is ostensibly susceptible to deeply damaging criticisms: that it's guilty of the ultimate republican heresy by agreeing to work partitionist arrangements; that it's guilty of dishonouring the memory of dead IRA volunteers (a charge that's most poignantly expressed in the emotive, rhetorical question – "is this what Bobby Sands", the first and most famous of the IRA hunger-strikers to die in prison in 1981, "died for: a cross-border body on fisheries?"); that it's guilty of acute naivete in expecting unionists to soften their intransigence and to treat republicans as equal political partners. So far Sinn Féin has managed to escape relatively unscathed from such attacks, not least because it has been able to offer counter-appeals that I'll mention shortly. But there's no doubt that such attacks restrict its official interpretive flexibility. For example, in line with its republican critics, Sinn Féin maintains the orthodoxies that all-Ireland support of the agreement does not constitute an act of self-determination by the Irish people, that a united Ireland is still a sacrosanct republican goal, and that realisation of the goal is historically inevitable. In maintaining these sorts of things, Sinn Féin continues to make noises that arouse unionist suspicions and fears and so inhibits the possibility of rapprochement. But, even so, what is notable is how Sinn Fein has managed to take the Agreement in its stride. Not only has Gerry Adams been able to deflect criticisms from his republican critics, but he has also made what seems like a pretty lousy deal for republicanism appear like another notch in Sinn Féin's belt. Sinn Féin remain upbeat, whatever the constraints their critics impose upon them: history is believed to be on their side.

By contrast, unionists whose interests arguably have been better served by the Agreement, at least in the short-term, are conspicuously down-beat. Even many pro-Agreement unionists think of themselves as losers and admit to having bought the present deal not because they liked it, but because it was the best they could now hope for. There is, then, a widely shared unionist pessimism, a reasonably common belief among unionists that they are swimming against the tide. And it's this that makes an already delicate unionist balance in favour of the Agreement extremely precarious. A real difficulty here is that pro-Agreement unionism doesn't possess an interpretive framework that differs markedly from anti-Agreement unionism. At most there are slight differences of emphasis and a greater propensity to pragmatism among pro-Agreement factions. But when we think of what is shared and, because of the almost even split in unionist ranks, how little scope pro-Agreement unionism has for making generous overtures to republicans even if it wanted to (which is debatable), then we may appreciate just how serious a difficulty that of interpretive constraint really is.

For instance, on practical issues, pro-and anti-Agreement unionists are opposed to any significant reform of Northern Ireland: both would prefer the RUC to remain unreformed, both are largely critical of any early release of prisoners, both dispute the necessity of any public recognition of an Irish identity within Northern society, and both shudder at the suggestion of sharing power with Sinn Féin. But Trimble is committed to working an Agreement which includes these sorts of provisions, whereas Paisley and McCartney aren't. Conceptually, it's hard to spot much difference between pro- and anti-Agreement unionists either. Both uphold as their principal political priority maintaining the Union; both are susceptible to the pull of cultural Protestantism as witnessed in the unified unionist defence of Orangemen's rights; and both are opposed to granting political entitlements to a nationalist identity. But, again, whereas it's easy to move within this sort of conceptual space and reject the Agreement, it's much trickier to move within it and somehow make the Agreement work. McCartney, in particular, grasps the predicament of pro-Agreement unionism here and tries to exploit it mercilessly. In doing so, he helps (unwittingly) to clarify the nature of pro-Agreement unionism's acute quandary: the new practices implied by the Agreement don't fit with the interpretative theories unionists rely upon. Sinn Féin has a similar problem, but it is nowhere near as sharp as that confronting the UUP.

Muddling Through and/or Interpreting Better?

What are we to make of the gloomy picture I've just been painting? How, if at all, is the problem of clashing interpretations to be overcome? Can the Agreement work regardless of this problem? I'd like quickly to try my hand at two sorts of answers to these questions. First, I'll suggest that the Agreement *may* still work in practice through a type of pragmatic muddling through. Second, I'll suggest that the problem of clashing interpretations *can* be overcome in principle by the adoption of an interpretation that is truer to the Agreement.

Pragmatic muddling through is conceivable if we judge that, although limited, the scope for political fudge exists to some extent. In its defence, a rationale with something like the following pitch may be invoked. Of course, republican and unionist interpretations of the Agreement clash, but what else would we expect. Pro-Agreement republicans and unionists have to appeal to hard-line constituencies and therefore cannot stray too far from their respective orthodoxies if they are to bring enough of their supporters with them. So, we shouldn't be too distracted by problems posed by clashing interpretations. What matters is that Sinn Féin and the UUP are committed to working the Agreement, and it's how they do this in practice that counts more than how they square various of their practices with their theories. Besides, both Gerry Adams and David Trimble can find enough in the Agreement to justify their support of it to relatively orthodox republicans and unionists.

For example, Adams can argue along these lines. Sinn Féin's willingness to embrace the changes outlined in the Agreement should be seen as a continuation of the policies the party has been pursuing to advance republican interests. Unlike the explicit militarism of the '70s, and unlike the mix of militarism and politics of the '80s, the '90s increasingly indicate that political strategies alone will aid the republican cause. It is now clear that there is no military solution to the problem of the North, and those republicans who think otherwise are kidding themselves. Republicanism is better served by Sinn Féin's participation in mainstream politics. The international support it can draw upon now illustrates the advantage of such participation: Adams and McGuinness are accepted as statesmen; with the silence of IRA guns and the antics of Orangemen, it's unionists who appear as the bad guys in the eyes of world opinion; there is a steady supply of financial support, especially from America; and there is the prospect of Sinn Féin becoming the largest nationalist party in the North. And all these advantages can be enjoyed without any forfeiting of republicanism's ultimate goals. Besides, since political realities dictate that there is not going to be a sudden end to partition, it makes perfect sense to contribute to its elimination from within the political system: by insisting upon an equality agenda within the North that makes the nature of society more republican-friendly; by working to extend areas of North-South co-operation to the point of making the border irrelevant; and by deriving hope from the fact that the unionist majority within the North is being slowly whittled away – with four out of six Northern counties now having a nationalist majority. These are the sort of counter-appeals at Adams' disposal which I earlier suggested help to explain why Sinn Féin hasn't been nearly as damaged by republican criticism as it might have been.

David Trimble, for his part, has also some arguments to offer to unionist supporters. The Agreement returns self-government to Northern Ireland and unionists will have a prominent, if no longer a dominant, role to play in it. The new Agreement replaces the loathed Anglo-Irish Agreement of 1985; it promises the kind of change to the Irish constitution that unionists have been advocating for years; it recognises British sovereignty in the North; and it guarantees that further constitutional change cannot legitimately be undertaken without deferring to the principle of consent (in other words, unionists now have a legally recognised veto insofar as they continue to be in a majority).

In a sense, then, we might ask who gives a cracker whether republicans believe that the Agreement leads to a united Ireland and unionists believe that it secures the Union. All that matters is that enough republicans and unionists consent to work it, for whatever reason. Keeping going the processes of pragmatic muddling through is what's of the essence, not becoming fixated on interpretive clashes and ideological incompatibilities. This is enough to aim at for now. The real task, then, is simply to capitalise on the fact that Adams and Trimble have both risked too much to back away from their commitments to making the Agreement work. And this is a task which we wouldn't expect either the British or Irish governments to shirk. We can be confident that both will be praising the virtues of pragmatism at every turn. In addition, the economic carrots being dangled in the event of peace being maintained are very tempting, and there is a growing tiredness in certain previously militant quarters which makes a return to conflict very unappealing.

Maybe the necessary ingredients are all here to see off the problems of overt opposition and clashing interpretations. Maybe all we should expect is a type of pragmatic muddling through that is able to be sustained by drawing on the sort of resources I have just mentioned: relatively plausible republican and unionist reasons for supporting the Agreement, the difficult-to-reverse commitments of the republican and unionist leaderships, pressure from the British and Irish governments, economic incentives, and general war-weariness. Maybe it is only a matter of time before unionists do find ways of working with republicans and of treating them as equal political partners, since the price of their not doing so may eventually be exorbitant. And if hope of lasting peace and political stability in Northern Ireland is realistically to be pinned on the pragmatic muddling through all of this suggests, it may yet prove more durable than the hopes raised by any other initiative in the last thirty years.

One nagging doubt about the sufficiency of such a pragmatic solution, however, is that it does very much depend upon the North's politicians developing, and quickly, the sort of political skills I previously suggested they lack. Another doubt concerns how long the Agreement can survive without the problem of clashing interpretations being tackled. For the uncomfortable fact is that the clashes involved aren't merely over matters of abstract doctrine; rather, they bear sharply upon how the new arrangements envisaged by the Agreement are to be worked. That's why it would be much better if republicans and unionists admitted that their interpretive frameworks weren't up to scratch and moved towards the adoption of an alternative framework which is more attuned to current realities. Part of what I'm driving at here may be gleaned by considering the recent remarks of Declan Kiberd:

The Belfast Agreement offers a postcolonial version of overlapping identities of a kind for which no legal language yet exists. It sees identity as open rather than fixed, a process rather than a conclusion. It leaves behind concepts of sovereignty, and nationhood, yet it will in effect be a working constitution for the next two decades. A common bond uniting all on the island who voted for it will be fidelity to the document, which will probably override their actual relation to their respective sovereign powers.

And, he concludes for good measure, "far from being nostalgists, the Irish may be the pragmatists of the postmodern, postcolonial world" (Kiberd, 1998: 14).

Kiberd's remarks may raise eyebrows. Certainly, it's hard to imagine anyone from Belfast sharing his confidence that the bond among the Agreement's supporters throughout Ireland will prove more powerful than their bonds to the British and Irish states. At any rate, I can't think of too many pro-Agreement unionists of whom this could possibly be predicted. And his anticipation of the Irish leaving behind their nationalism through pragmatic adjustment to the "postcolonial" and "postmodern" realities of our time presupposes a number of quite debatable things, including an implicit suggestion that the North's citizens will become as adept as the South's at shedding ideological baggage as political and economic circumstances dictate. But what Kiberd rightly draws attention to is how the Agreement plays on an idea of "overlapping" identities which transcends conventional notions of sovereignty and the nation-state, and for which no adequate legal language yet exists. And it is this idea, together with the set of practices it implies, that point to the redundancy of standard republican and unionist frameworks of interpretation. As I have argued elsewhere, adequate sense cannot be made of the Agreement on the terms of either traditional republicanism or traditional unionism (Porter, 1998b: 1-33; 1998a: vii-xix).

One attempt to make the sense required by the Agreement is

to say two basic things: that we need to redefine what Northern Ireland is; and that we need to identify political priorities that fit this redefinition. With regard to the first, Northern Ireland is unhelpfully thought of as merely a site of the Union or as merely the lost green field awaiting return to its proper owner. It is, rather, better depicted as a site where British and Irish factors intermingle and clash and demand mutual recognition. It is a site of "overlapping identities", to appropriate Kiberd's term. That is why there can be no exclusively British or Irish solution to the North, as the Agreement rightly acknowledges. Accordingly, the overriding political priority should be neither that of defending the Union nor that of hastening the arrival of a united Ireland. The priority should be to make Northern Ireland in all its complexity work. And that means highlighting the political goods of self-government and of citizen belonging. In other words, it is inconceivable that it can be made to work in the absence of public institutions guaranteeing that citizens of Northern Ireland have power over their own affairs, and institutions capable of commanding the allegiance of all citizens and not merely of one tribe. But, crucially, it is only as we concede the Britishness and Irishness of Northern Ireland, and so transcend typical unionist and nationalist constructions, that these sorts of goods and the priority of making the North work can be given their due.

The challenge is to unionists and nationalists, loyalists and republicans to adopt an interpretive framework, such as the one alluded to above, that is more in line with the Agreement they all subscribe to. Only thus may justice be done to the "totality of relationships" affecting life in the North and articulated in the three dimensions of the Agreement. And only thus may problems confronting the Agreement and the practices it requires be resolved in principle.

Afterword: Reconciliation and Its Unionist Critics

Introduction

After arriving back to live in Belfast in 1994 – two weeks before PIRA called its first ceasefire – I left to return to Australia in December 1999. Then for the years of 2002 and 2003, I had a research position at QUB which involved commuting between the vastly different worlds of Byron Bay in northern New South Wales and Belfast. During this period, I completed a book on reconciliation in Northern Ireland (*The Elusive Quest*). In 2004, I returned to live in Belfast again only to leave for Australia once more in 2006. Erratic behaviour some might say. Perhaps, but I do have other explanations. In part, the toing and froing between Northern Ireland and Australia reflected a tension in my family between the majority – a wife and two sons - who identified as Australian and the minority – a daughter and me – who identified more as (Northern) Irish. In larger measure, though, the intercontinental hopping about was due to life's uncertainties; or, more precisely, to instances of its rather nasty and fickle manifestations. This isn't the occasion to give detailed accounts of what I'm alluding to, but a vague indication may be appropriate in order to provide a backdrop which helps to make sense of other comments I'll make shortly.

By nastiness, I refer to the incursion of a (possibly unhinged) version of a loyalist paramilitary threat into the life of my family, which (my being regarded as a "Lundy" by some hard-nosed unionists and loyalists may or may not have encouraged and) resulted in one of my (terrified) sons retreating back to Australia to finish his high school education (and, by the way, he's still struggling with the trauma it caused, so thanks very much whoever you were). This prompted the family's departure a little later (1999). In the interim period between the two departures, I was having to modify my behaviour, since it was increasingly obvious that I was coming under scrutiny from some rather sinister figures, one of whom demanded that I prove my "loyalty" by addressing an upcoming loyalist prisoners' rally in the Park Avenue Hotel – fortunately, a much more amicable and reasonable loyalist intervened to prevent a potentially dangerous incident from developing.

By fickleness, I have in mind events (or, maybe more accurately, non-events) falling within the period of 2004-2006. I had returned to Belfast for several reasons, prominent among which was a belief that I was going to spearhead a new venture centred on the themes of reconciliation and citizenship. Funding had been agreed; commitments had been made (by those authorised to honour them) to me (and to others). And yet nothing eventuated, and no explanation was offered (I've since learned that it may have been because I was deemed at times to be keeping "disapproved" company – which intimates, quite bafflingly I think, that reconciliation's embrace isn't meant to extend to all actors in the North's politics). Fickle, indeed, are many of our words, and not least those of leading lights among "the great and the good" in Northern society. As for me, well, I was left hanging and forced eventually to conclude that this move back had been in vain and that my prospects were not likely to improve. I've never forgotten the last words spoken to me by (PUP leader) Davey Ervine – who sadly died prematurely not very long afterwards – "Norman", he said, "this is a very mean-spirited society; go to Australia and get on with your life". With more than a little disillusionment and regret I left Belfast for Australia again in 2006 – this time for my original Australian destination of Adelaide.

By way of completing background information which may usefully shed light on the main themes I'll soon be concentrating on in this Afterword, I should mention that during the mid-late 1990s I spent a lot of time working behind the scenes with political parties that had a history of paramilitary connections. This involved frequenting many bars, clubs and other venues with which I had no previous acquaintance, as well as accepting invitations to address audiences and participate in debates that took me far beyond my comfort zone. On occasions, I also organised clandestine gatherings which brought together (mostly senior) representatives of parties who tended to avoid one another in public. As a result, I developed an understanding of republican, loyalist and other activists which I wouldn't have had otherwise. This played a big role in my estimations of what was both needed and possible in the world of Northern politics; estimations that were radically out of kilter with mainstream unionist ones especially. Unsurprisingly, a lot of my behind-the-scenes activity was confidential, and, as such, constrains how many details I can divulge about it without betraying others' trust. Maybe I'm being over-scrupulous here given that we now know what some of us didn't know back then, namely that the parties and organisations I was dealing with were so infiltrated by spies and touts that it's highly unlikely that information I'm withholding isn't common knowledge, at least in certain circles. (As an aside, I received vague inklings of the reach of the peculiar world of surveillance when I was awoken one morning by a telephone call from a prominent IRA informer who was hiding away somewhere in England. This was my first and only communication with this person. To my amazement, he invited me to attend a weekend of discussions on unionism – involving among others David Trimble, Ian Paisley and Bob McCartney – at the country residence of a Tory member of the House of Lords. I declined the invitation, pointing out that the (loyalist) parties not invited to the weekend's talks were those I was concentrating attention on. He not only knew about that but, unprompted, proceeded to tell me that he was aware of my meetings with Sinn Féin – information unlikely to have come from republican sources given his ostracisation from Sinn Féin and PIRA for a period of years – and remarked that one of the republicans I was involved with was a particularly good guy. A few days, later an article appeared in a Sunday paper under the name of the informer basically pronouncing that there was no such thing as a good guy within the ranks of the Provisional movement. What a murky, strange, and topsy-turvy world we find ourselves inadvertently inhabiting at times, where words are frequently slippery and distinctions between appearance and reality often hard to fathom).

I've introduced these personal slants because I want to draw on aspects of them in the hope of reinforcing arguments I develop in the course of answering criticisms of my position on reconciliation. It's an odd thing for me to do. It's motivated principally out of despair that reasons alone are not enough to answer accusations that seem driven by deeper forces than a desire for clear thinking or a willingness to engage in fair debate. Without any faith that it'll make a difference, I thought I'd try here to intersperse my reasoning with examples gleaned from my practical political involvement. If all else fails, I aim to establish that a picture of my orientation to politics, sketched by academics and politicians who are unsympathetic to what I represent, is a distortion that can be sustained only through extreme ill-will.

For the remainder of this Afterword, I propose to concentrate on (some) criticisms of my book on reconciliation; ones emanating from unionist authors. Doing so enables me to complete my attempt to make sense of and redefine my relationship with unionism. More broadly, it also brings to a close my involvement in the politics of Northern Ireland and thus ends a pivotal chapter of my life (1994-2006) which, with an interruption in the middle, saw me return as a permanent resident to Northern Ireland and then leave again.

Reconciliation: A Quick Overview

The Elusive Quest. Reconciliation In Northern Ireland was published in 2003. The thrust of its argument may be discerned from Chapters eleven and twelve in this volume. It's important to stress that the argument was structured along the following lines: by considering a range of objections to the very idea of reconciliation as a political priority; by discussing various forms reconciliation might take in Northern Ireland ranging from "weak" to "strong"; by seriously entertaining the view that "weak" forms were all that could reasonably be expected and surmising that, if they were, they would be an improvement on the prevailing status quo in Northern society; by worrying nevertheless that, if such became accepted as our lot, some underlying sources of division would be left untroubled and would almost certainly return to haunt us; and by advocating, as a consequence, a "strong" conception of reconciliation on the grounds that it brought to explicit attention issues that made sense to avoid only in the short-term, but not in the long-term. My contention was that long-term thinking was advisable and that an ambitious notion of a reconciled society was an appropriate goal, albeit one that would undoubtedly meet with strenuous resistance and would be difficult to realise.

The main point of the book was to ask what it might mean to prioritise (strong) reconciliation, or at least to give it a place at the table alongside our other priorities, in order to encourage reflection on our sources of division by subjecting them to critical examination. I tried to articulate a series of arguments to the effect that many of our divisions, upon close inspection, needn't necessarily pose insuperable obstacles to reconciliation, especially if we allow them to be tempered by factors that we (potentially) hold in common. I did so by drawing on an understanding of reconciliation which, very tersely stated, recommended "embracing and engaging others who are different from us in a spirit of openness and with a view to expanding our horizons, healing our divisions and articulating common purposes" (Porter, 2003: 8). I tried to spell out the implications of this understanding over several chapters. At no point did it ever occur to me that I was proposing a model to be mechanically applied to the world of Northern politics, irrespective of its complexities. I have never thought that model-building illuminates political thinking (though I stand open to correction). Throughout the writing of the book, my thinking was influenced obviously by the type of political and philosophical assumptions that informed the writing of *Rethinking Unionism* (see Chapter five), but also by my various practical political involvements and my assessment of the possibilities they suggested.

The critics I'm now going to discuss, principally Arthur Aughey (again) and David Trimble, ignore almost everything I've just said. No attempt is made to engage with my actual arguments in order to show where my reasoning may be implausible, or where my case seems to break down. Rather, the almost irresistible impression conveyed is that my conclusions are considered disagreeable, and that the best way to refute them is to recreate (a mostly unrecognisable) version of my position which is then mercilessly pilloried.

Knowing how to organise my responses is a bit of a challenge, given the disparate nature of the various attacks to which I'm subjected. I'll try to bring order to the attacks by suggesting that they may be grouped under three stark claims: that I'm (1) often politically *naïve and* unfailingly politically *unrealistic*, that I'm (2) inappropriately *moralistic* and in ways that exacerbate the difficulties exposed in the first claim and that I'm (3) potentially (on occasions) politically *dangerous*.

Politically Naïve and Unrealistic?

The problem of political naïvety or impracticality is said to afflict me from the start; it originates in a misguided philosophical approach to politics which causes me to entertain preposterous expectations of the beleaguered members of Northern society. Not only that, but there are also, it seems, varying grades of naïvety, one of which doubles up as a sign of obtuseness. This issues in an unawareness of reconciliation's appropriate limitations which I demonstrate by stupidly (and it seems self-righteously) mischaracterising a position from which I've much to learn. And this is a fatal flaw which is compounded by a misconceived over-estimation of the role of dialogue in politics. Or so Aughey wants to inform me. Let's see what he has to say.

Abstract Philosophy

My approach to the North's politics is apparently crippled at a fundamental level due to its *over-reliance on philosophy*. Aughey seems to imagine that I start with what Michael Oakeshott called "a model laid up in heaven" (Aughey, 2005: 15) and later announces that my analysis "begins in philosophy and ends in mysticism" (Aughey, 2005: 75). I'll return to my mysticism later. For the moment, it appears that I gloss over most of the messy, complex realities of political life because I start at an abstract philosophical level which blocks out these realities and has me proposing courses of action that are irredeemably naïve or practically irrelevant. At any rate, I'm unable to get to grips properly with the conflictual inconveniences which defy my lofty philosophical appeals (my over-reliance on morality is also a problem here, as we'll see shortly); at best maybe, as Adrian Little seems to believe of my view of civil society, my approach possibly has (restricted) appeal to the extent that it only requires for its political application "the participation of middle class liberals rather than groups that are likely to conflict with one another" (Little, 2004: 124). So, I think I'm being told that my propensity to philosophise abstractly from the outset optimally finds an audience, if I'm especially lucky, only amongst the sort of people who are already nicely predisposed to get along with one another.

I've two sorts of responses here. The first I'll keep brief because I've already answered a similar line of criticism from Aughey (in relation to *Rethinking Unionism*) in Chapter six. Granted that we're referring in this context to *political philosophy* (and not, say, to metaphysics, epistemology or modal logic), I conceive of philosophy growing out of political life rather than being imposed on it. There are various ways of describing this via Aristotle or via hermeneutical phenomenology, and so on. Succinctly put, I'm maintaining that it's through reflecting on what we're about in our political practice that we may be led through the exercise of practical reason, for example, to call into question some things we've unreflectively taken for granted and to recommend other things we've barely thought of previously. The point is that I'm emphatically not proposing the advisability of model building prior to political involvement or the wisdom of thinking philosophically about politics from a disengaged stance; rather, it's reflection that is tied to social and political engagement all the way down that I'm practicing. And that's why it's much more accurate to say that I start with politics.

A second response underscores this through particular reference to political experiences that prompted the writing of *The Elusive Quest*. Some, such as my appearance at the Irish government-sponsored "Forum for Peace and Reconciliation" in Dublin, where I responded to questions from representatives of Ireland's non-unionist parties, and informal meetings with a range of British and Irish parties at locations such as Glencree in County Wicklow prompted me to think that more agreement may be possible between historical antagonists than unionism ever seems to allow. Other experiences reinforced that major obstacles stood in reconciliation's path and yet didn't eclipse its possibility altogether. Two of these, both as it happens in Derry, stand out. One was an occasion when I was invited to sit on a panel at a cross-community event to discuss ways of easing tensions between Derry's nationalist and unionist communities. Unfortunately, there had been serious rioting in Derry over the preceding weekend and the cross-community event turned into a single community gathering (nationalist/republican) and I found myself as the sole (political) representative of any form of unionism in the room. A specific incident highlighted the practical/political difficulty of easing tensions let alone pursuing ambitious plans of reconciliation. A rioter from the weekend's showdown with the RUC approached me brandishing a plastic bullet which he claimed "my police" had fired at him, and angrily demanded to know what I was going to do about it. The moment was more than a little uncomfortable. A second occasion occurred at a weekend event to mark the 25th anniversary of Bloody Sunday at a question-and-answer session in the Bogside Community Centre. As far as I could tell I was the only "unionist" present among many hundreds of republicans. In a scene reminiscent of the one I've just described (only this time without my being directly in the firing line), a very animated member of the audience informed all present of his passionate desire to rid the island of the likes of me – by forced drownings if that's what it took. A challenge for reconciliation indeed.

The point I now wish to underline through reference to these two incidents in Derry is that both prompted interesting discussions with leading figures of Sinn Féin who were present at one or other of the occasions. An upshot of these discussions was that far from drawing grim conclusions about reconciliation's prospects given the extremity of the political views on display, I left convinced that much more political room to manoeuvre was conceivable than appeared on the surface. And it was in these moments, of extraordinarily stark division which nonetheless bore glimmers of genuine hope, that my thoughts on reconciliation began to crystallise – and not when I was dreamily circumnavigating the heavens in search of a pristine model to impose on the North's hapless citizens or having cups of tea or passing the port in the right direction in suitably polite company. As I say, and whatever Aughey chooses to believe to the contrary, *The Elusive Quest* originated in politics, and in politics of a sharp and rudimentary kind at that.

Limitation-Obtuseness Problem

Even so, pointing this out isn't enough to offset my vulnerability to what I'll call the *limitation-obtuseness problem*. It apparently comes to light through my criticism of ATQ Stewart's appropriation of Joseph Conrad's diatribe against fraternity, which includes the line of the "Cain and Abel stuff" (fratricide) capturing fraternity's real meaning. I submit that this suggests misanthropy and contributes to treating division (and therefore sectarianism) in Northern society as given. Aughey lambasts the putative audacity of my interpretation of Stewart. Through my criticism, I am apparently accusing Stewart of "actively promoting division and desiring to prevent fraternity". And, he says, "Such a reading is quite perverse, confuses

Afterword: Reconciliation and Its Unionist Critics ~ 279

understanding with recommendation, limitation with inevitability, and reveals the historical ignorance at the heart of the moralizing vision"; then, for good measure, he adds that far from being an "unfortunate reading of our circumstances in Northern Ireland", as I claim, "it is only unfortunate in the sense that people must try to struggle against comforting illusions and falsehoods about Northern Ireland and even more comforting illusions about themselves" (Aughey, 2005: 15).

A few quick responses are in order. To clarify, (1) my claim wasn't that Stewart actively promoted division, but that his view "serves ... to reinforce division" (Porter, 2003: 268): these aren't identical claims, since one refers to intent and the other to effect and, contrary to Aughey's assertion, it is the latter claim that I am making. As to fraternity, well, it'd be hard not to surmise from Stewart's use of Conrad that he wasn't too keen on it, and I don't immediately grasp what is so intolerably naughty about making such an observation. Aughey is happy to relieve my ignorance: I confuse "understanding with recommendation". I agree (2) that there is a distinction to be drawn between understanding and recommendation, but often, as in this case, Stewart's "understanding" isn't neutral, especially when in other of his writings, quoted in *The Elusive Quest*, he refers to "all attempts to promote reconciliation as being singularly futile", to talk of reconciliation being "hot air" and to the "surrender" of one side or another as being the only way to end conflict (in Porter, 2003: 24). Stewart's "understanding" may not technically require recommending anything, but it constrains what it's apt to recommend not least through prescriptively loaded language aimed at that of which he disapproves – where "singularly futile" and "hot air" are apparently quite appropriate terms to describe reconciling endeavours. These unflattering terms are, in my opinion, used to jaundiced effect. So, I don't accept that I'm obtusely confusing anything here. But I'm not let off the hook so lightly, since I also confuse "limitation with inevitability" – to which charge I object, (3) that I'm not quite ready to confess guilt on this so-called confusion either because I disagree with Stewart (and obviously Aughey) about what counts as "limitation". Let's be clear, on their view most of what I support in the name of reconciliation overreaches what they see as proper limitation, but the disturbing thought remains that to concede to such limitation, in the context of Northern Ireland's history, is to pay a very high price – being hamstrung in the face of sectarianism and tacitly admitting its inevitability. Perhaps it's my imagination, but I get the impression that Aughey is much more riled by my meagre efforts at promoting reconciliation than he is by the sectarian shenanigans often practiced in the name of defending the Union. Whatever about that, I don't accept that sectarianism is inevitable, just as I don't buy the Stewart-Aughey notion of limitation, precisely because I think that humans have agency and aren't pre-determined to conform to morally repugnant modes of behaviour, even if there are powerful historical precedents for expecting them to do so.

In reasoning along these lines, however, I probably reveal, in Aughey's eyes, "the historical ignorance at the heart of the moralizing vision" which I'm brazenly advocating. I've a lot to say about his anti-morality point shortly, so I'll restrict myself for the moment to replying (4) that I evidently lack the faith that's necessary to receive this revelation – to reiterate, I'm simply saying that we have to be aware of our history but not necessarily constrained by it to the point of being little more than its victims; that there are opportunities in the present for overcoming some of our historical antagonisms, and, yes, that doing so would be a good thing. Why saying these sorts of things makes my position guilty of historical ignorance is puzzling. As to the jibe about those of us not enamoured by Stewart's analysis needing to face up to "comforting illusions and falsehoods" about Northern Ireland and "even more comforting illusions" about ourselves, I suggest (5) that Aughey shows little interest in playing the ball here and that indulging such gratuitous insults is close to being beneath contempt. Or, if I may put it this way, Aughey appears to have great difficulty understanding that bit of me that's in plain view in my writings, how much greater must his difficulty be in deciphering the bit of me that's hidden, namely my psyche to which he has no access? So better not to go there Arthur since your efforts – as amply demonstrated by your vague allusions to "even more comforting illusions" I entertain about myself (assuming that I am included among the "people" being referred to, which I take it I must be) – are unlikely to progress beyond the level of the infantile. Let's simply acknowledge that we disagree about politics and leave the other stuff out of it.

Dialogue Overrated

Without doubt my approach to reconciliation, and to politics in general, puts a heavy emphasis on the importance of dialogue. Aughey isn't happy about this. I'll reserve comment until later on what is, in my estimation, his most bizarre gloss on such an emphasis. For the moment, I'll pick up on his counters that dialogue is overrated because it tends "to be all process and no product" (Aughey, 2005: 73), and that participating in dialogue and having a voice doesn't guarantee being heeded: "the politically incorrect can speak all they like but they will only be listened to when they say what is required of them" (Aughey, 2005: 73). I have three responses. One is to concede a point to his latter counter but by turning it back on him. I agree that all the talk in the world is to little avail if what's being said is disapproved of by powerful interests such as the mainstream unionist ones Aughey represents and which I offend. Thus, by persistently misrepresenting my position, what I say is kept firmly on the margins. To make what's going on here seem a little less grubby, we could think of it as analogous to the Kuhnian claim about scientific research, namely that (as Steve Fuller comments) it "maintains the clarity of its research frontier, its forward momentum, by evaluating research solely in terms of its potential contribution to the dominant paradigm. Ideas, proposals and even findings that explicitly try to change the subject or overturn the paradigm are thus rarely welcomed (Fuller, 2005: 22). As I can attest, my arguments in *Rethinking Unionism* and *The Elusive Quest* are rarely welcomed among unionists; but worse, as Aughey keeps demonstrating, they are frequently twisted beyond recognition, which is, of course, one way of trying to fast-track their trip to the rubbish bin.

Another response is to say that this is hardly a convincing counter against dialogue as such. And it is not made any more impressive by Aughey's follow up claim that when we think we know everything that the other side is going to say (as Stewart and he fancy is the case in all unionist-nationalist/republican exchanges), then all our philosophical resources "turn out to be impotent in the resolution of conspicuous and divisive disagreement" (Aughey, 2005: 74). But what we have here, as in the first case, is a corruption of dialogue – either through a manipulative attempt to achieve only pre-approved outcomes which the powerful are in a position to secure, or through a determined bid to hold out against consequences which the wilfully obstinate are able to obstruct. A worrying feature of this argument is the absolute certainty that accompanies it, as if it merely reflects the way humans are programmed and so there's nothing that can be done about it. But this is all or nothing stuff. To observe that very often our best communicative efforts falter, or that they're susceptible to abuse, doesn't quite amount to a reason for abandoning them. And I don't accept for a moment Aughey's assertion that in our politics nobody ever listens to anyone they disagree with and that that's the end of the matter. Too much cynicism can be blinding: with listening it's a matter of degree – because we're not perfect and don't welcome being unsettled by hearing opponents presenting some inconvenient opinions or facts doesn't mean dialogue, listening and so on are simply dispensable. Small improvements in our appreciation of others' concerns remain a possibility that is being cynically dismissed as of no consequence because none of us can guarantee perfect dialogical conditions or outcomes. But that's an absurd requirement; one that I'm definitely not advocating. For all of his inveighing against the alleged impracticality of my more upbeat assessments of political co-operation's possibilities, it is Aughey's pessimistic appraisals that I find practically wanting.

A third response, which also addresses his complaint about dialogue being "all process and no product", is to draw upon another example from my political experience which I think tells against Aughey's cynicism. In early 1998, shortly before the Agreement was signed, I organised an "off-the-record" weekend of political discussions with prominent members of Sinn Féin and unionists of various descriptions. Without doubt it was the most illuminating of any such discussions I had experience of – a view shared by participants on both sides. There was an absence of the usual "whataboutery"; which was replaced by honest and direct interchanges in which interlocutors were prepared to concede faults and showed a willingness to develop better understandings of their opponent's position. Two seasoned participants on the unionist side, with whom I'd had no previous dealings, were deeply impressed by what they'd been part of, and one ventured that it had been the most illuminating experience of his political life. And I was informed that specific members of the republican contingent whom I was meeting for the first time were sufficiently enamoured by proceedings that they overcame their reticence about republicanism's political strategy and indicated that their full support of it could now be counted upon. Apparently, this was a big deal. Given the very delicate political circumstances of the time, such an outcome strikes me as a highly significant "product" of dialogue that defies Aughey's jibe about it being only "process". Moreover, this example illustrated what I already knew from my own interactions with republicans and loyalists – that pressing for the possibility of reconciliation through dialogue and so on isn't just a philosophically satisfying idea for the soft-hearted and weak-minded, but something capable of cutting through at the sharp end of politics. As I keep reiterating, my notions of reconciliation owe as much to my experience of politics as to my philosophy. There are possibilities at hand which most unionist politicians and their academic fellow travellers are unfortunately closed off from. They needn't be.

The Problem of Moralism in Politics

But then, of course, there remains the huge *problem of moralism* in politics to which David Trimble, in a review of my book in the *Times Literary Supplement*, also draws attention. From the musings of Aughey and Trimble there's a lot to disentangle.

Subtext and its Fallout

Let's start with Aughey's detection of the *subtext* of my moral vision: "the notion that if only nationalists would stop being nationalist and unionists would stop being unionist, then things would improve" (Aughey, 2005: 22). Since such a notion is doomed to failure on account of its disconnection to reality, the moral vision underlying it risks turning "into its opposite" – a "bitter denunciation" of the way things are because they don't match the vision's standards of "high-minded purity". And this yields "unconstructive" politics which, according to Aughey, Trimble exposes as a failure to admit "the messy, tension-filled business of political compromise". The assumption seems to be, then, that I am so attached to a lofty moral ideal ill-equipped to handle the realities of politics that I'll cling to it in the face of its inevitable disappointments to the extent of eschewing politics altogether. For, Aughey avers, my approach "can encourage apathy and disenchantment as it turns away from politics in order to preserve its righteousness" (Aughey, 2005: 22).

A problem with this extraordinarily fanciful line of thought is that its initial premise is false: there is no subtext which hinges on my asking anyone to stop being either nationalist or unionist. But I do suggest two things which Aughey finds disagreeable. One is that to the extent that it's feasible to envisage citizens working together in the North to sustain its post-Agreement institutions, it shouldn't be too far-fetched to imagine the *possible* emergence of a shared civic identity that sits alongside their identities as unionists or nationalists, or to intimate that if this were to occur it *may* help to ease tensions between them. Another is that acknowledging unionists as unionist and nationalists as nationalist, doesn't imply the impropriety of critically scrutinising what they take these things to mean in the context of contemporary Northern politics, of asking questions of their stances on issues of the day, or even, if we think there's a good case for doing so, of suggesting that the traditional (unionist or nationalist) fare on offer fails to offer enough to help us overcome our predicaments. Unionist and nationalist identities aren't hermetically sealed and fresh thinking, which obviously is frowned upon by those with a sceptical conservative outlook, doesn't have to be dismissed out of hand.

As for the tale Aughey spins from an incorrect premise, I'll restrict my comments to the bare minimum. I have more to say about Trimble shortly but, to clarify one point now, I may have criticised his tactics and priorities, but I never "dismissed the messy, tension-filled business of political compromise in favour of high-minded purity". The inability to grasp this is astonishing: disagreeing with someone's tactics and priorities doesn't equate with wishing to preserve high-minded purity, which I have no recollection of ever doing. Of course, it might help if any of *my* reasons were addressed, but alas that is too much to hope for. And, given my dealings with republicans, loyalists and others, the accusation that I'm unacquainted with the messy business of politics is amusing. The entirely speculative slurs that then follow are outrageous: when my purity is dashed on the rock of harsh reality (unionist recalcitrance presumably, since Aughey seems to regard these as synonyms even if he can't quite bring himself to say so), it risks turning into bitter denunciation. Pardon? I seriously doubt how any of my writings can be read as giving hint of something so toxic. Aughey is merely giving free rein to his imagination. Not content with that fiction, Aughey, in a flurry of inventive excitement, exults that for the sake of preserving righteousness, and through my inability to live with political messiness, I'm likely to encourage apathy, disenchantment and a turning away from politics. Really? Caricature abounds, no evidence is supplied and none of my arguments are consulted. In short, nonsensical attributions are just declared with assertive bluster. Meanwhile, back in the real world...

Against Civic Virtue

Unfortunately, I may not have the grip on this world that I suppose, as my moralism continues to obscure its proper nature not least when I stress the importance of civic virtues in politics. At least that's what I'm told. The real political world is impervious to such moralising because it's implausible to expect citizens to be "paragons of virtue, de-centred not self-centred" and so on (Aughey, 2005: 73). Yet again, as I noted earlier in his treatment of dialogue, we see Aughey play the trick of positing what I'm proposing as an impossible ideal beyond the reach of ordinary mortals in order to downplay the role of moral considerations in politics. In the case of civic virtues, expectations may indeed be implausible if perfection or being "a paragon" were the standard being set. But it's not. Civic virtues are character habits cultivated through experience and the extent to which any of us manifest them is a matter of degree. It's enough, in other words, to encourage even a minor association with civic virtue in an attempt to get going a debate about what's good for society as a whole, and not just what suits me and my political chums. Sure, if we are nothing more than self-centred all the way through then even that may be a tough request. But, if that's so, trust becomes a utopian dream, security a perpetual worry, stability a fragile experience and instrumental relations the only sort available. All political efforts at co-operation, not reducible to self-interest, must appear as a mirage, obviously including those I'm promoting through the cultivation of civic virtues and concern for the common good. And here's the rub: to accept Aughey's argument and its implications requires us to concede that self-centredness captures the "reality" of the human condition and determines political conduct. This is a mammoth requirement, which dismisses much of the tradition of Western moral and political thought and ignores huge tracts of human experience. More than dogmatic assertions – which are all that currently appear to be on offer – are needed if many of us are to be persuaded.

Regrettably, I can't yet take my leave of my unionist detractors. Looming ahead there awaits the core of the objection to my moralising approach to politics apparently delivered as a *coup de gras* by David Trimble's review of *The Elusive Quest*, which, Aughey effuses, pointed (in Trimble's own words) "to the void at its core" (Aughey, 2005: 109). So, let's see what the former law academic and (at the time) Northern Ireland's First Minister has to say. My definition of reconciliation "involves a merging of political and religious languages" through which I end up with "a highly moralistic approach to politics which makes high, not to say impossible, demands on a population which is emerging from thirty years of polarizing terrorist violence" (Trimble, 2003). I am without agencies to effect the "transformation" of Northern society that I advocate and thus the "void at the core of this book" is laid bare. Quite simply, I lack the agents capable of delivering my desired vision of transformation because I come up short in the numbers game: those political actors I might look to for assistance – Trimble names the PUP, Alliance Party and the Women's Coalition as potential candidates – are in decline and no match for the UUP (numerically speaking). And so, I'm left bereft as my "language of politics" becomes "submerged in that of religion and personal conversion". To add to my misery, a further problem is that though I wrongly apply a moral ideal to politics, my moral ideal is pretty suspect anyway as I don't use it to condemn terrorism and "a moral ideal which ignores the key question of who bears the responsibility for by far the greatest amount of death, injury and destruction over the period of the Troubles – the Provisional IRA – is a deeply flawed one". Furthermore, I'm feeble on the issue of decommissioning and I prove to be another "in a long-line of well-intentioned commentators who have been taken in" by the master dissemblers of the republican movement, about whom I'm far too nice anyway (Trimble, 2003). As Aughey tells me, in my narrative, "republicans are the good guys", those I deem to be "politically correct" (Aughey, 2005: 75).

Asking the Impossible

So once more I'm being told that in the name of reconciliation, I'm asking the impossible of people so recently traumatised by a generation of conflict. Too much too soon is being requested. I noted in Chapter seven that this is a familiar unionist refrain. Five years after the Agreement, with IRA weapons silent and now decommissioned,

Afterword: Reconciliation and Its Unionist Critics

I'm inclined to ask when it would ever be the right time to press a case for meaningful reconciliation, especially between unionists and republicans. One noticeable feature of Northern politics is that it's typically unionists who rail against reconciliation's intrusions into their world of victimhood; nationalists, the Alliance Party and other smaller parties not so much. It's as if unionist suffering is unique. An exception may be the sort of entrenched resistance to reconciliation also evident in the intra-communal hostilities that persist between different factions of both loyalism and republicanism. I want to cite an example of the latter which I think illuminates the issue Trimble raises, albeit indirectly.

Shortly after the publication of *The Elusive Quest*, I received a very animated dressing down by a Workers' Party (WP) stalwart who objected to my inclusion of the notion of forgiveness in politics and for very personal reasons. He recalled vividly events from 1975 during (what he and others believe was) an attempted "Pogrom" when PIRA made a concerted attempt to wipe out leading figures of the Official IRA (OIRA) in Belfast (who then retaliated in turn) – he survived the attacks but many of his comrades didn't. To expect him to forgive the Provos was not only unthinkable, but in his terms unconscionable – it was tantamount to asking him to betray the memory of past comrades. Knowing that forgiveness, which often carries religious connotations, was a delicate card to play in this instance – one which carried the potential to inflame things further, given that his atheism was worn proudly and enthusiastically – I treaded warily. I invoked Hannah Arendt's point (which is the one I stuck to in the book) about forgiveness being required to break the cycle of revenge. I knew he respected Arendt, but he wasn't accepting her point. I then proffered the thought that in steadfastly refusing to countenance forgiveness, the risk of being consumed by bitterness was exacerbated, and this I submitted was scarcely an edifying prospect. Wrong! Bitterness, he insisted, was the engine driving resistance to forgiveness; it was the necessary condition for keeping alive memory of his comrades and ensuring they received the respect they were due. Rather than accept my view that bitterness could become all-consuming and twist and distort one's personality, he almost saw it as a virtue. At about roughly this point in our (at times "interesting") discussion we looked at each other, shrugged and ordered another pint. He wasn't convincing me, and I wasn't convincing him, but we weren't going to fall out over it.

Three points are relevant here from the encounter I've just described. (1) Some imperatives of reconciliation (such as forgiveness) aren't guaranteed to become easier with time. My WP interlocutor's point wasn't Trimble's – you're asking too much too soon – it was rather, you're asking too much period. His rage was as fierce on the day I spoke to him as it had been over a quarter of a century earlier. (2) Trimble's equivocal logic which hints, but stops short of guaranteeing, that a time may come when reconciliation isn't asking too much of unionists doesn't convincingly escape entanglement in the unequivocal language of the former OIRA veteran – for some people, reconciliation's time is never going to be right, which, as befitted the man, he made painstakingly clear in his own inimitable and brutally honest fashion. (3) Whether ambivalently or non-ambivalently expressed, and however sensitively we should handle the pain and sense of injustice sometimes informing opposition to reconciliation, I'm not persuaded by appeals to put reconciliation's requirements on the back-burner. In reference to the example I cited, I definitely don't buy the suggestion of bitterness being a virtue; to think otherwise is to invite unbearable corrosive consequences for human relations and society. And that is true of other blocks to reconciliation's message, including fear, indifference and so on.

There is still plenty left to confound me, however, including a sequence of related claims: I *lack agents* capable of delivering strong reconciliation; a problem highlighted by the fact that those I might look to for support here *lack the numbers* required to be of assistance; and, as a consequence, I'm reduced to relying rather pathetically on *religion and private conversion* to do my heavy lifting.

Where are the Agents?

The manner in which agency emerges as a problem in this context is a little baffling. If I were making claims about historical destiny – such as Aughey's notion of integration as "an idea whose time has come" (see Chapter four) or republicans' belief in the inevitability of Irish unity, then it'd be appropriate to scrutinise my text for hints of possible agents of delivery. But I'm not. Nor am I proposing a blueprint for a way forward which promises the arrival of a new Jerusalem if only I can drum up enough electoral support – another instance which would legitimately invite questions about agency. So, let's get a bit of perspective. I've written a book read by a handful of people (some of whom seem not to have understood it). I wrote it as a citizen offering reasons to other citizens as to why we might give more attention to reconciliation in order to improve the quality of Northern social and political life. I hoped, at best, to get a discussion going among a very small sub-group of citizens who were sufficiently educated and/or politically motivated to bother reading it. And that's it. I don't need to fret over the paucity of agents prepared to take up cudgels for strong reconciliation; I wasn't expecting to be flooded by volunteers. The most I hoped for was that a few citizens might see the point of what I was driving at and take it on board as they saw fit. So, this whole line of critique is in my view utterly misconceived.

Quantitative Morality?

It does, however, raise curious considerations. One of these is that it's appropriate to think that lack of numbers sounds the death knell for a moral ideal such as reconciliation. As Trimble helpfully informs me, my potential support in Northern Ireland is on the wane. Why that impugns the validity of the ideal is a mystery. I'm curious to know how morality is decided by numbers. I'm reminded here, of a similar sort of argument once put to me on a different topic and under very different circumstances. One evening at a social event in Blackfriars, Oxford – more years ago than I care to remember – a celebrated Dominican thinker (renowned for his mastery of Aquinas, Marx and Wittgenstein, among others) took me aside to inform me that Protestants were to be pitied. Why so? Well, I was told, because Catholics possessed the truth, as was confirmed by their having the numbers – "and so many people can't be wrong". Not one of his finer arguments admittedly, but, despite its crude reduction of truth to quantitative calculations, clemency in judgement was readily available on the "impeccable" grounds that liquor had been taken. As far as I can tell, the argument for making morality similarly subject to quantitative calculations has no such escape clause; it seems to have been submitted in a state of sobriety. As it stands, it's not even an entertaining distraction but merely a dull irrelevance.

Relying on Religion?

That still leaves, of course, the charge that my pitch for reconciliation is reduced to "relying on religion and personal conversion". If this charge is meant to sting, it fails. It makes me smile. Now I acknowledge that the ways of providence are often hard to fathom, and that the operations of the Spirit can't be predicted, but I'd guess that personal conversion to the cause of strong reconciliation would not come through "a leap of faith", as Aughey conjectures, (Aughey, 2005: 109) but through being convinced by the argument of *The Elusive Quest* – which would make me as chirpy as a proverbial chipmunk. I'm unaware of having offered any specifically religious or theological arguments for reconciliation in my book (though there are plenty to be made), but I'd like to think that there were some that might appeal to those of a religious disposition. So, if I can count on a bit of religious sympathy for my position then I find that gratifying, especially since I know that there are religious types from whom I can count on opposition.

But Trimble and Aughey (who, as I've indicated, also weighs in on this topic) are accusing me of something more: that my political or philosophical language has taken on a religious hue. I rely on "a huge voluntaristic act of will" (Trimble), peddle "a civil religion", end up in "mysticism" (Aughey), and so forth. Unsurprisingly, not a single argument from my book is given as evidence of these claims. If I thought it'd serve any worthwhile purpose, I'd explain at length what's so misinformed about these attempted put-downs. I don't. Thus, I'll settle for saying only this: (1) it's impossible to give credence to the accusations as they don't reflect anything I've written in my book; (2) to accuse me of voluntarism is to betray theological/philosophical illiteracy – lying behind my insistence on giving reasons (which I scarcely thought relevant to mention earlier) is an ultimate rejection of the voluntarism that entered Western theology and philosophy through thirteenth century Franciscanism (Duns Scotus, William of Ockham); and (3) as for mysticism all I can say to Aughey is tell me more, since I've no idea what you're talking about but, rather than be repelled, I could be interested if you can assure me that dialogical rationality is alive and well at some mystical academy I ought to know about.

The further religiously tinged attributions of civic faith, secular religion and the like to my view of strong reconciliation invite giggling but since they're seemingly trotted out with the serious intent of ridiculing a position by saddling it with religious connotations (where these connotations at least in politics mean excessive, undesirable and probably oppressive), I'll take the opportunity to offer a simple reply. Religion in public space, whether civic or otherwise, doesn't instantly send alarm bells ringing; precisely because I'm not a proceduralist in the manner of Rawls or Habermas (though the latter has shifted his views somewhat), I maintain that religious views are entitled to expression in debates about what sort of a society we wish to live in; and my only proviso is that they're not entitled to special pleading by summoning (their interpretation of) divine authority as a clinching argument. Aughey's snide ascriptions of religious intent to my position are designed to discredit and arouse fearmongering; they are not only unworthy but tellingly shallow.

An Inadequate Moral Ideal

Now for a nice little twist to the argument against strong reconciliation. For all the extensive palaver about the inappropriateness of pursuing moral ideals in politics, I'm told my problem, which comes to the fore through my treatment of republicanism, is that I'm operating with an *inadequate moral ideal of reconciliation*; one that's soft on terrorism, lax on decommissioning, elicits gullibility to republican dissembling and proves its distastefulness by regarding republicans as the good guys.

According to Trimble, "a moral ideal which ignores the question of who bears the responsibility for by far the greatest amount of death, injury and destruction over the period of the Troubles – the Provisional IRA – is a deeply flawed one." So, to clarify, moral ideals may be okay in politics as long as they're the right ones –

Afterword: Reconciliation and Its Unionist Critics

those that show "us" in a positive light and "them" in a negative one. As I remarked in chapter seven, the language of moral condemnation is an important part of unionism's arsenal when dealing with republicans. So, please let's be honest about it – some prominent unionists don't like the ways in which I describe and apply reconciliation as a moral ideal. Right, then, what's wrong with it? *Soft on terrorism* is the first answer. Here Trimble offers two points, viz., that "terrorism" doesn't feature in the book's index and that I don't condemn the Provisional IRA. Regarding the index, I should point out that other things also don't feature (the B-Specials, for example). Regarding condemnation, I don't condemn loyalist paramilitaries or the British Army either. The central issue that's being missed here is that I'm not buying into the blame game of who bears most responsibility for conflict in the North because I'm focusing on how we may fashion a future beyond conflict in a post-Agreement society. I have little doubt that republicans have abandoned militarism and, in the context of political circumstances in which guns are overwhelmingly silent, I see little virtue in dragging up horrors from the past. Anyway, Trimble is skating on much thinner moral ice than he supposes (given the morally dubious actions for which unionism has historically been responsible) when he effectively says to republicans that until they do as we (unionists) insist there can be no reconciliation. And the notion that saying this sort of thing is political realism in action is comical.

Which brings us to *decommissioning* about which I'll say the following. First, I have consistently maintained that ridding Northern Ireland of paramilitary weapons is an important goal of peace. But, in the early throes of a post-conflict situation, that doesn't mean that making decommissioning a pre-condition of other political developments is a wise move. Second, the lack of any decommissioning of loyalist weapons hasn't in the past or the present prevented the UUP from entering into political arrangements with loyalist parties. Yet the UUP continues to balk at developing arrangements with Sinn Féin, even after the decommissioning of PIRA weapons. Third, for all the rhetoric, it's not clear what made decommissioning a specifically unionist concern, or its prioritisation a virtual badge of unionist orthodoxy. Unionism's past hardly contains the answer. And pointedly, neither the Alliance Party nor the SDLP – parties whose commitments to peace and constitutional politics are beyond reproach – became fixated on decommissioning in the way that mainstream unionist parties did. Taking the high ground on decommissioning seems somewhat contrived.

Another story may help. Shortly following the "unofficial" weekend of discussions between republicans and unionists that I referred to earlier, I was approached by a member of Sinn Féin who asked if I could arrange a follow-up gathering focused on the topic of decommissioning. He explained that republicans thought that the issue of decommissioning had the potential to wreck the possibility of any agreement being reached and suggested that it may be possible to bridge the gap with unionism on this issue if a meeting could be arranged behind closed doors, where it'd be easier to engage in frank and honest discussion. He said that for such an event any one, or all three, of Sinn Féin's political leadership – Adams, McGuinness and McLaughlin – would willingly attend if there were comparable representation on the unionist side (that is, unionists with the authority to deliver on any deal that may be reached). I put out feelers within the ranks of unionism, including with one of the participants in the earlier discussions and his initial response was enthusiastic. Then I received word that under no circumstances would such an event be approved by the UUP leadership and that any participation by a party member would be frowned upon. My initially enthusiastic unionist suddenly went quiet and hasn't yet returned my calls! When I reported the news back to Sinn Féin the response was simple: "well, we all know what that means".

Indeed, we did. Trimble, it seems, calculated that the UUP's interests wouldn't be best served by a quiet resolution of the issue; not when he could use it as a stick with which to beat republicans and, with luck, have them denied political office. This isn't to say that had the event taken place it would've led anywhere. But, even so, I find it difficult to treat Trimble's pontifications on decommissioning with anything other than huge pinches of salt. Which reinforces a much bigger point: sure, it's impossible to envisage reconciliation with historical antagonists once it's decided that you're not going to try. But to extrapolate from the particular example of what I see as unionist recalcitrance to a general conclusion of reconciliation's impossibility – which allegedly makes my proposals ludicrous – is itself more than faintly ridiculous.

On the other issues of *gullibility* and treating republicans as "politically correct" good guys, short answers are more than adequate. When it comes to accepting or not accepting republicans' *bona fides*, I'm hardly going to defer to politicians who don't appear to care for their company and have had minimal direct dealings with them. I came to know a lot of republicans over several years and in various situations. And, while I'm happy to listen to advice on how I should regard them, I will ultimately back my own judgement – which, I have found, is typically more informed than the judgements of those presuming to warn me against trusting any of them. So, I'm very content to ignore Trimble's spiel about how my delusional faith in reconciliation makes me susceptible to republican spin and dissembling.

Does this confirm, then, as Aughey asserts, that I regard republicans as politically correct good guys (understanding that if I do I condemn myself as an enemy of unionism)? No. Aughey is mischief making. Consider this, I've never supported armed struggle in Ireland, I've never advocated a united Ireland and I'd invite anyone who thinks I'm "soft" on republicanism to read what I've written about it in my book (Porter, 2003: 232-255). I do, however, believe that Sinn Féin should be treated with respect and accepted as equal political partners in the quest to make Northern society as reconciled as possible. And for this I refuse to apologise.

Politically Dangerous?

Now we descend into truly farcical stuff, which, while worth a mention, doesn't warrant much attention.

From Anti-Political to Dangerously Political

Whereas previously Aughey was contending that my moralism ended up being quite anti-political, he is also keen to argue that it may be politically dangerous. Take the following chain of assertions. The form of deliberative rationality integral to my moral ideal involves "crushing conformity"; I propose a "catechism of civic faith" which treats "politics as a secular religion" – the central message of which is that "Northern Ireland must be born again" though strong reconciliation; but since, as Trimble pointed out, I lack any transformative agency I merely "bless the politically correct" (republicans) and anathematise the "incorrect" (unionists); working away in all of this is my use of philosophy which is properly understood as really part of "a shadow game" concerned to assert "authority" and which culminates in my abandonment of philosophy for "mysticism"; also at play here is a disturbing affliction of hubris which displays itself through my treating political opponents as though they're unable to present their arguments in "a fully moral or rational way"; thus my celebration of dialogue isn't what it seems – I don't reason with my opponents but seek to "re-educate them"; and this creates a threatening scenario giving off "a whiff of authoritarianism" (Aughey, 2005: 75).

It's difficult to know how to respond to a chain of assertions that, as far as I can tell, derive from Aughey's imagination and nowhere else. It's as if once Aughey says it's so, it must be so. Except it isn't. A more comprehensive misreading of anything I've written would be hard to concoct. I've nothing to add to remarks I've already made about the quasi-religious allusions he makes. And I'm not sure I can do much more than wonder how he detects "crushing conformity" in a notion of reconciliation which insists on respecting differences between citizens, giving others due recognition and engaging them in dialogue. I'll just make two short responses to his endeavour to render my account of reconciliation as authoritarian.

Philosophy as a Shadow Game?

One of his strategies here is to assert, in blatant contradistinction to my own philosophical elucidations, that I employ philosophy as part of a shadow game designed to assert authority. This reads to me as an attempt to fit what I'm doing within a Schmittian paradigm. But, since I'm not smitten by Schmitt, I don't treat concepts as weapons. And I don't think of philosophy as a tool to be deployed in political combat, or as part of a "shadow game" preoccupied with asserting "authority", because I don't work within a friend/enemy framework. It's as if Aughey has to superimpose his *modus operandi* on others (in this case me) as he doesn't quite grasp that there are other ways to think about politics. My use of philosophy here is closer to the Gadamerian ambition of "fusing horizons" which fosters epistemic humility rather than hubris by envisaging us being opened up to different views, engaging with them, potentially being extended by, and learning from, them, and maybe adjusting our own position as a consequence. Unsurprisingly, a Gadamerian take on doing philosophy makes dialogue central in a manner that's foreign to Schmitt and Aughey.

Dialogue and Authoritarianism?

But Aughey's suspicions are unlikely to be allayed by my reference to dialogue given that he infers that I deploy it to advance nefarious ends, such as re-education and authoritarianism. As a riposte, I'd like here to quote what I say about dialogue in *The Elusive Quest*.

Dialogue presupposes engagement. Interpretations are its stuff, as are nuances, shades of meaning and ambiguities...Through dialogue we may aim to become clearer about things – our confusions, misunderstandings, and so on; we may try to figure out how we can together work through our difficulties, as we strive for better interpretations of our problems, circumstances, and respective positions. But our various attempts to become clearer...are always provisional. They are never absolute.

On dialogical terms...language does not function as a tool over which we have complete mastery; and risk, vulnerability and uncertainty cannot be expunged without dialogue ceasing to be dialogue (Porter, 2003: 130).

I hope it's sufficient to point out that the above dialogical emphases on working together, striving for better interpretations, provisionality, lack of mastery, risk, vulnerability and uncertainty do not square with Aughey's accusations about denying opponents' rational capacities and wanting to re-educate them in threatening ways that smack of authoritarianism. And when he pronounces (unbelievably) that I don't give reasons to those with whom I disagree, I think it's time to take my leave. A splendid joke Arthur, but I fear my humour is fading.

Conclusion

Responding to Aughey's criticisms of my book on reconciliation and my earlier book on unionism (Chapter six) has been a strange experience. I am left pondering whether if I didn't exist Aughey would have had to invent me. The disconcerting thought is that I do exist and yet he has still had to invent me. The 'Norman Porter' to whom he refers in his writings is mostly a stranger to me; someone I may have had a fleeting acquaintance with somewhere I can't quite remember, but otherwise an alien. Eventually, frustration with such an abnormal situation reaches a limit; and when it becomes obvious that one's interlocutor stubbornly persists in refusing to hear what one is saying and to respond in good faith, it's probably time to shrug, smile and move on.

References

Arendt, Hannah, 1959, *The Human Condition* (Chicago, University of Chicago Press).
— 1968, *The Origins of Totalitarianism*, 3rd ed (New York, Harcourt, Brace Jovanovitch).
— 2000, "What is Freedom?" in *The Portable Hannah Arendt*, ed., Peter Baehr (New York, Penguin).
Aughey, Arthur, 1989, *Under Siege: Ulster Unionism and the Anglo-Irish Agreement* (Belfast, Blackstaff Press).
— 1995, "McCartney in the Wings", *Fortnight*, no. 340 (June).
— 1996, "Norman Conquered", *Fortnight*, no. 355 (November).
— 1997, "A State of Exception: The Concept of the Political in Northern Ireland", *Irish Political Studies*, vol. 12, no. 1.
— 2005, *The Politics of Northern Ireland. Beyond the Belfast Agreement* (London, Routledge).
Berlin, Isaiah, 1969 *Four Essays on Liberty* (Oxford, Oxford University Press).
Bew, Paul, et al, 1979, *The State in Northern Ireland 1921-72* (Manchester, Manchester University Press).
Coulter, Colin, 1996, "Direct Rule and the Unionist Middle Class", in Richard English and Graham Walker (eds), *Unionism in Modern Ireland. New Perspectives on Politics and Culture* (Dublin, Gill and MacMillan).

English, Richard, 1997, "The Northern Ireland Peace Process Reconsidered", *Eire-Ireland. An Interdisciplinary Journal of Irish Studies*, vol. 31, nos. 3 and 4.

Fuller, Steve, 2005, *The Intellectual* (Cambridge, Icon).

Kiberd, Declan, 1998, "Romantic Ireland's Dead and Gone", *Times Literary Supplement*, (June).

Little, Adrian, 2004, *Democracy and Northern Ireland. Beyond the Liberal Paradigm?* (New York, Palgrave).

McCartney, Robert, 1985, *Liberty and Authority in Ireland*, Field Day Pamphlet, No. 9 (Derry, Field Day).

— 1995a, *Belfast Telegraph* (19 January).

— 1995b, *News Letter*, (7 March).

— 1997, *Belfast Telegraph*, (14 May).

Mill, John Stuart, 1910, *Utilitarianism, Liberalism and Representative Government* (London, Dent).

O'Malley, Padraig, 1983, *The Uncivil Wars. Ireland Today* (Belfast, Blackstaff Press).

— 1990, *Biting at the Grave. Irish Hunger Strikes and the Politics of Despair* (Belfast, Blackstaff Press).

Pollock, Andy, ed., 1993, *A Citizens' Inquiry. The Opsahl Report on Northern Ireland* (Dublin, Lilliput Press).

Porter, Norman, 1996, *Rethinking Unionism. An Alternative Vision for Northern Ireland* (Belfast, Blackstaff Press).

— ed., 1998a, *The Republican Ideal. Current Perspectives* (Belfast, Blackstaff Press).

— 1998b, *Rethinking Unionism*, updated edition (Belfast, Blackstaff Press).

— 2003, *The Elusive Quest. Reconciliation in Northern Ireland* (Belfast, Blackstaff Press).

— 2020, *Political Theology. A Radical Idea and an Alternative*, rev. ed., (Independently Published).

Schmitt, Carl, 1995, *The Concept of the Political*, trans. George Schwab (Chicago, University of Chicago Press).

Trimble, David, 2003, "The Long hard Road to Reconciliation," *Times Literary Supplement* (15 April).

Walker, Brian, 1996, *Dancing to History's Tune. History, Myth and Politics in Ireland* (Belfast, Institute of Irish Studies).

Walzer, Michael, 1983, *Spheres of Justice. A Defence of Pluralism and Equality* (Oxford Blackwell).

www.ingramcontent.com/pod-product-compliance
Lightning Source LLC
Chambersburg PA
CBHW022036290426
44109CB00014B/870